Rick Stein Coast to Coast

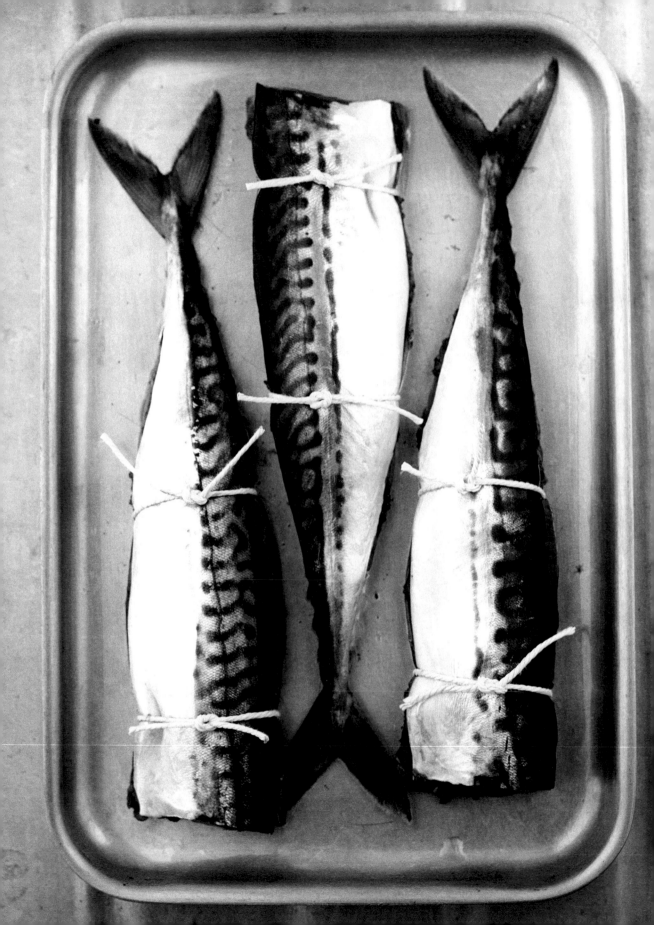

Rick Stein
Coast to Coast

Food from the land &
sea inspired by travels
across the world

BOOKS

10 9 8 7 6 5 4 3 2 1

Published in 2008 by BBC Books, an imprint of Ebury Publishing
A Random House Group Company

Photographs by James Murphy
Photographs on pages 6, 12, 54, 70, 71, 96, 138, 168, 191, 206, 238, 239 and 248 by Noel Murphy
Photography copyright © Woodlands Books Ltd 2008

The Random House Group Limited Reg. No. 954009

Addresses for companies within the Random House Group can be found at
www.randomhouse.co.uk

A CIP catalogue record for this book is available from the British Library

ISBN 978 1 846 07614 5

The Random House Group Limited makes every effort to ensure that the
papers used in our books are made from trees that have been legally sourced
from well-managed and credibly certified forests. Our paper procurement
policy can be found on www.randomhouse.co.uk

Commissioning editor: Shirley Patton
Project editor: Eleanor Maxfield
Home economist: Debbie Major
Design and art direction: Smith & Gilmour, London
Production controller: Bridget Fish

Colour origination by Altaimage, London
Printed and bound in Germany by Firmengruppe APPL,
aprinta druck, Wemding

CONTENTS

In 1955, when I was just eight, my father took the whole family, in a pale blue Jaguar Mark VII and a Rover 90, to a hotel called the Carlos V on La Salve beach at Laredo, between Santander and Bilbao, on the north coast of Spain. I don't remember a great deal about the holiday except that everywhere we went the Spanish were full of awe of the mighty Jaguar, which they called the Haguar. I recall too the presence of many Guardia Civil with their curious black three-corned hats, particularly holding back the crowds at the Battle of the Flowers festival in the town, held every August. There was a military prison at the far end of the very long beach and not much else except the hotel. It had different coloured tiles on each floor: red on the ground, yellow on the first, then green, and finally and most intriguingly blue on the top floor, a source of much satisfaction to myself and my sister Henrietta. We both drank Coca-Cola for the first time – I think we were only allowed one bottle a day – and it came in slightly green-tinted glass bottles, which was completely fabulous to us both. Even more extraordinary was the food, particularly squid, which came in a black ink stew with tomato, olive oil and garlic. I remember that this was the first realisation I had that food abroad was exotically different to what we had at home and I believe that that's when my 'wanderlust' to travel from coast to coast across countries around the world started.

Since then my greatest enthusiasm in life has been finding dishes that change my perception of cooking, that reveal a whole new vista of flavour combinations. I think we all enjoy that. Just like that squid in black ink, I can still remember the first time that I tasted the salty, hot, sweet and sour flavours of Thai cooking – the combination of fish sauce, bird's eye chillies, palm sugar and lime juice. I just couldn't believe anything would ever taste so good again.

Really good local dishes tell me more about the thoughts, habits and enthusiasms of a foreign country than museum visits or a walk round a famous cathedral. More than that, finding out what dishes people hold dear is, in my opinion, the best way of getting to know them. When I have such conversations, I experience a sort of thrill of recognition. This is a realisation that you have so much in common with people who speak entirely unfamiliar languages and have quite a different history. One of the most enjoyable experiences for me on this subject was meeting the Japanese Ambassador to London, Mr Yoshi Nogami. A few years ago I cooked a gratin of Cornish crab with spinach at a banquet celebrating the investiture of the, then, new Lord Mayor of the City of London, David Brewer. Like me, David comes from Cornwall and wanted something local. He introduced me to Ambassador Nogami, pointing out that while a great admirer of my TV programmes, the Ambassador thought I had one or two lessons to learn about the finer points of sushi and sashimi. He'd seen a programme where I joined a mackerel fishing trip out of Padstow and had filleted and sliced the fish on board and served it on some sushi rice to the slightly astonished group of dads and small boys. He had enjoyed the film, but said that in Japan they never use raw mackerel, it's always cured. I was a bit embarrassed, but soon got over it when he said he'd already been to

Padstow and thoroughly enjoyed the fish soup at my restaurant, but what he really liked was our fish and chips. It turned out that he spent a lot of his free weekends travelling around the British Isles finding places that served the best Lancashire hot pot, steak and kidney pies and, most importantly, roast beef with Yorkshire pudding because, as he pointed out, we don't do roasts in Japan, we don't have the ovens. I went to Japan and learnt how to make good sushi and sashimi, both recipes of which are in the book, but more importantly to me, I discovered how essential good food is in Japanese life and how incredibly respectful they are of seasonality and how they have an almost religious sense of the importance of eating certain foods at certain times of the year. It's not going too far to say that my series of conversations with him made me realise that the appreciation of good food is endlessly subtle and rewarding.

Ever since that first trip to Spain, my enthusiasm for finding good food and thereby discovering so much about people from other countries has continued unabated and all the chapters in this book reflect that. The fish curries of southern India were another sort of right of passage for me. I remember in the late 80s the editors of *The Good Food Guide* used to pontificate quite sternly about sticking to one's roots in food, keeping menus regional, keeping one's respect for local dishes. They argued that poor copies of other countries' foods on a British restaurant menu were an indication of our feelings of inferiority about our own cooking. I did my best to cook British but, when I started going to Goa and eating dishes like the *Mussel, cockle and clam masala* on page 152, or the *Mackerel recheado* on page 140 I began to wonder. I think it was probably the *Monkfish vindaloo* on page 160 which I had at Bagga beach which did it. It came with slightly charred naan bread perfumed with garlic and warm from the tandoor oven, chunky slices of cucumber much more bitter than our own, sprinkled with lime juice and coriander and a salad of beautifully sweet tomatoes with thinly sliced sharp onions and spiced with chilli and cumin and a trace of sourness from palm vinegar. That was it. I could not prevent myself from bringing them home and putting them on the menu in Padstow. My chef friend in Goa, Rui, had introduced me to the taste of real vindaloo, rather than the absurdly hot and over-spiced version you often get in Britain. Each time I went to Goa he sent me home with a big pot of home-made vindaloo paste, which always leaked into my luggage. It was the taste of those pastes in conjunction with the recipes which he gave to me for vindaloo and other fish curry bases that led me to think that if I could get the dishes right and indeed produce a really good version of them, what was so wrong with putting them on my own menu alongside grilled Dover sole, cod in parsley sauce, gulls eggs with celery salt and prawn cocktails? Looking back, of course, I shouldn't have worried about those food guide writers, but at the time I wanted to be recognised and felt I'd have to hide my own enthusiasms. One of the few pluses of getting older is you tend to do what you want and not care what other people think.

These days the menus of most restaurants in the UK will have dishes from all over the world. It's the same in countries like Holland, Denmark and Germany; the eclectic style prevails. Part of the reason for this is that we don't need the rather substantial food that our forbears ate as fuel dishes and look to cuisines from hotter climates which tend to be lighter and simpler in their cooking.

This would include countries like Spain, and all the countries around the Mediterranean, not to mention further afield: India, South-east Asia, Japan and China. The other reason for the mixing of dishes is that everyone travels, and styles of cooking from far away are no longer too unfamiliar to be ordered. It's the same in the USA, Canada, South Africa, Australia and New Zealand; all have this predilection for potpourri menus. On this subject, I recall a conversation with an Australian couple in my restaurant a few years ago, where they explained that they had come to live in the Home Counties, and complained how boring English food was when compared to Australian. I said that if they were talking about traditional Australian food, which I took to mean the cooking brought over from Britain and the only food available when I first went there in the mid 60s, I would speak up in favour of the British version any day. What they were actually referring to was the food of the more recent immigrants to Australia: Italian, Greek, Vietnamese, Thai, Lebanese and many more. The same is now true of the larger cities in the UK. London has cooking from most of the countries in the world. The fact is, these days my enthusiasm for travelling from one coast to another in different countries is reflected in the food we all love to eat in this country. At some point you have to say it's all British food. When you consider that in a recent survey two of the most popular foods were spaghetti Bolognese and curry, it has to be accepted that this is true.

I'm just someone with an enthusiasm for food and a curiosity that's sent me sniffing around all over the place looking for lovely dishes in all corners of the globe. I think that with the ease and relative cheapness of travel and the enormous amount of information easy to get hold of on the internet, most of us will continue to gain a greater awareness of what's going on all over the world. I was recently in Germany, where my father's family came from, and talking to a cousin, now in her late 60s, about her memories of the Second World War. The overwhelming impression I got from her was a sense of Germany's isolation from the rest of the world that went back to the end of the First World War, when the country was left almost as a punishment to recover itself, a policy which led to the rise of Hitler. As soon as the Second World War ended, her father sent her away all over the world, including a trip to our farm in Oxfordshire. He did the same with all his children, so keen was he for them to learn about the world out there and impress on them the need to be outward-looking, trying in a family way, to avoid what had happened before.

I feel that celebrating great food from all over the world is a very effective way of communicating with people everywhere. From the comforting star anise fragrance of the broth and texture of the rice noodles in a *Vietnamese pho* (see page 200) to the pleasure of crisp, early summer vegetables in a *Salade tourangelle* (see page 64); from that most perfect of sweets, the soft crust of a perfectly turned out *Pavlova with cream and passion-fruit* (see page 241) from Australia, to a thick fillet of *Grilled salted cod with beer bacon and cabbage* (see page 44) from a pub in Suffolk enjoying food from everywhere is how we can best get on with each other on this overcrowded planet.

Britain & Ireland

When I was making a TV programme set in France called *Rick Stein's French Odyssey*, a few years ago, I began to realise to my surprise that a lot of French regional food was no better or worse than our own. I was thinking particularly about cassoulet, the haricot bean, pork, duck confit and Toulouse sausage stew. I thought it like our own Lancashire hot pot. The difference is that the French are very good at selling what they produce. They are also good at packaging what they make. Whether it be in pretty jars with lids topped with rustic paper and hand-written labels or fresh from the boulangerie in blackened baking trays, they have an ability to turn any local food into a cause for celebration. We don't seem so clever at that and yet we have great regional food, which at long last is being recognised, not only in farmers' markets and farm shops but even supermarkets now sell plenty of local food. I was scanning a menu at a new chop house in the City of London the other day and thought how attractive a menu of all British and Irish food could look: chops, roasts, oysters, cockles and laver bread, champ and Irish stew – my mouth was watering.

I've tried in this chapter to pull together not so much the classics but dishes that mean a lot to me as good examples of our own cooking. Some are my own, many of the others I picked up on journeys around Britain and Ireland, notably whilst making two series of *Food Heroes*. In these programmes, I sought out small producers of excellent quality food who in many cases were not making great money out of what they were doing but were fired with a sense of purpose. One of them I revisted only yesterday – Great Keiro Farm where Nigel and Jax Buse grow the asparagus that we use in our restaurants in Padstow. It looks over the Camel Estuary at St Minver, but the asparagus fields are actually in Trebetherick and are still owned by the Betjeman family and were originally rented to them by Sir John Betjeman himself. Standing there in the beds, helping myself frequently to bites of raw asparagus which taste more like peas until cooked, with the red flag of the 13th green at St Enedoc golf course and the idiosyncratically stunted spire of St Enedoc Church beyond, in mid-May when everything was green and mild around, with Jax complaining about the predation of the asparagus from the many rabbits around, I was filled with a warm feeling of pleasure in great local produce yet again. You might like to try the *Chicken and creamy asparagus soup* on page 18.

The chapter is full of favourites. There's fish cakes and a classic recipe for Cornish pasties and perhaps the most popular dish of lemon sole we serve at the restaurant, *Goujons of lemon sole with parmesan breadcrumbs* (see page 28). I suspect too that there's universal affection from all British people for *Cauliflower cheese* (see page 22) and *Treacle tart with clotted cream ice cream* (see page 49). These are the sorts of dishes that I would proudly point out as examples of why British food is often underrated.

The Padstow deli crab sandwich with parsley, chilli, lemon and rocket

If crab came out of its shell in lovely firm pieces like lobster, I wouldn't be surprised if it fetched more money, because I often think it's got a better flavour. Fortunately, it's not enormously expensive and it's really good in sandwiches. This is a great favourite at our deli. I can't resist mayonnaise with crab – it's one of my favourite combinations. I've also added a little chilli and some rocket, parsley and sea salt. Although I've specified slices of wholemeal bread with the recipe, it's also very special in a baguette.

MAKES 6

12 thin slices of wholemeal bread (each weighing about 40 g/1½ oz)
75 g (3 oz) butter, softened
5 tablespoons *mayonnaise* (page 280)
1 teaspoon lemon juice
½–1 red chilli, depending on heat, seeded and finely chopped
500 g (1¼ lb) fresh hand-picked white crab meat
2 tablespoons chopped flat-leaf parsley
50 g (2 oz) rocket
Sea salt

Butter the slices of bread and put them to one side.

Put the mayonnaise (see page 280) into a small bowl and stir in the lemon juice and chilli. Put the crab meat and parsley into another bowl and lightly stir through the mayonnaise mixture. Season to taste with a little salt.

Put 4 slices of the bread, buttered sides up, on a board and spoon over the crab mixture. Cover with a generous layer of the rocket leaves and then top with the remaining slices of bread. Cut each sandwich diagonally into halves or quarters and serve at once.

Hugo's breakfast fishcakes

I was once asked to rename this recipe but couldn't possibly because it's Hugo's. He runs a brilliant guesthouse just outside Padstow called Woodlands, *where he cooks special breakfasts.*

SERVES 4

400 g (14 oz) floury main-crop potatoes, such as Desirée,
    peeled (350 g/12 oz prepared weight) and cut into large chunks
300 g (10-oz) fillet of white fish, such as pollack, gurnard, cod
    or haddock, cut into small chunks
225 ml (8 fl oz) full-cream milk
1 pared strip of lemon zest
1 bay leaf
40 g (1½ oz) butter
1 teaspoon olive oil
1 small onion, finely chopped
A handful of curly-leaf parsley leaves, chopped
1 teaspoon lemon juice
25 g (1 oz) plain flour
1 large egg, beaten
100 g (4 oz) fresh white breadcrumbs
Sea salt and freshly ground black pepper
Soured cream and chives, to serve

Cook the potatoes in boiling, salted water for 20 minutes or until tender. Drain well, tip back into the pan and mash until smooth. Set aside.

Meanwhile, put the fish, milk, lemon zest, bay leaf and some black pepper into a pan. Cover, bring to the boil and simmer for 4 minutes or until the fish has just cooked through. Remove and discard the bay leaf and lemon zest, lift the fish on to a plate and reserve the poaching milk. Remove and discard any skin and bones from the fish and leave the fillet to cool slightly.

Melt 15 g (½ oz) of the butter in a medium-sized saucepan, add the olive oil and onion and cook gently for 6–7 minutes, until soft and translucent but not brown. Add the mashed potatoes, allow them to warm through slightly; then add the fish, parsley, lemon juice and 2 tablespoons of the poaching milk and mix together well. The mixture should be neither dry nor so wet that it is difficult to handle. Leave to cool.

Meanwhile, season the flour with some salt and pepper and sprinkle it on to the work surface. Put the egg into a shallow dish and the breadcrumbs into another. Using slightly wet hands, form the mixture in the flour into 8 small fish cakes, which are about 1 cm (½ inch) thick. Dip them into the beaten egg and then the breadcrumbs, put on to a baking tray and chill them for 1 hour (or better still overnight) in the fridge.

Melt the remaining butter and a teaspoon of olive oil in a large, non-stick frying pan, add the fish cakes and fry them gently for about 5 minutes on each side until golden. Serve with some soured cream and chives on the side.

Creamy chicken and asparagus soup

Everybody should have an asparagus soup in their repertoire. There's so much flavour in the stalks, including the fibrous ends that most people chop off and discard, and I think it's a shame to waste good food if you can find a way not to. I blanch the tips and add them to this soup, made creamy and slightly tart with crème fraîche.

SERVES 8

1 small chicken, weighing about 1¼ kg (2¾ lb)
The other ingredients for making *chicken stock* (page 278)
200 g (7 oz) bunch thin asparagus
75 g (3 oz) butter
1 small onion, finely chopped
100 g (4 oz) thinly sliced leek
100 g (4 oz) fennel, chopped
50 g (2 oz) plain flour
200 ml (7 fl oz) crème fraîche
Sea salt and freshly ground white pepper

Remove the breasts from the chicken, skin and set them to one side. Use the remaining chicken carcass and the legs to make the stock (see page 278).

Bring the stock to the boil, add the chicken breasts, cover and leave to simmer gently for 15 minutes. Lift the chicken out on to a plate, cover and leave until cool enough to handle. Meanwhile, measure how much stock you have left. You want 2¼ litres (4 pints) so, if you have less, top it up with a little water or extra chicken stock. If you have slightly more, boil it until it is reduced to the required amount. When the chicken is cool enough to handle, tear it into fine shreds. Cover with cling film and set aside with the stock.

For the soup, cut 2½ cm (1 inch) off the tips of the asparagus and set to one side. Roughly chop the remainder. Melt the butter in a clean pan, add the onion, leek, fennel and asparagus stalks and cook gently for 10 minutes, until soft but not browned. Stir in the flour, then gradually stir in the reserved chicken stock and bring to the boil. Cover and simmer for 10 minutes until the vegetables are very tender.

Meanwhile, drop the asparagus tips into a small pan of boiling, salted water and cook for 2 minutes. Drain, refresh under cold water, and set aside.

Remove the soup from the heat and leave to cool slightly. Then liquidise in batches until smooth, and pass through a sieve into a clean pan. Bring back to a simmer and then stir in the crème fraîche, shredded chicken and asparagus tips and season to taste with salt and some freshly ground white pepper. Serve with some crusty fresh bread.

Pea and ham soup with bacon butties

As an accompaniment, a bacon buttie is a zillion times better than putting chips with everything as they do in most pubs in Great Britain. I mean, who really wants soup with chips?

SERVES 4

75 g (3 oz) butter
225 g (8 oz) onions, chopped
25 g (1 oz) plain flour
900 g (2 lb) fresh or frozen peas
Salt and freshly ground white pepper

FOR THE HAM STOCK:

450 g (1-lb) piece of smoked gammon, or 1 small smoked ham hock
1 large onion
2 large carrots
3 celery sticks, sliced
3 bay leaves
½ teaspoon black peppercorns
A pinch of crushed dried chillies
2 litres (3½ pints) water

FOR THE BACON BUTTIES:

8 slices of medium-thick white bread
A little salted butter, at room temperature
1 tablespoon canola or sunflower oil
8 slices rindless smoked back bacon

For the ham stock, put all the ingredients into a pan, and bring to the boil, skimming off the scum as it rises to the surface. Lower the heat and leave to simmer for 1 hour. Strain, discarding the vegetables but reserving the piece of gammon. You want 1½ litres (2½ pints) of stock so, if you have slightly more, return to a clean pan and simmer until reduced to the required amount.

For the soup, melt the butter in a pan, add the onions, and cook gently for about 10 minutes, until soft but not browned. Stir in the flour and cook gently for 1 minute, then gradually add the stock and bring to the boil. Add the peas, bring back to the boil and simmer for 3 minutes. Meanwhile, skin the piece of gammon and chop the meat into small pieces. Remove the soup from the heat and leave to cool slightly. Then blend in a liquidiser, in batches if necessary, until smooth. Pour back into the pan and stir in the gammon and some seasoning to taste. Place the soup over a low heat and leave to reheat gently.

For the bacon butties, lightly butter the slices of bread. Heat the oil in a non-stick frying pan, add the bacon rashers and fry over a medium-high heat until the edges are just turning golden. Push the bacon to the side of the pan and briefly dunk the buttered side of 4 slices of the bread in the bacon fat. Cover these slices of bread with the rashers of bacon, cover with the second slices of bread and cut in half – not into triangles! Spoon the soup into warmed soup plates and serve with the bacon butties.

Oven-dried tomato and thyme tart with Blue Vinny, olive oil and rocket

Of all blue cheeses, Blue Vinny is perhaps the leanest, as it is made with skimmed milk; it is the produce of thrifty Dorset farmers looking to make extra money from the remains of the milk after the prized cream has been skimmed off. It's good for cooking with, though, because sometimes a relatively low-fat cheese is just what's required. I think of this tart as being a light first course or lunch. It also works very well when made with other blue cheeses, and with robustly flavoured sheep's milk cheeses such as feta or pecorino. I like the veining in Vinny, though; it gives the dish a sort of faint taint which I find pleasing.

SERVES 8

750 g (1½ lb) vine-ripened or plum tomatoes
450 g (1 lb) puff pastry
100 g (4 oz) Blue Vinny cheese, thinly sliced
1 teaspoon thyme leaves
1 tablespoon extra virgin olive oil, plus extra to serve
A handful of wild rocket leaves
Sea salt and freshly ground black pepper

Preheat the oven to its highest setting. Cut the tomatoes in half lengthways and place them cut side up in a lightly oiled, shallow roasting tin. Sprinkle over 1½ teaspoons of sea-salt flakes and some black pepper and roast for 15 minutes. Lower the oven temperature to 150°C/300°F/Gas Mark 2 and roast them for a further 1¼–1½ hours, until they have shrivelled in size but are still slightly juicy in the centre. Remove and set aside.

Increase the oven temperature to 200°C/400°F/Gas Mark 6. Roll out the pastry on a lightly floured surface into a 30 x 37½ cm (12- x 15-inch) rectangle. Lift it on to a lightly greased baking sheet, prick here and there with a fork and bake blind for 18–20 minutes, until crisp and golden. Remove from the oven, carefully turn it over and bake for a further 5 minutes.

Arrange the tomatoes haphazardly over the tart base, leaving a narrow border free around the edge. Crumble over the slices of Blue Vinny, sprinkle over the thyme leaves and drizzle over the olive oil. Return the tart to the oven for 5–6 minutes or until the cheese has melted.

Remove the tart from the oven and scatter the rocket over the top. Cut it into 8 pieces, sprinkle with a little extra virgin olive oil and serve.

Cauliflower cheese

Cauliflower cheese is precisely the sort of British dish that most people secretly adore, but which is so often massively overcooked and under-cheesed that it is regarded as a typical example of how bad our food can be. Imagine, though, if this dish was called something like chou-fleur au tomme de Savoie fermière *and was made from the famous mountain cheese from Savoy: it would probably be a local speciality. A cauliflower cheese that uses good mature cheddar and where the cauliflower is not overcooked and plenty of the pale-green inner leaves are used is a joy.*

SERVES 4

1 large, very fresh cauliflower, weighing about 1 kg (2 lb 4 oz)
Hot-buttered wholemeal toast, to serve
FOR THE CHEESE SAUCE:
1 small onion, peeled and halved
4 cloves
450 ml (¾ pint) full-cream milk
1 bay leaf
½ teaspoon black peppercorns
30 g (1 oz) butter
30 g (1 oz) plain flour
175 g (6 oz) mature cheddar cheese, coarsely grated
3 tablespoons double cream
1 teaspoon English mustard
Salt and freshly ground white pepper

For the cheese sauce, stud the onion halves with the cloves and put them into a pan with the milk, bay leaf and black peppercorns. Bring to the boil, then remove from the heat and set aside for 20 minutes to infuse.

Bring a large pan of well-salted water, 1 teaspoon per 600 ml (1 pint), to the boil. Strain the milk into a jug and discard the flavouring ingredients. Melt the butter in a non-stick pan, add the flour and cook over a medium heat for 1 minute. Remove from the heat and gradually beat in the milk. Return to the heat and bring to the boil, stirring. Leave to simmer very gently for 10 minutes, giving it a stir every now and then.

Meanwhile, preheat the grill to high. Cut the cauliflower into large 7½ cm (2½-inch) florets, discarding the thick cone-shaped core and the larger, tougher green leaves. Drop the cauliflower florets and young green leaves into the boiling water and cook for 8 minutes (this includes the time it takes for the water to come back to the boil) until tender. Drain and leave briefly for the steam to die down.

Remove the sauce from the heat and stir in 100 g (4 oz) of the grated cheese together with the cream, mustard and some seasoning to taste. Arrange the cauliflower leaves and florets in a warmed shallow ovenproof dish and pour over the cheese sauce. Scatter over the rest of the cheese and slide under the grill for 3–4 minutes until golden and bubbling. Serve with plenty of hot, buttered wholemeal toast.

John Dory chowder with mussels and cider

I love white chowders, the creamy fish soups from New England. It's the combination of salt pork (in this case smoked bacon), onion, cream and milk, potato and parsley with some local seafood that is so satisfying. Here, my Cornish version contains some local cider, mussels (perfect if you can gather some from a beach somewhere as they are always pleasingly salty) and John Dory, which is firm, well-flavoured and a very special fish from the West Country. Indeed, so much do I revere the fish that we use it as our restaurant logo.

SERVES 4

500 g (1 lb 2 oz) live mussels, cleaned (page 283)
150 ml (¼ pint) Cornish cider
25 g (1 oz) butter
100 g (4-oz) piece of rindless smoked streaky bacon,
    cut into small cubes
1 small onion, finely chopped
20 g (¾ oz) plain flour
1 litre (1¾ pints) full-cream milk
2 potatoes (about 225 g/8 oz in total), peeled and cubed
1 bay leaf
225 g (8 oz) John Dory fillet, cut into short, chunky strips
120 ml (4 fl oz) double cream
A pinch of cayenne pepper
2 tablespoons chopped parsley
Salt and freshly ground white pepper

Put the cleaned mussels (see page 283) and cider into a medium-sized pan over a high heat. Cover and cook for 2–3 minutes or until they have just opened, shaking the pan occasionally. Then tip them into a colander set over a bowl to collect the juices. Leave to cool slightly and then remove the meats from the shells, cover and set aside. Discard the shells.

Melt the butter in another pan, add the bacon and fry until lightly golden. Add the onion and cook gently for 5 minutes or until the onion has softened.

Stir in the flour and cook for 1 minute. Gradually stir in the milk and then add all but the last tablespoon or two of the mussel cooking liquor (the last drops might be a bit gritty), the potatoes and bay leaf and 1 teaspoon of salt and leave to simmer gently for 10 minutes or until the potatoes are just tender.

Remove the bay leaf, add the pieces of John Dory and simmer for 2–3 minutes or until the fish is just cooked.

Stir in the cream and season to taste with cayenne pepper, salt and white pepper. Remove from the heat and stir in the mussels, to warm them through just briefly, and most of the chopped parsley. Serve in warmed bowls, sprinkled with the rest of the parsley.

Salad of Lancashire cheese with pancetta in balsamic vinegar and chilli beetroot

I call this my 'ladies who lunch' salad. It's absolutely necessary these days to list a few big plates of salad on our menus for those who don't want to eat too much, normally for dieting reasons and normally, therefore, for girls. Most of the women I know would choose something like this at lunch with low-calorie ingredients. In this case, a small amount of pancetta and cheese is tossed with lots of salad leaves and thinly sliced beetroot pickled in a garlic and chilli vinegar. Mrs Kirkham's Lancashire cheese is perfect for this, being quite surprisingly piquant, but, if you can't get it, parmesan is very good too. At the restaurant we also do this as a vegetarian dish and change the pancetta to thinly sliced aubergine, which we lightly salt, steep in olive oil and thyme leaves, and chargrill.

SERVES 4

2 x 50 g (2 oz) cooked beetroot
3 tablespoons sherry vinegar
A small garlic clove, finely chopped
1 teaspoon caster sugar
¼ teaspoon dried chilli flakes
225 g (8 oz) Lancashire or parmesan cheese
4 tablespoons extra virgin olive oil
75 g (3 oz) thinly sliced smoked pancetta
1 tablespoon balsamic vinegar
100 g (4 oz) mixed baby salad leaves, such as lambs'
    lettuce, baby beet leaves and rocket
Sea salt and freshly ground black pepper
A few small flat-leaf parsley leaves

Halve the beetroot and cut it into thin slices. Put them into a small bowl, with the sherry vinegar, garlic, sugar, chilli flakes and ½ teaspoon of salt, and leave for 1 hour.

Thinly slice the cheese and crumble it into smallish pieces. Put a little olive oil in a heavy-based frying pan and fry the pancetta (in batches if necessary) on each side until crisp and golden. Add the balsamic vinegar and allow it to bubble away to nothing. Remove the pancetta from the pan, leave it to cool, and then break it into small, chunky pieces.

To serve, toss the salad leaves with the remaining olive oil and a little seasoning to taste. Pile on to 4 large plates and tuck the bacon, beetroot and cheese in amongst the leaves. Sprinkle over the parsley leaves and serve immediately.

Poached salmon with cucumber and dill salad

The point of this dish is the exact cooking of the salmon. It is so much better when it is slightly undercooked, so I've given very precise instructions. It goes without saying that the salmon should be of the highest quality, wild or organically farmed, and perfectly fresh. The cucumber and dill salad is a memory of my childhood. I don't know why it is, but I can never completely recapture the flavours of my mother's cooking; maybe it's got something to do with nostalgia.

SERVES 8

1 kg (2¼ lb) salmon fillet
FOR THE *COURT-BOUILLON*:
3 litres (5¼ pints) water
100 g (4 oz) bulb fennel, sliced
1 onion, sliced
3 bay leaves
1 teaspoon black peppercorns
300 ml (½ pint) white wine
1 tablespoon salt
FOR THE SALAD:
2 cucumbers
4 tablespoons white wine vinegar
2 tablespoons chopped dill
1 tablespoon caster sugar
½ teaspoon salt

For the *court-bouillon*, put all the ingredients into a saucepan and bring to the boil. Leave to simmer for 10 minutes and then strain into a deep roasting tin in which the fish fillet will fit. Place directly over the heat, bring up to the boil and then slide in the salmon, skin side up. Bring back to a simmer, simmer for just 1 minute and then turn off the heat and leave the fish to poach in the cooling liquid.

By the time the liquid has cooled down the fish will be cooked – it should register about 50°C at the centre of the thickest part. Carefully lift the fish out, drain away the excess liquid and then place on an oval serving plate. Peel away the skin and then cover the fish with cling film. Keep it cool, but do not refrigerate it.

For the salad, peel the cucumbers and cut them into thin slices. Place a layer of the cucumber slices over the base of a shallow portable dish and sprinkle with a little of the vinegar, chopped dill, sugar and salt. Continue to layer up the cucumber slices like this until all the ingredients are used up. Cover and chill until ready to serve the salmon.

Goujons of lemon sole
with parmesan breadcrumbs

I can't think of a better fish for goujons than lemon sole – its flavour seems to compliment speedy deep-frying in a breadcrumb coating perfectly – but all of the cheaper flat fish, such as flounder, plaice and dab are almost improved by deep frying. The word 'goujon' is French for the small freshwater fish the gudgeon, which is approximately the right size for them. Incidentally, they are kept in large tanks in water-quality laboratories, as they can detect impurities in water like no other and change sex if things aren't to their liking.

SERVES 4

450 g (1 lb) skinned lemon sole fillets
100 g (4 oz) fresh white breadcrumbs
25 g (1 oz) parmesan cheese, finely grated
½ teaspoon cayenne pepper
Sunflower oil, for deep-frying
50 g (2 oz) plain flour
3 eggs, beaten
Sea salt
Lemon wedges, to serve

Cut each lemon sole fillet diagonally across into strips about the thickness of a man's finger – about 2½ cm (1 inch) across. Mix the breadcrumbs with the grated parmesan and cayenne pepper and set aside.

Heat some oil for deep-frying to 190°C/375°F or until a cube of day-old bread will brown in about a minute. Line a baking tray with plenty of kitchen paper.

Coat the goujons a few at a time in the flour, then in beaten egg and finally in the breadcrumb mixture, making sure that they all take on an even coating and remain separate.

Drop a small handful of goujons into the oil and deep-fry for about 1 minute until crisp and golden. Lift out with a slotted spoon on to the paper-lined tray to drain and repeat with the remainder, making sure the oil has come back to temperature first.

Pile the goujons on to 4 warmed plates and garnish with the lemon wedges. If you like, serve with a mixed whole leaf or herb salad, dressed with a little extra virgin olive oil and some seasoning.

Roast chicken with parsley and tarragon, poached Puy lentils and roasted vine tomatoes

I wrote this recipe as a way of making a simple roast chicken something a bit more memorable for a special occasion. A lot of the time, poultry recipes call for some sort of aromatic stuffing, but I don't think this really imbues the flesh with flavour. Far better to work a flavoured butter of garlic, parsley, tarragon and chives under the skin. It also looks extremely attractive when you slice the roast chicken with a band of green next to the moist white meat. I've accompanied the dish with some roasted tomatoes with olive oil and thyme and some puy lentils into which I've stirred the cooking juices from the chicken.

SERVES 4

1¾ kg (3¾ lb) free-range chicken
5 tablespoons mixed chopped parsley, tarragon and chives
2 garlic cloves, crushed
½ teaspoon salt
2 teaspoons lemon juice
Coarsely ground black pepper
60 g (2 oz) softened butter

FOR THE PUY LENTILS:
25 g (1 oz) butter
60 g (generous 2 oz) finely chopped onion
2 garlic cloves, finely chopped
250 g (9 oz) Puy lentils
½ teaspoon salt
450 ml (¾ pint) *chicken stock* (page 278)
1 teaspoon thyme leaves

FOR THE ROASTED TOMATOES:
450 g (1 lb) small vine-ripened tomatoes, still on the vine
2–3 tablespoons olive oil
Sea salt flakes and coarsely ground black pepper

Preheat the oven to 220°C/425°F/Gas Mark 7. Mix the chopped herbs, garlic, salt, lemon juice and black pepper into 50 g (2 oz) of the butter. Starting at the neck end of the chicken, slip your fingers beneath the skin and carefully loosen it over the breasts, taking care not to tear it. Push the herb butter under the skin, spreading it as evenly as you can over the meat of each breast. Truss the chicken into a neat shape. Melt the rest of the butter and brush over the chicken and the base of a small roasting tin. Put the chicken into the tin, season with salt and pepper and roast for 15 minutes. Then lower the oven temperature to 200°C/400°F/Gas Mark 6 and continue to roast for 1 hour and 15 minutes (15 minutes per 450 g/1 lb plus 15 minutes), covering loosely with a sheet of foil once it is nicely golden. Because the skin has been detached from the rest of the bird it tends to brown a little more quickly than usual.

Meanwhile, for the lentils, melt the butter in a medium-sized pan. Add the onion and garlic and fry gently until soft and lightly golden. Add the lentils, salt and stock, cover and simmer for 20 minutes. Add the thyme leaves, recover and continue to cook for a further 5 minutes until tender.

When the chicken is cooked, remove it from the oven and increase the oven temperature to 240°C/500°F/Gas Mark 9. Pour the juices from the chicken cavity into the roasting tin, transfer the chicken to a baking tray, cover loosely with foil and leave somewhere warm to rest for 15 minutes before carving.

Put the vine tomatoes, still attached to the stalk, into another small roasting tin and rub with the olive oil. Sprinkle with the salt and pepper and roast on the top shelf of the oven for 5 minutes.

Meanwhile, separate the butter from the chicken juices and stir 2 tablespoons of it into the lentils. Discard the rest. Pour the juices into a small pan and bring to a gentle simmer. Carve the chicken, divide it between 4 warmed plates and spoon over some of the juices. Serve with the Puy lentils and roasted tomatoes.

North Atlantic prawn pilaf

This uses ingredients you can get from any fishmonger or supermarket. I really want this book to be used every day. This is a nice, gentle dish, ideal for supper with a glass of New Zealand Chardonnay.

SERVES 4

800 g (1 lb 12 oz) unpeeled, cooked North Atlantic prawns
50 g (2 oz) butter
1 small onion, chopped
1 small carrot, roughly chopped
½ teaspoon tomato purée
900 ml (1½ pints) *chicken stock* (page 278)
350g (12 oz) basmati rice
2 shallots, finely chopped
1 garlic clove, very finely chopped
3 cloves
3 green cardamom pods
1 cinnamon stick, broken into 4 pieces
¼ teaspoon ground turmeric
3 tablespoons chopped coriander
3 plum tomatoes, skinned, seeded and diced (page 283)
Sea salt and freshly ground black pepper

Peel the prawns but keep the heads and shells. Put the prawns on a plate and set aside.

Heat 25 g (1 oz) of the butter in a large pan, add the onion and carrot and fry over a medium heat for 6–7 minutes, until lightly browned. Add the prawn heads and shells and continue to fry for 3–4 minutes. Add the tomato purée and chicken stock, bring to the boil and simmer for 15 minutes. Strain into a measuring jug; if there is more than 600 ml (1 pint), return it to the clean pan and boil rapidly until reduced to this amount.

Meanwhile, rinse the rice in a few changes of cold water until the water runs relatively clear. Cover with fresh water and leave to soak for 7 minutes. Drain well.

Melt the rest of the butter in a saucepan and add the shallots, garlic, cloves, cardamom pods, cinnamon stick and turmeric and fry gently for 5 minutes. Add the rice and stir well to coat the rice with the spicy butter. Add the stock to the pan, season with salt and bring to the boil, then turn the heat right down to the slightest simmer, put a lid on the pan and leave to simmer for 10 minutes. Don't lift the lid during this time.

Uncover and gently stir in the peeled prawns, coriander, diced tomatoes and some seasoning to taste. Re-cover and leave for 5 minutes to warm through. Then spoon into a warmed serving dish and serve.

Smoked haddock and leek tart

I can never enthuse enough about smoked haddock, but you have to have a good supplier because good smoked haddock is only very lightly cured in salt and therefore doesn't keep for a particularly long time. But when it is good, it is sublime. Curiously enough, the idea for what is essentially a quiche came on one of my Food Heroes trips to Ireland, when we were following up a story about the popularity around Belfast of a vegetable soup made with leeks, carrots, herb celery, dried peas, pearl barley and lentils called, rather prosaically, 'soup veg soup'. I was standing in a field of leeks, marvelling at the thickness of them and thinking deeply about the indefinable affinity that they have with seafood, when my mind then wandered over to a time when I spent a couple of weeks wandering around various food producers in West Cork and Kerry. I remember visiting a number of smokeries and marvelling at the smoked haddock there, and the idea of combining smoked haddock and leeks in a pleasingly comforting Irish sort of dish came to mind. I'm very happy to report that two of those suppliers are still doing very well: Frank Hederman from Cobh and Sally Barnes of Woodcock Smokery in Castletownshend.

SERVES 6-8

20 g (¾ oz) butter
225 g (8 oz) leeks, washed and thinly sliced
350 g (12 oz) undyed smoked haddock
A small bunch of chives, chopped
3 large eggs
300 ml (10 fl oz) double cream
15 g (½ oz) parmesan cheese, finely grated
Sea salt and freshly ground black pepper

FOR THE RICH SHORTCRUST PASTRY:

225 g (8 oz) plain flour
½ teaspoon salt
65 g (2½ oz) chilled butter, cut into pieces
65 g (2½ oz) chilled lard, cut into pieces
1½ –2 tablespoons cold water

For the rich shortcrust pastry, sift the flour and salt into a food processor or mixing bowl. Add the pieces of chilled butter and lard and work together until the mixture looks like fine breadcrumbs. Stir in the water with a round-bladed knife, until the mixture comes together into a ball and then turn out on to a lightly floured work surface and knead briefly until smooth.

Roll out the pastry thinly on a little more flour and use to line a 4 cm (1½-inch) deep, loose-bottomed 25 cm (10-inch) flan tin. Prick the base here and there with a fork and chill for 20 minutes.

Meanwhile, melt the butter in a large pan, add the leeks and some seasoning and cook gently, uncovered, for 15 minutes, giving them a stir every now and then, until they are very tender. Adjust the seasoning if necessary.

Bring some water to the boil in a large shallow pan. Add the smoked haddock and simmer for 4 minutes, until the fish is just cooked. Lift the fish out on to a plate and leave until cool enough to handle. Then break it into flakes, discarding any skin and bones.

Preheat the oven to 200°C/400°F/Gas Mark 6. Line the pastry case with greaseproof paper and baking beans and bake blind for 15 minutes. Remove the paper and beans and return to the oven for 5 minutes, until lightly golden. The pastry case, leeks and smoked haddock can all be prepared in advance to this stage. Leave the pastry case to cool and then store in an air-tight container and keep the leeks and smoked haddock chilled until needed.

To cook the tart, preheat the oven to 190°C/375°F/Gas Mark 5. Stir half the chopped chives into the leeks and spoon them over the base of the pastry case. Toss the rest of the chives through the flaked smoked haddock and scatter it over the top. (This helps to stop all the chives from floating to the top during cooking.) Beat the eggs with the cream, parmesan cheese and some salt and black pepper and pour over the leeks and smoked haddock. Bake the tart for 30–35 minutes, until just set and lightly browned on top. Remove from the oven and leave to cool slightly before serving.

Haddock and Cornish Yarg pie
with a potato pastry crust

Fish pies are always incredibly popular. This one is a result of my continuing attempts to try and produce some genuinely local dishes. Here I've used all local fish and vegetables and that excellent cheese, Cornish Yarg, which is mild and firm and particularly suited to a pie like this. If you can't get Cornish Yarg, use a mild Cheddar.

SERVES 6

600 ml (1 pint) milk
300 ml (10 fl oz) *fish stock* (page 279)
750 g (1½ lb) haddock fillet
275 g (10 oz) leeks
65 g (2½ oz) butter
50 g (2 oz) carrot, finely diced
50 g (2 oz) celery, finely diced
50 g (2 oz) onion, finely chopped
40 g (1½ oz) rindless smoked streaky bacon,
    thinly sliced
50 g (2 oz) plain flour
100 g (4 oz) cooked, peeled prawns
100 g (4 oz) Cornish Yarg cheese, grated
Freshly grated nutmeg
Sea salt and freshly ground black pepper
FOR THE *BOUQUET GARNI*:
1 bay leaf
A small bunch of parsley, with stalks
Leaves from the centre of 1 head of celery
1 small sprig of thyme
FOR THE POTATO PASTRY CRUST:
325 g (12 oz) floury potatoes such as Maris Pipers,
    peeled and cut into chunks
225 g (8 oz) self-raising flour
1 teaspoon salt
175 g (6 oz) cold butter, cut into small pieces
2 tablespoons cold water
1 egg, beaten
Freshly ground black pepper

For the pastry, cook the potatoes in boiling, salted water until tender. Drain well and either mash or pass through a potato ricer. Leave to cool.

Meanwhile, put the milk and fish stock (see page 279) into a large pan and bring to the boil. Add the haddock and simmer for 5–7 minutes, until firm and opaque. Lift the fish out on to a plate and, when cool enough to handle, break the flesh into large flakes, discarding any skin and bones.

Clean the leeks, finely dice 50 g (2 oz) of them and set aside. Thinly slice the remainder. Melt 25 g (1 oz) of the butter in a clean pan, add the sliced leeks and fry gently for 2–3 minutes, until just cooked. Lift out with a slotted spoon and set aside.

Add the diced leek, carrot, celery, onion and bacon to the pan with a little more of the butter if necessary. Fry over a gentle heat for 10 minutes without letting them brown. Add the remaining butter to the vegetables, stir in the flour and cook for 1 minute. Remove the pan from the heat and gradually add the cooking liquid from the haddock, stirring all the time to make a smooth sauce. Bring to the boil, stirring. Tie together all the ingredients for the *bouquet garni* and add to the pan. Simmer gently for 30 minutes, then remove the *bouquet garni* from the pan and season the sauce with nutmeg, salt and pepper.

Stir the flaked fish, reserved leeks, prawns and Cornish Yarg into the sauce, spoon into a deep 1¾-litre (3-pint) pie dish and push a pie funnel into the centre of the mixture. Set aside to cool.

Meanwhile, for the pastry, sift the flour, salt and pepper into a bowl. Add the butter and rub it in with your fingertips until the mixture looks like fine breadcrumbs. Add the cold potato and lightly mix into the flour, then add the water and stir with a round-bladed knife until everything starts to stick together. Form it into a ball, turn out on to a lightly floured work surface and knead briefly until smooth. Chill for 20–30 minutes.

Preheat the oven to 200°C/400°F/Gas Mark 6.

Roll out the pastry on a floured surface until it is slightly larger than the top of the pie dish. Cut a thin strip off the edge of the pastry, brush with a little water and press it on to the rim of the pie dish. Brush with a little more water. Make a small cut in the centre of the remaining pastry and then lay it over the pie so that the pie funnel pokes through the cut. Press it on to the rim of the dish and crimp the edge decoratively with your fingers. Brush the top with beaten egg and decorate with leaves cut from the pastry trimmings if you wish. Bake in the oven for 35–40 minutes, until the pastry is crisp and golden.

Stein's classic Cornish steak pasty

If you don't wish to make the pastry, use 1 kg (2 lb 4 oz) of ready-made puff pastry instead.

150 g (5 oz) peeled swede
250 g (9 oz) peeled floury potatoes
150 g (5 oz) onion, chopped
400 g (14 oz) chuck steak, cut into 1cm (½-inch) pieces
1 egg, beaten
Salt and freshly ground black pepper
FOR THE PASTRY:
150 g (5 oz) strong plain flour
300 g (10 oz) plain flour
½ teaspoon salt
50 g (2 oz) butter
225 g (8 oz) chilled white vegetable shortening,
    cut into very small pieces
225 ml (8 fl oz) cold water

For the pastry, sift the flours and salt into a bowl, add the butter and rub it in with your fingers to fine crumbs. Stir in the vegetable shortening, followed by the water and bring everything together into a soft dough. Knead briefly until smooth, wrap in cling film and chill for 30 minutes.

Unwrap the dough and roll it out on a lightly floured surface into a long, thin rectangle about 1 cm (½ inch) thick. Fold up the bottom one third and then fold down the top one third and roll out once more. Repeat this process until all the pieces of fat have disappeared. Fold up the dough once more, wrap it in cling film and chill for another 30 minutes.

For the filling, cut the swede and potatoes into 1 cm (½-inch) thick slices, then each slice lengthways into 1 cm (½-inch) thick 'chips'. Cut these across into 5 mm (¼-inch) thick pieces. Mix the swede, potatoes, onion and steak together in a bowl with 1 teaspoon of salt and ¾ teaspoon freshly ground black pepper.

Roll out the dough once more on a floured surface until it measures 3 mm thick and cut out six 20 cm (8-inch) discs. Spoon one sixth of the mixture into the centre of each pastry disc and lightly brush the edge of one half of the pastry disc with water. Bring the edges together over the top of the filling and press together well. Then, working from left to right, fold in the corner and then fold 2½ cm (1¼ inches) of the edge inwards. Fold over the next 2½ cm (1¼ inches) and continue like this along the edge, to create a rope-like design which will seal the pasty. Chill for 1 hour.

Preheat the oven to 180°C/350°F/Gas 4. Transfer the pasties to a greased baking sheet and brush them with beaten egg. Bake for 1 hour, turning them around after 30 minutes so that they all brown evenly. Serve warm.

Warm salad of pan-fried pheasant breasts with watercress and potatoes

The particularly peppery tang of watercress is what makes this salad such a pleasure, that and the use of pheasant breasts. A good game butcher should be able to supply them.

SERVES 4

225 g (8 oz) small floury potatoes, such as Maris Piper
15 g (½ oz) butter
3 tablespoons olive oil
2 x 175–225 g (6–8 oz) pheasant breasts
75 g (3 oz) watercress sprigs
½ small red onion, thinly sliced
1 tablespoon chopped chives
Sea salt and freshly ground black pepper

FOR THE DRESSING:
1 small shallot, finely chopped
½ garlic clove, finely chopped
2 tablespoons sherry vinegar
2 teaspoons walnut oil
2 tablespoons olive oil
1 teaspoon chopped chives

Peel the potatoes, cut them in half lengthways and then cut each half across into 5 mm (¼-inch) thick slices. Drop them into a pan of boiling salted water and cook for 2–3 minutes, until just tender. Drain well.

Heat the butter and 1 tablespoon of the olive oil in a heavy-based frying pan, add the potato pieces and sauté until golden brown and sandy on the outside. Season with some salt and pepper, remove from the pan and keep warm.

Brush the pheasant breasts on both sides with the remaining olive oil and season with some salt and pepper. Heat the cleaned frying pan over a high heat. Add the pheasant breasts, skin side down, and sear briefly on both sides until they have taken on a good colour. Then lower the heat to medium, cover and cook gently for 5–6 minutes on each side until just cooked through. Lift on to a plate, cover and leave to rest for 5 minutes.

For the dressing, add the shallot and garlic to the pan and fry for just a few seconds, then add the vinegar and loosen all the caramelised juices from the base of the pan with a wooden spoon. Tip the mixture into a bowl and whisk in the walnut oil, olive oil, chives, ½ teaspoon of salt and some black pepper.

Lift the pheasant breasts on to a board and carve each one into thin slices.

To assemble the salad, place a few sprigs of watercress and some slices of onion in the centre of 4 plates. Add a few slices of the pheasant and a few sautéed potatoes. Scatter over some more watercress and onion, drizzle over the dressing and sprinkle with some chopped chives. Serve immediately.

Roast rib of beef with Yorkshire puddings and roasties

The method for roasting any joint of meat is always the same. Start it in a very hot oven for half an hour or so, to brown and flavour the surface, then reduce the temperature to about 160°C/325°F/Gas Mark 3 to complete the roasting. Cooking at this lower temperature reduces the amount of moisture loss, giving you much juicier slices of beef. It is also very important to remember to rest your joint for between 15 minutes and half an hour before carving it. This allows the moisture in the beef to settle back into the meat.

SERVES 8

2-rib of beef, weighing about 2½ kg (5½ lb), chined but not trimmed
1 onion, thickly sliced
Oil, for brushing
1½ teaspoons plain flour
Sea salt and freshly ground black pepper
Horseradish sauce, to serve
FOR THE YORKSHIRE PUDDINGS:
225 g (8 oz) plain flour
½ teaspoon salt
4 eggs
300 ml (½ pint) full-cream milk
150 ml (¼ pint) water
FOR THE ROAST POTATOES:
1¾ kg (4 lb) floury potatoes, such as Maris Piper or King Edwards, peeled
250 g (9 oz) goose fat

Preheat the oven to 230°C/475°F/Gas Mark 8. Put the potatoes into a pan of well-salted water (1 teaspoon per 600 ml/1 pint), bring to the boil and simmer for 8–10 minutes, until soft on the outside but still slightly hard in the centre. Drain off the cooking liquid, reserving 600 ml (1 pint) for the gravy, and leave the potatoes aside to dry off. Meanwhile, put the goose fat in a large roasting tin in which the potatoes will fit in a single layer and slide it on to the bottom shelf of the oven for 5 minutes to become hot. Return the potatoes to the pan, cover with a lid and shake gently to rough up their edges a little. Remove the roasting tin of hot fat from the oven, add the potatoes and turn them over once or twice until they are all well coated. Drain away any surplus fat from the tin and return to the oven.

Now weigh the joint of beef and calculate the cooking time, allowing 10 minutes per 500 g (1 lb 2 oz) for very rare, 12 minutes per 500 g (1 lb 2 oz) for rare, 15 minutes for medium and 20 minutes for well done. Put the onion into the centre of another roasting tin. Rub the joint of beef with oil and season all over with ½ teaspoon salt and pepper. Place on top of the onion and put it on to the top shelf of the oven. Roast for 30 minutes to brown the meat well.

Swap the beef and potatoes around so that the potatoes are now on the top shelf and lower the oven temperature to 160°C/325°F/Gas Mark 3. Continue to roast for the calculated cooking times – so 50 minutes for a 2½ kg (5½ lb) joint that is to be served very rare.

After the beef has been cooking at the lower temperature for 20 minutes, make the Yorkshire pudding batter. Sift the flour and salt into a bowl, make a well in the centre, break in the eggs and, using a wire whisk, beat them together well, gradually beating in the milk and water to make a smooth batter, making sure that it is free of lumps and has the consistency of double cream. Set aside for 30 minutes.

Remove the beef from the oven and lift it on to a carving board. Increase the oven temperature to 220°C/425°F/Gas Mark 7. Cover the beef with foil and leave it to rest in a warm place for 30 minutes. Pour the excess fat from the roasting tin into a small bowl. Spoon ½ teaspoon of the beef fat into each compartment of a 12-hole muffin tray. Move the roast potatoes again, to a lower shelf and slide the muffin tray on to the top shelf (remember that the Yorkshires will rise a lot so you may need to lower the shelf a bit). Leave for 5 minutes until the fat is very hot and then remove carefully and pour enough batter into each hole to fill it three-quarters full. Return the tray to the oven and cook for 25–30 minutes until puffed up and golden. Don't open the door for at least the first 15 minutes!

Now make the gravy. Place the beef-roasting tin directly over a medium heat on the hob and, if the onions are not already richly caramelised, cook them for a few more minutes until they are. Sprinkle in the flour, stir well and then add a little of the reserved potato cooking water and scrape the base of the tin with a wooden spoon to release all the caramelised cooking juices. Gradually add the rest of the potato water and simmer until reduced to a well-flavoured gravy. Strain into a clean pan, season to taste and keep hot.

Uncover the beef and pour any juices from the carving tray into the gravy. Carve the beef into thin slices. Carving a joint of beef on the bone is not as difficult as it may seem. If you like, first remove the thinner, fatty flap of meat from the top of the joint. Then run your knife between the bones and the eye of the meat, in an L-shaped motion, and remove it in one piece to a board for slicing, along with the thinner flap. Alternatively, if you like carving at the table, it looks much more theatrical if you carve the meat off the bone, in which case cut between the meat and the chine bone (backbone) and remove this bone. Now slice between the meat and the rib bones to release it but leave the bones in place. You will now be able to cut away neat slices of meat.

Serve the roast beef on warmed plates with the Yorkshire puddings, roast potatoes, ideally some type of brassica, the gravy and some horseradish sauce.

Grilled salted cod with beer, bacon and cabbage

This recipe comes from a chef who has, sadly, left us to run a pub and restaurant in the Home Counties. His name is Jason Fretwell and he was a very inventive chef who was keen on British food. This was one of his best dishes. He also had a great recipe for a steamed fish pudding, which I must get from him some time. You could also make this with haddock or hake and it also works quite well with really thick fillets of plaice or lemon sole, folded over themselves to look like one thick fillet.

SERVES 4

4 x 175 g (6 oz) pieces of unskinned, thick cod fillet
50 g (2 oz) butter
1 small Savoy cabbage, weighing about 750 g (1½ lb),
   cored and thinly sliced
2 tablespoons sunflower oil
75 g (3 oz) rindless smoked streaky bacon,
   cut into thin strips
1 onion, finely chopped
1 garlic clove, very finely chopped
300 ml (10 fl oz) *chicken stock* (page 278)
300 ml (10 fl oz) pale ale
2 tablespoons chopped parsley, plus extra to garnish
Sea salt and freshly ground black pepper

Place the cod skin side down on a plate and sprinkle heavily with salt. Leave for 20 minutes and then rinse the salt off and dry on kitchen paper. Melt 25 g (1 oz) of the butter. Brush the cod with a little of the butter and sprinkle the skin with salt and pepper.

Put the cabbage into a large pan of boiling, salted water and bring back to the boil. Drain and refresh under cold running water.

Heat the oil in a large, heavy-based pan, add the bacon and fry over a high heat until crisp and lightly golden. Add the rest of the melted butter, onion and garlic and fry for 5 minutes, until the onion is soft and lightly browned. Add the chicken stock and beer to the pan and reduce the volume of liquid by three-quarters over a high heat. Add the cabbage and the rest of the butter and cook gently for a further 5 minutes until the cabbage is tender. Season to taste with salt and pepper, add the parsley and keep warm.

Preheat the grill to high. Grill the cod for 8 minutes on one side only, until the skin is crisp and the fish is cooked through. Put the cabbage in 4 large, warmed soup plates. Sprinkle the skin of the cod with a little sea salt, coarsely ground black pepper and chopped parsley, place on top of the cabbage and serve.

Raspberry cranachan

I was asked to cook dinner for the Queen and the Duke of Edinburgh at 10 Downing Street a few years ago as part of the Golden Jubilee celebrations. I was, however, somewhat stumped by the request for one of the courses to have a golden theme. Perhaps dourade royale – gilt-headed bream – or something with gold leaf in it? Not really me, I felt. Then I remembered the Scottish whipped cream, oatmeal and honey dessert called cranachan which often has a little touch of whisky in it, and so I thought to use Chivas Regal and then make it with golden raspberries. It's equally good made with ordinary red raspberries and a drop of single malt, such as Springbank.

SERVES 4

50 g (2 oz) medium oatmeal
300 ml (10 fl oz) double cream
3 tablespoons clear honey, heather if possible
2 tablespoons whisky
350 g (12 oz) raspberries

Preheat the grill to medium. Spread the oatmeal on a grilling tray and toast, turning occasionally, until golden brown. Remove and leave to cool.

Whip the cream in a large bowl until it just begins to thicken, then whisk in the honey and whisky until the mixture forms very soft peaks. Fold in most of the oatmeal and then lightly fold in most of the raspberries, so that some of them still show through the cream.

Spoon the mixture into 4 glasses and then sprinkle with a little more oatmeal. Serve immediately.

Treacle tart with clotted cream ice cream

There's not a lot to say about the raw materials in my treacle tart – it's just fresh breadcrumbs, lemon juice, golden syrup and shortcrust pastry. The success of a good treacle tart is getting the right ratio of fresh white breadcrumbs to syrup and the right amount of lemon juice. That and a good ice cream, like a Cornish clotted cream ice cream. I have a wistful memory of making treacle tarts. In the very early days of The Seafood Restaurant, I would always leave the making of them to the last minute; not a great idea but typical of me, I'm afraid. I remember on one occasion, after a particularly busy lunch, I had to make three of them immediately after I'd finished service, for that evening. They were on the wires of the old six-burner cooker, which was the only stove I had when we started, when Roger, a builder friend of mine, came into the kitchen and yelled something at me. I turned round and dropped all three tarts. I was so exhausted at the time that I've never forgotten it. Another memory is of a perfect lunch in the 60s at the Shipwrights Inn in Padstow – a large kipper followed by sublime treacle tart with clotted cream and a pint of St Austell Ordinary.

SERVES 8-10

725 g (1½ lb) golden syrup
Juice of ½ lemon
175 g (6 oz) coarse fresh white breadcrumbs
FOR THE PASTRY CASE:
225 g (8 oz) plain flour
½ teaspoon salt
65 g (2½ oz) chilled unsalted butter, cut
    into pieces
65 g (2½ oz) chilled lard, cut into pieces
1½–2 tablespoons cold water
FOR THE CLOTTED CREAM ICE CREAM:
600 ml (1 pint) full-cream milk
225 g (8 oz) clotted cream
1 vanilla pod, slit open lengthways
6 egg yolks
75 g (3 oz) caster sugar

For the ice cream, put the milk and clotted cream into a pan. Scrape out the seeds from the vanilla pod, add the pod and seeds to the milk and cream and almost bring to the boil. Set aside for 20 minutes.

Cream the egg yolks and sugar together in a bowl. Bring the milk and cream back to the boil, strain on to the egg yolks and whisk in. Strain the mixture once more back into a clean pan and cook over a gentle heat, stirring consistently, until the mixture has thickened and lightly coats the back of a spoon. Pour into a bowl and leave to cool; then chill in the fridge until quite cold (overnight if possible).

Churn the mixture in an ice cream maker until smooth. Transfer to a plastic box, cover and freeze for 6 hours or until needed.

For the pastry, sift the flour and salt into a food processor or a mixing bowl. Add the pieces of butter and lard and work together, either in the food processor or with your fingertips, until the mixture looks like fine breadcrumbs. Stir in the water with a round-bladed knife (or process very briefly) until it comes together into a ball, then turn out on to a lightly floured surface and knead briefly until smooth. Roll out and use to line a loose-bottomed flan tin that measures 23 cm (9 inches) across the base and is 4 cm (1¾ inches) deep. Chill for 20 minutes.

Preheat the oven to 200°C/400°F/Gas Mark 6. Line the pastry case with a crumpled sheet of greaseproof paper and a thin layer of baking beans and bake blind for 15 minutes. Remove the paper and beans and return to the oven for 5–6 minutes or until the edges are biscuit-coloured. Remove and lower the oven temperature to 180°C/350°F/Gas Mark 4.

Stand the tin of golden syrup in a pan of hot water until it has gone liquid and then measure out your required amount into the dried-out pan. Stir in the lemon juice. Tip the breadcrumbs into the pastry case and spread them out evenly. Carefully spoon over the warm syrup and allow it to sink in and saturate the bread. Bake for 25–30 minutes, until set and golden brown. Leave to cool in the tin for 15 minutes. Transfer to a serving plate and serve, cut into wedges, with scoops of the clotted cream ice cream.

Blackberry and toasted oatmeal dacquoise

A dacquoise is a three-layer meringue gateaux sandwiched together with whipped cream, blueberries and blackberry purée. It's normal to flavour the meringue with toasted nuts, but I've found that oatmeal is a delightful alternative here.

SERVES 8

FOR THE OATMEAL MERINGUE:
50 g (2 oz) pinhead oatmeal
175 g (6 oz) caster sugar, plus 2 tablespoons
3 large, very fresh egg whites
Icing sugar, for dusting

FOR THE FILLING:
450 g (1 lb) blackberries
75 g (3 oz) caster sugar
300 ml (½ pint) double cream

Preheat the oven to 180°C/350°F/Gas Mark 4. Spread the oatmeal out on a baking tray and sprinkle with the 2 tablespoons of caster sugar. Toast in the oven for 15 minutes until golden. Transfer to a plate and leave to cool. Lower the oven temperature to 110°C/200°F/Gas Mark ¼.

Line 1 large or 2 smaller baking sheets with non-stick baking parchment and mark a 20 cm (8-inch) circle on each. In a large bowl, whisk the egg whites into stiff peaks. Gradually whisk in the rest of the sugar to make a stiff, glossy meringue, then fold in all but 1 tablespoon of the toasted oatmeal.

Divide the meringue equally between the baking sheets and spread the mixture out within the marked circles to make 2 discs. Sprinkle one disc with the rest of the toasted oatmeal. Bake for 2 hours, then turn off the oven and leave them to go cold inside the oven.

Fill the dacquoise 1–2 hours before serving. Put 300 g (11 oz) of the blackberries into a liquidiser or food processor with the sugar and blend until smooth. Then press through a sieve into a bowl to remove all the seeds.

Whip the cream into soft peaks. Put the plain meringue disc on a flat serving plate and spread with the whipped cream. Scatter with the blackberries and then drizzle over 4 tablespoons of the blackberry purée. Cover with the oatmeal-covered disc and chill in the fridge for 1–2 hours, to allow time for the meringue layers to soften slightly.

To serve, dust the top lightly with icing sugar and cut into thin wedges with a sharp, serrated knife. Serve with the remaining blackberry purée and some extra pouring cream if you wish.

The blueprint for my main restaurant in Padstow, *The Seafood Restaurant*, is to be found in any of those small places you find on the coast of Brittany or Normandy. It tries to recall the joy of finding a little village somewhere near Brest where they have plates of moules, *fines de claire* oysters, John Dory, maybe with with boulangère potatoes, or perhaps some Normandy turbot with a cider sauce and always a platter of *fruits de mer*. This is a collection of molluscs, like mussels and clams, winkles and whelks, with crabs, prawns and lobster, served up with a thick mustard mayonnaise, made with vegetable oil, never olive oil, and a little bowl of red wine vinegar and finely chopped shallots. The food of our nearest neighbours has had, not unnaturally, the most influence on me. In spite of all my roaming, I still feel that French food is the most satisfying of all the great cuisines. It's become popular to remark that it isn't what it used to be due to the encroachment of convenience food, which affects us all, but it can still be breathtaking. The cooking of Western Europe is what I like to eat most. Indeed the menu at our bistro *St Petroc's* is built around this affection: *Carbonnade of beef* (see page 65), *Gravlax* (see page 56), risottos, comforting soups like *Garbure béarnaise* (see page 77) or *Soupe au pistou* (see page 59), Spanish dishes such as *Chorizo and butter bean stew* (see page 78), Portuguese dishes such as the *Barbecued sardines with piri piri oil* (see page 66), and puddings such as *Coeurs à la crème* (see page 89) or *Beignets soufflés* (see page 92), are all the sort of familiar European dishes which demand a good bottle of Muscadet, Beaujolais or Sauternes and are to be found in this chapter.

If I were asked to name a favourite from this chapter, I would probably answer diplomatically 'they are all favourites', but in truth the *Fore-rib of beef with béarnaise sauce* (a côte de boeuf) (see page 68) would be it. The first time that came into my life was, curiously enough, not in France, but in Oxford. Shortly after I left the university, the chef Raymond Blanc opened his first restaurant in north Oxford called *Le Quat' Saisons*. It was in the Banbury Road in a shop that I believe was formerly a hairdresser. At the time in the early 70s, the idea of opening a smart restaurant in a shopping precinct was audacious. I've never forgotten the excitement of that restaurant and nothing summed it up better than the service of the côte de boeuf brought to the table on a rugged wooden chopping board on a trolley by professional-looking French waiters in blue aprons along with a deep bowl of fluffy béarnaise sauce and another bowl of exquisite frisée salad and chips, maybe fried in duck fat then and expertly carved for two of us at the table and washed down with probably a St Amour or a Moulin á Vent. I still can't resist a côte de boeuf whether I'm in one of those large bustling brasseries in Paris like *Chartier*, *La Coupole* or *Bofinger*, or *La Tupina* in Bordeaux where they grill the beef over a log fire.

Gravlax (dill-cured salmon)

I like to add coarsely crushed white peppercorns to my cure of salt, sugar and fresh dill. You might not care for it, but it gives it an almost dusty flavour which appeals to me. I think black peppercorns are very good too. Lots of recipes don't include either, but I like a thick, green crust of dill and peppercorns, as it looks so appetising when thinly sliced on a plate with some of the mustard and horseradish sauce. You might like to serve the gravlax with some boiled new potatoes to make a more substantial course; they often do so in Scandinavia.

SERVES 6

2 x 750 g (1½ lb) unskinned salmon fillets
A large bunch of dill, roughly chopped
100 g (4 oz) coarse sea salt
75 g (3 oz) white sugar
2 tablespoons crushed white peppercorns

FOR THE HORSERADISH AND MUSTARD SAUCE:

2 teaspoons finely grated horseradish (fresh or from a jar)
2 teaspoons finely grated onion
1 teaspoon Dijon mustard
1 teaspoon caster sugar
2 tablespoons white wine vinegar
A good pinch of salt
175 ml (6 fl oz) double cream

Put one of the salmon fillets, skin side down, on to a large sheet of cling film. Mix the dill with the salt, sugar and crushed peppercorns and spread it over the cut face of the salmon. Place the other fillet on top, skin side up.

Tightly wrap the fish in 2 or 3 layers of cling film and lift it on to a large, shallow tray. Rest a slightly smaller tray or chopping board on top of the fish and weight it down. Refrigerate for 2 days, turning the fish every 12 hours so that the briny mixture that will develop inside the parcel bastes the outside of the fish.

For the horseradish and mustard sauce, stir together all the ingredients except the cream. Whip the cream into soft peaks, stir in the horseradish mixture, cover and chill.

To serve, remove the fish from the briny mixture and slice it as you would smoked salmon. Arrange a few slices of the gravlax on each plate and serve with some of the sauce.

Soupe au pistou

I was listening to a programme on Radio 4 one day, which was trying to assess the relative importance of vision over hearing in building up memory. In the end, the experts were forced to admit that this was as yet unquantifiable, as was the importance of smell; all I can say is that the memory of my first real encounter with basil is as vivid as anything else. It was during a long, warm September in the early 80s in a friend's garden that ran down to the River Fal. The basil was nearly three feet high. Amazingly, looking back now, basil didn't feature much in my cooking before then, but it was at this same time that I came across Elizabeth David's recipe for soupe au pistou. Though my version is now slightly modified, I can still remember the intense aroma of parmesan, garlic, basil and olive oil in the mortar and pestle and the complete exhilaration of this wonderful vegetable soup after tasting it, green with pistou. Pistou is, of course, very closely related to the Genoese pesto, since Nice, where this soup comes from, and Genoa are so close but, unlike pesto, it doesn't include pine nuts and often uses a little chopped tomato.

SERVES 6–8

100 g (4 oz) dried white beans, such as cannellini or haricots blanc, soaked in cold water overnight

4 tablespoons olive oil

1 garlic clove, finely chopped

A *bouquet garni* of bay leaves, thyme and parsley stalks

1 onion, chopped

1 leek, washed and cut into small dice

2 carrots, cut into small dice

675 g (1½ lb) courgettes, cut into small dice

450 g (1 lb) vine-ripened tomatoes, skinned, seeded and chopped (page 283)

2 medium-sized potatoes, peeled and cut into small dice

100 g (4 oz) fine green beans, topped, tailed and cut into 3–4 pieces each

100 g (4 oz) fresh or frozen peas

75 g (3 oz) dried spaghettini, broken into small pieces, or small pasta shapes

Sea salt and freshly ground black pepper

FOR THE PISTOU:

A good bunch (about 50 g/2 oz) of basil leaves

3 fat garlic cloves, peeled

1 vine-ripened tomato, skinned and chopped (page 283)

75 g (3 oz) parmesan cheese, freshly grated, plus extra to serve

150 ml (5 fl oz) olive oil

Drain the soaked beans. Heat 2 tablespoons of the oil in a medium-sized pan, add the garlic and the *bouquet garni* and cook gently for 2–3 minutes.

Add the drained beans and 1¼ litres (2 pints) of water, bring to the boil, cover and leave to simmer for 30 minutes–1 hour, or until just tender. Add ½ teaspoon of salt and simmer for 5 more minutes. Set to one side.

Heat the rest of the oil in a large pan. Add the onions, leeks and carrots and cook gently for 5–6 minutes, until soft but not browned.

Remove and discard the *bouquet garni* from the beans and add the beans and their cooking liquor to the pan of vegetables. Add the courgettes, tomatoes and potatoes, another 1¼ litres (2 pints) of water, 2 teaspoons of salt and some pepper. Bring to the boil and simmer, uncovered, for 20 minutes.

Add the green beans, peas and pasta to the pan and simmer for another 10 minutes or until the pasta is cooked.

Meanwhile, for the pistou, blend the basil, garlic, tomato and cheese together in a food processor. Then, with the machine still running, gradually add the olive oil to make a mayonnaise-like mixture. Season to taste with salt and pepper.

Remove the pan from the heat and stir in the pistou. Adjust the seasoning and serve in warmed bowls, with some extra grated parmesan cheese.

Classic fish soup with rouille and croûtons

I've always thought that a good fish soup is the best way to test the quality of a good fish restaurant. It's all to do with the depth of flavour that comes from using lots of fish and shellfish with saffron, tomatoes, red peppers, fennel, garlic and, always for me, orange peel.

SERVES 4

900 g (2 lb) mixed fish, such as gurnard, conger eel, dogfish, pouting, cod and grey mullet
1.2 litres (2 pints) water
The other ingredients for making *fish stock* (page 279)
85 ml (3 fl oz) olive oil
75 g (3 oz) each onion, celery, leek and fennel, roughly chopped
3 garlic cloves, sliced
Juice of ½ orange plus 2 pared strips of orange zest
200 g (7 oz) can of chopped tomatoes
1 small red pepper, seeded and sliced
1 bay leaf and 1 sprig of thyme
A pinch of saffron strands
100 g (4 oz) unpeeled, cooked North Atlantic prawns
A pinch of cayenne pepper
Sea salt and freshly ground black pepper
1 quantity of *rouille* (page 281)
FOR THE CROÛTONS:
1 mini French baguette
Olive oil, for frying
1 garlic clove
25 g (1 oz) parmesan cheese, finely grated, to serve

Fillet the fish and use the bones with the water to make a fish stock (see page 279).

Heat the olive oil in a large pan, add the vegetables and garlic and cook gently for 20 minutes, or until soft but not coloured. Add the orange zest, tomatoes, red pepper, bay leaf, thyme, saffron, prawns and fish fillets. Cook briskly for 2–3 minutes, then add the stock and orange juice, bring to the boil and simmer for 40 minutes. Meanwhile, for the croûtons, thinly slice the baguette and fry the slices in the olive oil until crisp and golden. Drain on kitchen paper and rub one side of each piece with the garlic clove.

Liquidise the soup and pass through a conical sieve into a clean pan, pressing out as much liquid as possible with the back of a ladle. Return the soup to the heat and season to taste with the cayenne, salt and pepper.

Ladle the soup into a warmed tureen and put the croûtons, parmesan cheese and rouille into separate dishes. To serve, ladle the soup into warmed bowls and leave each person to spread some rouille on to the croûtons, float them on their soup and sprinkle them with some of the parmesan cheese.

Moules marinière with cream, garlic and parsley

I was leafing through a new BBC poetry book, The Nation's Favourite Poems of Desire, *and I came across a poem by Elizabeth Garrett that subtly ties together the sensuality of eating mussels with your fingers. She describes cooking the mussels as follows:*

'I pour on wine; it seems they beg for more,
The beaked shells yearning wide as if in song –
Yet dumb – and lewdly lolling parrot-tongues.
Cream licks the back of a spoon and drawls a slur
Of unctuous benediction for this feast.
We smooth our cassocks; bow our heads; and eat.'

SERVES 4

1¾ kg (4 lb) live mussels, cleaned (page 283)
1 garlic clove, finely chopped
2 shallots, finely chopped
15 g (½ oz) butter
A *bouquet garni* of parsley, thyme and bay leaves
100 ml (3½ fl oz) dry white wine
120 ml (4 fl oz) double cream
A handful of parsley leaves, coarsely chopped

Soften the garlic and shallots in the butter with the *bouquet garni*, in a large pan big enough to take all the mussels – it should only be half full. Add the mussels and wine, turn up the heat, then cover and steam them open in their own juices for 3–4 minutes, giving the pan a good shake every now and then.

Remove the *bouquet garni*, add the cream and parsley and remove from the heat. Spoon into 4 large warmed bowls and serve with lots of crusty bread.

Salade tourangelle

This is rather more like a platter of hors d'oeuvres than a single tossed salad. It's a paean of praise to the delights of early-summer vegetables: artichoke hearts, asparagus, celery and green beans, all dressed separately and arranged on a large platter.

SERVES 6

4 globe artichokes
Juice of 1 lemon
400 g (14 oz) asparagus tips
400 g (14 oz) fine green beans
225 g (8 oz) chestnut mushrooms, wiped clean
4 celery stalks
16 walnuts in the shell, or 100 g (4 oz) walnut halves
2 small shallots, finely chopped
A small bunch of parsley, finely chopped
½ teaspoon Dijon mustard
1 teaspoon chopped tarragon
2 tablespoons double cream
The leaves from 3 small sprigs of chervil
2 teaspoons lemon juice
Sea salt and freshly ground black pepper
1 quantity of *walnut vinaigrette dressing* (page 281)

To prepare the artichokes, break off the stems and discard. Cut off the top half of each globe and then bend back the green leaves, letting them snap off close to the base, until you reach the hairy choke at the centre. Slice this away with a small knife, close to the heart, or scrape it away with a teaspoon. Trim away the darker green bases of the leaves, so that you are left with just the paler convex-shaped heart. Drop them into a bowl of cold water mixed with the lemon juice as you prepare each one. Steam or boil for 4–5 minutes, until just tender, then leave to cool. Slice thinly and set aside.

Cook the asparagus and green beans separately in well-salted boiling water until just tender – about 1 minute for the asparagus and 2 minutes for the beans. Drain well, refresh under cold water, and set aside.

Trim the stalks of the mushrooms and then slice them thinly. Thinly slice the celery stalks. Shell the walnuts, trying to keep the halves intact.

Put the artichoke hearts, asparagus, green beans, mushrooms and celery into 5 separate bowls. Add half the chopped shallots, 1½ tablespoons of the dressing and 1 tablespoon of the chopped parsley to the asparagus; the rest of the shallots, the rest of the parsley and another 1½ tablespoons of the dressing to the beans; mix the mustard into another tablespoon of the dressing and add to the artichokes with the tarragon; add the double cream, the rest of the dressing and the chervil leaves to the mushrooms; finally add the lemon juice to the celery. Season each of the salads with some salt and pepper. Arrange the salads around the edge of a serving platter and pile the walnuts in the centre.

Carbonnade of beef à la flamande

I don't think we cook enough with beer in Britain. Our beer, with its body and fragrant hoppiness, is ideal for cooking. You'd have thought that a carbonnade, though from Belgium, would be found in many a pub because a good British beer would be the obvious thing to drink with a carbonnade, but sadly it isn't. My carbonnade is made with slices of shin of beef. Though this requires long, slow cooking, the meat acquires a beguiling succulence in the process.

SERVES 4

2 tablespoons sunflower oil
900 g (2 lb) sliced shin of beef
750 g (1½ lb) onions, thinly sliced
50 g (2 oz) butter
2 tablespoons flour
2½ tablespoons Worcestershire sauce
600 ml (1 pint) hoppy beer, such as Adnams Suffolk ale
600 ml (1 pint) deep, rich-coloured *beef stock* (page 278)
A *bouquet garni* of 2 bay leaves, 2 thyme sprigs and
    a small bunch of parsley
Salt and freshly ground black pepper

Preheat the oven to 160°C/325°F/Gas Mark 3. Heat the oil in a flameproof casserole, add the slices of shin and brown well on both sides. Lift them on to a plate, add the onions and butter to the casserole and cook over a low heat for 15 minutes, stirring often, until soft and well coloured.

Stir in the flour and cook for a minute or two. Return the shin of beef to the pan and lift some of the onions on top. Add the Worcestershire sauce, beer, stock, *bouquet garni*, 1 teaspoon of salt and 20 turns of the black pepper mill. Cover and cook in the oven for 2 hours. Serve with braised red cabbage and baked potatoes.

Portuguese barbecued sardines with piri-piri oil

This recipe came about as a result of an evening spent at the Portuguese club in St Helier on the island of Jersey. The Portuguese serve these sardines on thick slices of bread. It's the perfect al fresco dish as, to eat it, you lift the fillets off the bones, eat the fillets and throw away the bones, then eat the bread, which by now is soaked with oil, adding some salad, if you like.

SERVES 4

12–16 fresh sardines
Crusty bread, thickly sliced, to serve
FOR THE PIRI-PIRI OIL:
1 garlic clove, finely chopped
Finely grated zest and the juice of 1 small lemon
½ teaspoon dried chilli flakes
120 ml (4 fl oz) olive oil
FOR THE SALAD:
4–6 large, vine-ripened tomatoes, thinly sliced
1 red onion, thinly sliced
2 small *roasted red peppers* (page 280), thinly sliced
50 g (2 oz) well-flavoured black olives
Sea salt and freshly ground black pepper.
Extra virgin olive oil and red wine vinegar, to serve

To prepare the sardines, rub off the scales with your thumb, working under cold running water, then gut them and trim off the fins.

To make the piri-piri oil, simply mix all the ingredients together and season with a little salt and pepper.

If you are using a charcoal barbecue, light it 30–40 minutes before you want to start cooking. If using a gas barbecue, light it 10 minutes beforehand.

Meanwhile, for the salad, arrange the sliced tomatoes over a large serving plate and sprinkle with the sliced onion and roasted peppers. Season with salt and pepper, scatter over the olives and drizzle with a little oil and vinegar.

When you are ready to cook, the charcoal should be covered in a layer of white ash. Make 3 shallow slashes on either side of each fish and then brush generously inside and out with the piri-piri oil. Cook them on the barbecue for 3 minutes on each side, until the skin blisters and chars a little bit and the eyes turn opaque. Serve them on the slices of bread with some of the salad to follow.

Fore-ribs of beef with béarnaise sauce

I am looking for the taste of the fire here. The meat should be slightly burnt on the outside yet very rare in the centre and the only way to do this is on a barbecue. Because this cut of meat, a côte de boeuf, contains a lot of fat, it needs a great deal of attention and, unless you have quite a sophisticated barbecue that can dampen down the effects of a lot of flaring fat, it's probably best to start cooking the ribs on the barbecue and then transfer them to your oven once they have taken on a good dark-brown colour. You can buy ribs on the bone that have been trimmed right down to what is now called the rib eye. These are much more controllable on the barbecue, but I think something is missing if the outer fattier and tougher muscle of the rib is missing. In the winter, I always have a wood-burning stove alight in the kitchen. I leave the wood to burn down to hot ash and then rest a simple cast-iron grill rack on the fire box. This is perfection: a char-grilled joint with a faint hint of wood smoke. Serve with the cheesemaker's salad, so named because cheesemakers in the Auvergne region of France like to dress their salads with fresh cream which is naturally readily available and then sharpen it with thin rings of shallots softened in red wine vinegar.

SERVES 4

2 chined fore-ribs of beef, separated
Sea salt and freshly ground black pepper

FOR THE BÉARNAISE SAUCE:
1 tablespoon chopped tarragon
2 shallots, finely chopped
50 ml (2 fl oz) white wine vinegar
3 tablespoons water
225 g (8 oz) unsalted butter
2 egg yolks
½ teaspoon salt
Freshly ground black pepper

FOR THE CHEESEMAKER'S SALAD:
2 shallots, thinly sliced into rings
1 tablespoon good red wine vinegar
1 mild, delicately-flavoured green lettuce,
   such as butterhead or hothouse,
   washed and dried

Preheat your barbecue to high. For the béarnaise sauce, put the tarragon, shallots, pepper, vinegar and 1 tablespoon of the water into a small pan and boil rapidly until it has reduced to 1 tablespoon. In another small pan, clarify the butter: melt it and pour off the golden clear part, leaving the milky solids in the pan. Set the reduction and the clarified butter aside.

Season the ribs well on both sides with salt and pepper. Cook them on the barbecue for 5 minutes on each side for rare or 6½ minutes on each side for medium-rare, or until the temperature in the centre reaches 47°C. Remove, cover and leave to rest for 15 minutes.

For the salad, put the shallots and vinegar into a large shallow salad bowl. Toss together and set aside for 20 minutes to soften the shallots.

Meanwhile, finish the béarnaise sauce: put the egg yolks and remaining water into a bowl set over a pan of simmering water, making sure that the bowl is not touching the water, and whisk vigorously until the mixture is voluminous and creamy. Then remove the bowl from the pan and gradually whisk in the warm clarified butter. Stir in the tarragon and shallot reduction and salt.

Add the salad leaves to the bowl with a pinch of salt and the cream and toss together gently to coat all the leaves.

To serve, cut off the bone and carve the meat across into long, thin slices. Serve with the béarnaise sauce, chips fried in goose fat and the salad.

Sole Véronique

There's a nice story attached to the naming of this classic French dish. The chef-saucier of the Ritz in Paris, Monsieur Malley, left work after a busy lunch having instructed a young commis chef to add some tiny green Muscat grapes to the sole with white-wine sauce that was to be served that evening. On his return for service he discovered the young chef in a state of excitement; his young wife had just given birth to their first child, Véronique, and Monsieur Malley named the dish after her.

SERVES 4

8 x 75 g (3 oz) Dover sole fillets, skinned
600 ml (1 pint) *fish stock* (page 279), or *chicken stock* (page 278)
85 ml (3 fl oz) dry vermouth, such as Noilly Prat
300 ml (10 fl oz) double cream
A squeeze of lemon juice
25–30 seedless green grapes, preferably Muscat, halved
Sea salt and freshly ground white pepper

FOR THE FLEURONS GARNISH:
250 g (9 oz) puff pastry
A little flour, for rolling out
A little beaten egg, for glazing

For the fleurons, preheat the oven to 200°C/400°F/Gas Mark 6. Roll the pastry out thinly on a lightly floured surface and cut out eight 7½ cm (3-inch) discs using a pastry cutter. Then, using the pastry cutter again, cut away one side of each disc to make a crescent-moon shape. Put on to a greased baking sheet and chill for 20 minutes. Then brush with beaten egg and with the tip of a small, sharp knife, lightly score a criss-cross pattern on each one. Bake for 20 minutes, or until puffed up and golden. Remove and keep warm. Lower the oven temperature to 180°C/350°F/Gas Mark 4.

Season the sole fillets lightly on both sides, then fold them in half, skinned side innermost, and place side by side in a buttered shallow ovenproof dish. Pour over the stock, cover with foil and bake for 20 minutes.

Remove the fish from the dish and put on a warmed serving plate. Cover with foil and keep warm. Pour the cooking liquor into a saucepan, add the vermouth, then bring to the boil and boil vigorously until reduced to about 6 tablespoons. Add the cream and a squeeze of lemon juice and simmer until it has thickened to a coating consistency.

Add the grapes to the sauce and warm through gently. Season the sauce to taste, pour it over the fish and garnish with the puff pastry fleurons. Serve immediately.

Baked guinea fowl with garlic beans and smoked sausage

I think guinea fowl has a particularly satisfying flavour. It's probably as far into game as many people want to go and I think it's very successful in this dish, which has the idea of cassoulet as its theme.

SERVES 4

225 g (8 oz) dried haricot beans, soaked in cold water overnight
1 tablespoon olive oil
1½ kg (3 lb) guinea fowl
2 heads of garlic, broken into individual cloves and peeled
25 g (1 oz) butter
50 g (2 oz) smoked bacon lardons (short, fat strips)
The leaves from a large sprig of rosemary
225 g (8 oz) smoked sausage, cut into chunky slices
150 ml (5 fl oz) *chicken stock* (page 278)
Sea salt and freshly ground black pepper

Drain the beans, put them into a saucepan and cover with plenty of fresh cold water. Bring to the boil and simmer gently for 30 minutes–1 hour (this will depend on the age of your beans), until just tender, adding 1 teaspoon of salt 5 minutes before the end of cooking. Drain and set aside.

Preheat the oven to 200°C/400°F/Gas Mark 6. Heat the olive oil in a medium-sized flameproof casserole. Season the guinea fowl, add it to the casserole and brown it on all sides. Turn the bird breast side up and add the garlic cloves, butter, bacon lardons and rosemary to the casserole. Cover with a tight-fitting lid, transfer to the oven and cook for 30 minutes.

Add the beans, smoked sausage, chicken stock, ½ teaspoon of salt and some black pepper to the casserole and stir once or twice to coat everything in the cooking juices. Continue to cook, covered, for a further 30 minutes or until the guinea fowl is tender and cooked through.

To serve, lift the guinea fowl on to a board, cut off the legs and cut each one in half at the joint. Cut the breast meat away from the carcass in 2 whole pieces and slice on the diagonal. Divide the beans between 4 warmed, deep, bistro-style plates and place one piece of leg and some of the sliced breast meat on top.

Grilled cod with aïoli and butter beans

This is a hot version of the classic Provençal dish aïoli garni. I would suggest a Côtes de Provence rosé, a Portuguese white Dâo or a white Corbières from south-western France to go with this.

SERVES 4

50 g (2 oz) dried butter beans
2 eggs
1 fennel bulb
4 fillets of cod, skin on, each weighing about 175–200 g (6–7 oz)
Melted butter, for brushing
6 basil leaves, thinly sliced
1 teaspoon sea salt
Freshly ground black pepper
1 quantity *aïoli* (page 278)

FOR THE SAUCE:

225 g (8 oz) finely chopped mixed carrot, leek, celery and onion
50 g (2 oz) unsalted butter
1 tablespoon cognac
10 g (¼ oz) dried mushrooms
1 tablespoon balsamic vinegar
¼ medium-hot red chilli, seeded and chopped
2 tablespoons olive oil
1 teaspoon Thai fish sauce (nam pla)
600 ml (1 pint) *fish stock* (page 279)
½ teaspoon salt
4 fresh basil leaves, finely sliced

Bring the butter beans to the boil in a large pan of salted water. Simmer gently until very soft. Remove from the heat and keep warm in the cooking liquid.

To make the sauce, sweat the mixture of carrot, leek, celery and onion in a large pan with half the butter, until soft. Add the cognac and let it boil. Then add all the rest of the sauce ingredients, except the remaining butter and the basil leaves. Simmer for 30 minutes. Then pass the sauce through a fine sieve. Bring it back to the boil and simmer until reduced to about 150 ml (5 fl oz).

Boil the eggs for 7 minutes. Drain, remove the shells and keep warm.

Remove the outer leaves of the fennel but don't cut off the tops. Slice into thin sections then cook in salted water until just tender. Drain and keep warm.

Preheat the grill to high. Brush the pieces of cod on both sides with melted butter and place, skin side up, on a greased baking tray or the rack of the grill pan. Grill for 8 minutes or until just cooked through. This will depend on the thickness of the fillets. Place the cod on 4 warmed plates. Drain the butter beans and divide between the plates. Add the fennel, then cut the eggs in half and put one half on each plate. Add a spoonful of aïoli to each serving.

Bring the sauce to the boil and whisk in the last 25 g (1 oz) of butter, then add the basil leaves. Pour the sauce over the beans and fish and serve.

Goats' cheese and thyme soufflé

I wrote this, not to be cooked in little soufflé dishes, but in a large, oval, earthenware one, brought to the table all puffed up and brown and sprinkled with thyme. A perfect illustration of generous, hearty cooking.

SERVES 4

1 small onion, halved
3 cloves
300 ml (10 fl oz) full-cream milk
300 ml (10 fl oz) double cream
1 bay leaf
½ teaspoon black peppercorns
75 g (3 oz) butter
40 g (1½ oz) plain flour
5 large eggs
The leaves from 2 large sprigs of thyme, plus a few leaves to garnish
150 g (5 oz) soft, fresh goats' cheese, such as Irish St Tola, Welsh
    Pant-Ysgawn or French Crottin de Chavignol, crumbled
25 g (1 oz) hard goats' cheese, such as English Village Green,
    or parmesan cheese, finely grated
¼ teaspoon cayenne pepper
Sea salt and freshly ground black pepper

Stud the onion halves with the cloves and put them into a pan, with the milk, cream, bay leaf and black peppercorns. Bring to the boil and then remove from the heat and set aside for 20 minutes to infuse.

Strain the milk and cream through a sieve and discard the flavouring ingredients. Melt the butter in a non-stick pan, add the flour and cook over a medium heat for 1 minute. Gradually beat in the milk and cream and bring to the boil, stirring. Simmer very gently over a very low heat for 10 minutes, giving it a stir every now and then. Pour into a mixing bowl and leave to cool slightly.

Preheat the oven to 200°C/400°F/Gas Mark 6. Separate the eggs and put the whites into a large mixing bowl. Mix the egg yolks into the sauce and then stir in half the thyme leaves, the crumbled fresh goats' cheese, the grated hard goats' cheese or parmesan, cayenne pepper, ¾ teaspoon of salt and some black pepper. Whisk the egg whites until they form soft peaks and fold them into the mixture.

Lightly butter a shallow oval ovenproof dish measuring 30 x 18 cm (12 x 7 inches) and about 5 cm (2 inches) deep. Pour in the soufflé mixture, sprinkle with the remaining thyme leaves and bake for 30 minutes, until the top is puffed up and golden but the centre still soft and creamy. Garnish with a few thyme leaves and serve with a green salad.

Garbure béarnaise

Garbure is a warming ham, duck confit and vegetable soup from the Pyrenées, which has been on and off our menu at St Petroc's for ten years. I think the particular excitement of this soup is the saltiness of the duck confit and smoked ham hock, combined with the sweetness of the cabbage that goes in at the end. Like all these hearty meat and vegetable soups and stews, it improves with being reheated the following day.

SERVES 8-10

1 smoked ham hock, weighing about 1¼ kg (2½ lb)
225 g (8 oz) dried haricot beans, soaked in cold water overnight
2 carrots
2 leeks
2 celery sticks
100 g (4 oz) slice of swede
1 large onion, chopped
450 g (1 lb) large, floury potatoes, such as Maris Piper,
    peeled and cut into 1 cm (½-inch) dice
6 garlic cloves, chopped
A *bouquet garni* of bay leaves, thyme and parsley stalks
½ Savoy cabbage, thickly sliced
2 legs of *duck confit* (page 279)
Sea salt and freshly ground black pepper
TO SERVE:
1 small baguette, thinly sliced
1 garlic clove, peeled
A small handful of coarsely chopped parsley, to garnish

Put the ham hock into a snugly fitting pan and add enough cold water to cover it by about 5 cm (2 inches). Bring to the boil, skimming off any scum as it rises to the surface, then lower the heat and simmer for 1 hour. Drain the haricot beans, add them to the pan and simmer for 30 minutes.

Cut the carrots, leeks and celery lengthways into quarters and then cut across into thin slices. Cut the swede into similar-sized pieces.

Add the carrots, leeks, celery, swede, onion, potatoes, garlic, *bouquet garni*, 1 teaspoon of salt (if your hock is not very salty) and some pepper to the pan and simmer for 25 minutes.

Remove the *bouquet garni* from the pan, add the cabbage and duck confit (see page 279) and cook for a further 30 minutes. Then take the ham hock and duck confit out of the pan, remove the meat from the bones and discard the skin and bones. Pull the meat into small pieces with 2 forks and return to the pan.

To serve, lightly toast the slices of baguette and rub them with the peeled garlic clove. Put three slices of bread into each soup bowl, ladle over the soup and serve sprinkled with the parsley.

Chorizo and butter bean stew with garlic and thyme

I buy the chorizos and butter beans for this from a company called Brindisa *(see page 283), which specialises in Spanish produce, but I know that you can get both at many supermarkets, too. The quality of the chorizo is all-important and I would recommend* Brindisa's *parrilla chorizo picante. The butter beans I use, called judiónes de La Granja, are also sensational.*

SERVES 4

350 g (12 oz) dried judión butter beans,
    soaked overnight
225 g (8 oz) hot chorizo for cooking,
    such as parrilla chorizo picante
50 ml (2 fl oz) olive oil
5 garlic cloves, thinly sliced
½ medium onion, finely chopped
175 ml (6 fl oz) red wine
400 g (14 oz) can of chopped tomatoes
1 tablespoon thyme leaves
2 tablespoons chopped flat-leaf parsley
Sea salt

Put the butter beans into a large pan with lots of water, bring to the boil and simmer for 1 hour or until tender. Drain and set aside.

Cut the chorizo sausages into thin slices. Put the olive oil and garlic into a pan and heat over a medium-high heat until the garlic begins to sizzle. Add the chorizo and cook until the slices are lightly browned on both sides, then add the onion and continue to cook until it has softened.

Add the red wine and cook until it has reduced to almost nothing. Add the canned chopped tomatoes, thyme, butter beans and ½ a teaspoon of salt and simmer for 15 minutes.

Scatter over the parsley, spoon the stew into deep, warmed bowls and serve with some crusty fresh bread.

Arroz a la banda
(saffron rice and squid served with allioli)

I actually prefer this to paella because the enduring problem with paella is that some of the ingredients are always overcooked. Arroz a la banda, which means 'rice served apart', allows for the rice and seafood to be cooked separately and then served together – to me, a much better arrangement, especially when accompanied by a searing-hot garlic allioli.

The recipe makes just a small amount of this exceptionally pungent sauce, and a teaspoon or so is all you will need per person, just like mustard. If you favour something less demanding, try the garlicky mayonnaise aïoli instead (see page 278). I have purposely written this recipe using ingredients you can get anywhere, except perhaps for the smoked paprika called La Chinata. The rich fish stock uses small, cheap fish such as gurnard or whiting, or steaks of bigger fish. If I'm making this in Cornwall, I'll bung in a few shore crabs, prawns or lobster shells, too, to add flavour.

SERVES 4

2 tablespoons extra virgin olive oil

2 good pinches of paprika

450 g (1 lb) cleaned squid (page 283), cut across into rings
    and the tentacles cut into 7½ cm (3-inch) pieces

Sea salt and freshly ground black pepper

1 quantity of *allioli* (page 278)

FOR THE FISH STOCK:

4 tablespoons olive oil

4 garlic cloves, sliced (no need to peel)

A large pinch of dried chilli flakes

2 strips of pared orange zest

1 onion, sliced

1 red pepper, sliced (no need to seed)

1 fennel bulb, sliced

675 g (1½ lb) cheap, but well-flavoured small fish,
    such as gurnard, cleaned but left whole, or steaks
    or fillets of fish such as ling and pollack, cut into
    slightly smaller pieces

2 tomatoes, sliced

1½ litres (2½ pints) water

A small handful of oregano leaves

A large pinch of saffron strands

FOR THE RICE:

2 tablespoons extra virgin olive oil

1½ teaspoons paprika

A large pinch of smoked paprika, preferably La Chinata (optional)

2 garlic cloves, finely chopped

500 g (1 lb 2 oz) paella rice, such as Calasparra

First make an aromatic fish stock to flavour the rice. Heat the olive oil in a large pan, add the garlic, chilli flakes and orange zest and fry until the garlic is just beginning to colour. Add the onion, red pepper and fennel and fry until soft. Now add the fish and tomatoes and continue to fry for 5 minutes or so, stirring occasionally.

Add the water and oregano and bring to the boil. Reduce the heat and simmer for 40 minutes. Then strain the stock. The best piece of equipment to use for straining a rich stock like this is a conical strainer, as it allows you to force as much flavour as possible through with the back of a ladle. If you don't have one, press the cooked fish and vegetables against the side of a sieve. Add the saffron and ½ teaspoon of salt to the stock, set aside and keep hot.

For the rice, heat the oil in a shallow pan in which you can serve it (I use a shallow Le Creuset casserole, 30 cm/12 inches in diameter), with the paprika, the smoked paprika, if using, and the garlic. As soon as the garlic starts to colour, add the rice and stir-fry for about 2 minutes. Add the hot stock, 1 teaspoon of salt and some black pepper and bring to the boil, stirring occasionally. Reduce the heat a little and cook, uncovered, without stirring, for 8 minutes. Then reduce the heat right down to low and cook for a further 7 minutes, again without stirring. Now test the rice; it should be tender but still have a slight bite to it. Remove the pan from the heat, cover and leave for 5 minutes. When you take the lid off, the rice should look marvellous – each grain separate and the top an appetising yellow-brown with flecks of saffron.

While the rice is cooking, make the allioli (see page 278). Transfer to a small bowl.

To cook the squid, heat the olive oil in a large frying pan. Toss in a pinch of paprika and half the squid and fry over a high heat for 2 minutes, until lightly coloured. Season with salt, remove and repeat with the remaining squid. Serve the rice with the stir-fried squid and allioli.

Beef Stroganoff with matchstick potatoes

I have a considerable affection for this dish, as I learnt to cook it this way a long time ago, in the 60s, when I was a trainee chef at the Great Western Royal Hotel at Paddington Station. The thing that impressed me was the speed with which you could turn it out and the practicality of the dish, which uses the tail end of the fillet. These were too thin for the tournedos that were the main use of beef fillet in that traditional, but actually very well run, kitchen. For success with matchstick potatoes, you need Maris Pipers, and they must be starchy ones and not have been mishandled, as this causes the starch to turn into sugar. This is my girlfriend Sarah's favourite dish, although she thinks it's better made with fresh cream rather than soured.

SERVES 4

675 g (1½ lb) beef fillet, preferably cut from the tail end
65 g (2½ oz) unsalted butter
1½ tablespoons paprika (hot Hungarian, if you like a little subtle heat)
1 large onion, very thinly sliced
350 g (12 oz) button mushrooms, thinly sliced
3 tablespoons sunflower oil
300 ml (10 fl oz) soured cream
2 teaspoons lemon juice
A small handful of parsley leaves, finely chopped
Sea salt and freshly ground black pepper
FOR THE MATCHSTICK POTATOES:
450 g (1 lb) floury potatoes, such as Maris Pipers, peeled
Sunflower oil, for deep-frying

Cut the steak into slices 1 cm (½ inch) thick, then cut each slice across the grain into strips 1 cm (½ inch) wide.

For the matchstick potatoes, cut the potatoes by hand into short sticks 3 mm (¼ inch) thick, or use a mandolin. Set aside in a bowl of cold water. Heat some oil for deep-frying to 190°C/375°F or until a cube of day-old bread rises to the surface and browns within 1 minute.

Melt the butter in a large frying pan, add the paprika and onion and cook slowly until the onion is soft and sweet but not browned. Add the mushrooms and fry gently for 3 minutes. Transfer to a plate and keep warm.

Drain the matchstick potatoes and dry thoroughly in a clean tea towel or a salad spinner. Plunge into the hot oil and fry for 3 minutes, until crisp and golden. Drain briefly on kitchen paper and keep hot in a low oven.

Heat half the oil in the pan until very hot, add half the fillet steak and fry quickly, seasoning and turning it as you do so, for just over 1 minute. Transfer to a plate and repeat with the rest of the steak.

Return the onion mixture to the pan and pour in the soured cream. Bring to the boil and simmer for a minute or so, until thickened, then return the steak to the pan and heat very gently for 1 minute; the beef should not be cooked any further. Stir in the lemon juice and parsley and serve with the potatoes.

Lamb Champvallon

This is a very pleasant dish, similar to Lancashire hot pot but with three important differences. Firstly, it is flavoured with lots of thyme. Secondly, it contains plenty of garlic, which naturally the British version doesn't. Thirdly, and perhaps most interestingly, it's probably named after Françoise de Champvallon, who witnessed the marriage between Louis XIV and his mistress, Madame de Maintenon. Whether the name of the dish is correctly ascribed or not doesn't matter, it's just that the French have a charming ability to make their dishes sexy. I love the British bluntness of Lancashire hot pot, but it doesn't quite have the same romantic ring to it.

SERVES 6

1 x shoulder of lamb, boned
4 tablespoons olive oil
600 ml (1 pint) *chicken stock* (page 278)
1 large onion, halved and thinly sliced
2 garlic cloves, thinly sliced
1 teaspoon thyme leaves
1 kg (2 lb 2 oz) floury potatoes, such as Maris Pipers, peeled
50 g (2 oz) butter
Sea salt and freshly ground black pepper

Trim away the excess fat from the shoulder of lamb to leave you with approximately 1.2 kg (2½ lb) of lean lamb. Cut the meat into two smaller pieces, slice each one across into 1 cm (½-inch) thick slices and season with a little salt and pepper. In a flameproof casserole or large saucepan, brown the meat in 3 batches in 1 tablespoon of the oil, deglazing the pan between each batch with a little of the chicken stock and returning it to the jug. This releases the caramelised juices from the base of the pan, giving the stock more flavour and preventing them from becoming burnt.

Heat the remaining tablespoon of oil in the pan, add the onion and garlic and fry until soft and nicely golden. Return the lamb to the pan with the stock and thyme leaves, ½ teaspoon of salt and some freshly ground black pepper. Cover and leave to simmer for 1 hour, or until tender.

Preheat the oven to 200°C/400°F/Gas Mark 6. Slice the potatoes quite thinly. Melt 25 g (1 oz) of the butter in a 24 cm (8-inch) cast-iron casserole dish and neatly overlap half of the potatoes over the base of the pan. Season lightly and cook over a medium heat until they are golden brown on the underside. Then lift the lamb and onions out of the cooking juices with a slotted spoon and spoon in an even layer on top of the potatoes. Spoon away the excess fat from the top of the cooking juices, adjust the seasoning if necessary and pour 500 ml (18 fl oz) back over the lamb.

Neatly overlap the remaining potatoes over the top of the lamb, pour over the remaining cooking juices and season lightly. Melt the remaining 25 g (1 oz) of butter, drizzle over the potatoes and bake, uncovered, for 1 hour. Serve at the table, straight from the casserole.

Lulu's roast chicken with ginger, pasta, tomatoes and the roasting juices

Debbie Major, without whom these cookery books wouldn't happen on account of how I'm an idle dreamer, found this recipe in a book that I've long cherished but failed to notice myself, written by Richard Olney – Lulu's Provençal Table.

SERVES 4

450 g (1 lb) vine-ripened tomatoes
1½ kg (3 lb) free-range chicken
1 tablespoon finely grated fresh ginger
3 tablespoons olive oil
Juice of 1 lemon
50 ml (2 fl oz) dry white wine
350 g (12 oz) penne or small, tubular-shaped pasta
2 garlic cloves, bruised and then chopped
A large handful of basil leaves, finely shredded
Sea salt and freshly ground black pepper

Preheat the oven to 230°C/450°F/Gas Mark 8. Skin, seed and chop the tomatoes. Toss them in a colander with ½ teaspoon of salt and set aside for 1 hour.

Season the chicken's cavity with salt and pepper and then smear the inside with the grated ginger. Put the bird into a roasting tin, rub all over with a little of the olive oil and season with some salt and pepper. Roast the chicken for 20 minutes. Lower the oven temperature to 180°C/350°F/Gas Mark 4. Pour the excess fat from the roasting tin and pour a little lemon juice over the bird. Return to the oven and roast for a further 45 minutes, basting now and then with the rest of the lemon juice and then the white wine, until the juices from the thigh run clear when pierced with a skewer.

About 15 minutes before the chicken is ready, cook the pasta in plenty of well-salted boiling water (1 teaspoon salt per 600 ml/1 pint water) for about 12 minutes, until *al dente*.

Meanwhile, put the rest of the olive oil and the garlic into a large frying pan and place it over a high heat. As soon as the garlic starts to sizzle, add the tomatoes and toss over a high heat until a lot of the excess juice has evaporated and they give off a nice, slightly caramelised smell. Add the basil, toss again and remove from the heat.

Drain the pasta well. Remove the chicken from the oven, lift it on to a board and pour away any excess fat from the tin if necessary. Now tip any juices from the cavity of the chicken back into the roasting tin. Add the tomatoes, cooked pasta and a little black pepper to the roasting tin and turn everything together well in order to release all the roasting juices from the base of the tin.

Carve the chicken and divide between 4 warm serving plates. Spoon some of the pasta alongside and serve with a light green salad.

Braised fillet of turbot with slivers of potato, mushrooms and truffle oil

I originally devised this recipe using fresh black truffles but these are pretty impossible (and pretty expensive) to get, especially outside the restaurant business. However, the flavour of truffles is so good that it seemed a shame not to try to incorporate them somewhere. Then I found an Italian olive oil flavoured with white truffles. It is fantastic and quite easy to get in any good delicatessen. A little bottle is also fiendishly expensive but it goes a long way.

SERVES 4

600 ml (1 pint) *chicken stock* (page 278)
175 g (6 oz) waxy main-crop potatoes, such as Wilja
100 g (4 oz) unsalted butter
1 thin slice of cooked ham, weighing about 25 g (1 oz),
 cut into very fine dice
25 g (1 oz) shallots, finely chopped
85 ml (3 fl oz) dry vermouth, such as Noilly Prat or Martini
100 g (4 oz) button mushrooms, thinly sliced
2 teaspoons lemon juice
1 tablespoon truffle oil
750 g (1½-lb) turbot fillet, skin on, cut into 8 pieces
1 tablespoon chopped parsley
Sea salt and freshly ground black pepper

Put the chicken stock into a pan to boil until reduced by half. Set aside. Peel and slice the potatoes as thinly as you can and then cut them across into thin matchsticks. Melt half the butter in a frying pan that is large enough to hold all the pieces of fish in one layer. Add the potatoes, ham and shallots and cook gently for 4–5 minutes. Add the vermouth and reduced chicken stock and simmer for about 8 minutes, until the potatoes are almost, but not quite, cooked. You can prepare the dish to this stage some time in advance if you wish.

Stir the mushrooms, lemon juice, truffle oil and some salt and pepper into the pan and then rest the pieces of turbot on top, skin side up. Cover and simmer for about 6 minutes or until the fish is cooked through. Lift the fish on to a plate and keep hot. Add the remaining butter to the pan and boil rapidly for 10 minutes or until the sauce has thickened and the potatoes are just beginning to break up.

To serve, peel the skin off the turbot and place the fish on 4 warmed plates. Stir the parsley into the sauce and spoon it on top of the fish.

Coeurs à la crème with raspberries

I'd forgotten the charm of these little hearts of cream cheese, which I used to make in the 70s and 80s, until I went to the Stilton factory in Colston Bassett and renewed my sense of wonder at the way curds and whey separate with the addition of so little rennet. The making of your own cream cheese is a source of great satisfaction, I think; something to be proud of when it's turned out of the muslin-lined, perforated, heart-shaped moulds, covered with cream and sugar, and served with just a handful of perfect raspberries. One addition I used to make back then was to pare the zest off a couple of lemons and grind it with lots of sugar, in a coffee grinder kept especially for this purpose, into a lemon-flavoured icing sugar for sprinkling over the hearts.

SERVES 4

600 ml (1 pint) full-cream milk
1 tablespoon rennet
½ teaspoon salt
150 ml (5 fl oz) double cream
15 g (½ oz) caster sugar
Single cream and fresh raspberries, to serve

Put the milk into a pan and bring it up to 37°C (98°F). Pour it into a bowl, stir in the rennet and set it aside somewhere cool, but not in the fridge, until set.

When the mixture is firm, break it up into pieces and stir in the salt. Pour it into a large, muslin-lined sieve set over a bowl, cover and leave somewhere cool to drain for 8 hours or overnight, but again, do not refrigerate.

Tip the cheese-like mixture out of the muslin cloth into the sieve and press it through into a clean bowl. Lightly whip the cream and sugar together in another bowl into soft peaks and gently fold it into the cheese-like mixture.

Line 4 coeur à la crème moulds with small squares of damp muslin. Spoon in the mixture and lightly level the tops. Cover and chill in the fridge for 2–3 hours.

Turn them out on to small plates and pile some raspberries alongside. Sprinkle over some sugar, pour around a little cream, and serve.

Beignets soufflés in cinnamon sugar with hot chocolate sauce

Sweets like this are where my heart really lies – uncomplicated, yet requiring the best materials: free-range eggs for the choux pastry, fresh oil, and good dark chocolate. Even something as apparently unvarying as ground cinnamon needs attention. There's a vast difference in taste between freshly bought cinnamon and the stuff that's been in the cupboard far too long and is like dust. Every time I go through my drawers and cupboards and look at the dates on spice jars, I'm amazed how time nips along nicely. I hang on to things. There's a lovely idea in one of Anne Tyler's books, A Patchwork Planet, *where the central character's job is cleaning out people's attics, removing the things they want to but can't get rid of.*

SERVES 6

75 g (3 oz) unsalted butter
225 ml (7½ fl oz) cold water
95 g (3¾ oz) plain flour, well sifted
3 large eggs, beaten
Sunflower oil, for deep-frying
50 g (2 oz) caster sugar
¾ teaspoon ground cinnamon
FOR THE CHOCOLATE SAUCE:
200 ml (7 fl oz) double cream
90 g (3½ oz) good-quality plain chocolate, broken into small pieces

For the chocolate sauce, put the cream and chocolate pieces into a small pan and stir over a low heat until the chocolate has melted and the sauce is silky-smooth. Keep warm over a very low heat.

For the beignets, put the butter and water into a pan and leave over a low heat until the butter has melted. Turn up the heat, bring to the boil and then add the flour and beat vigorously until the mixture is smooth and leaves the sides of the pan. Leave to cool slightly and then gradually beat in the eggs to make a smooth, glossy choux pastry.

Heat a large pan of oil for deep-frying to 190°C/375°F. Drop about 6–8 heaped teaspoons of the choux pastry into the oil, taking care not to overcrowd the pan, and cook for 5 minutes, turning them over now and then, until they are puffed up, crisp and golden. Don't be tempted to lift them out too soon – they will continue to expand in size as they cook for the full 5 minutes, which allows sufficient time for the choux pastry in the centre to cook. Lift them out with a slotted spoon on to a tray lined with kitchen paper and drain briefly, then keep hot in a low oven while you cook the rest.

Mix the caster sugar and cinnamon together in a shallow dish, add the beignets a few at a time, and toss them gently until they are well coated.

To serve, arrange 4 of the beignets in the centre of warm plates and drizzle some of the chocolate sauce over them. Serve immediately, while still warm.

Crème brûlée ice cream

This ice cream was invented quite by accident, when Christine Hope, who once worked for us, curdled a rich custard intended for a crème brûlée and asked me whether she should throw it away and start again. 'No,' I said, 'it would be a waste. Sprinkle it with sugar, burn the top as you would normally under a grill and then bung it in the ice cream machine and we'll see what happens.' And what happened was that it turned into the most superbly flavoured and textured ice cream, because the caramel broke up into exquisite little crunchy pieces. We normally serve it with pears poached in port and cinnamon, or just a pile of fresh berries and maybe a little fruit coulis and a sprig of mint.

SERVES 8

200 ml (7 fl oz) milk
375 ml (13 fl oz) double cream
1 teaspoon vanilla extract
5 egg yolks
120 g (4½ oz) caster sugar

Put the milk, cream and vanilla extract into a pan and bring slowly to the boil.

Meanwhile, beat the egg yolks with 50 g (2 oz) of the caster sugar until pale and creamy. Gradually beat in the hot milk and cream, then return the mixture to the pan and cook over a gentle heat until it is thick enough to coat the back of the spoon. Do not let it boil or it will curdle.

Pour the custard into a shallow ovenproof dish – it should be about 2½ cm (1 inch) deep and come near the top of the dish. Leave to cool; then cover and chill for 6 hours or until set.

Preheat the grill to its highest setting. Remove the custard from the fridge and sprinkle with the remaining caster sugar. Put it under the grill for about 5 minutes, until the sugar has caramelised. Alternatively, if you have a blowtorch, you can achieve the same results by playing the flame across the top of the sugar. Remove and leave to cool.

Break up the caramel topping here and there with the handle of a kitchen knife and stir the pieces into the creamy mixture below. Transfer to an ice cream maker or a plastic container and freeze for 3 hours, or until firm.

Mediterranean & Middle East

My most recent book was was called *Mediterranean Escapes*. One of the thoughts that went through my mind all the while I was writing this was how can an area so gastronomically vast that it covers Spain, France and Italy right round to North Africa be identified as having the same gastronomic features? In the end I did feel that the food common to the whole region did unify it: olive oil and olives, capers, lemon, tomatoes, garlic, an enthusiasm for fish, saffron, red peppers, Provençal herbs such as rosemary, thyme, oregano, basil, and quite a lot of chilli and of course wine, mostly white. It all adds up to a recognisable style of cooking. The dish in this chapter *Fillet of John Dory with olives, capers and rosemary* (see page 110) is my attempt to sum up Mediterranean cooking in one dish. It's been on our restaurant menu for at least ten years and is really a warm salad with fish, a combination which I use quite often, where I arrange fillets of fish in and amongst salad leaves. It works because all the ingredients are delicately mixed together at the last minute, including the fish, which is cut into finger-sized slices and cooked quickly under a grill. I sometimes think it's embarrassingly simple, but it has the essential points of a good Mediterranean dish; in addition to the ingredients in the title, it also includes wedges of small tomatoes and warm new potatoes and parsley. In Mediterranean dishes I'm always looking for vibrant colours and flavours, which I think the John Dory dish has. Another dish with the same attraction in this chapter would be the *Warm poached skate with the sunny and aromatic flavours of Morocco* (see page 105). Here I've accompanied the fish with tomatoes, saffron, garlic and chilli and, as it is north Africa, some shredded coriander and mint, but the combination of the deep yellow of the saffron and the bright red of the tomato in the sauce again reminds me of the lively colours of the region.

The cooking of the Mediterranean region most commonly features food which is quickly assembled and cooked: salads, pasta dishes like the *Linguine with porcini, garlic and truffle oil* (see page 128), risottos like the simple and delicious risotto milanese which accompanies the *Osso bucco* on page 120 and antipasti like the *Beef carpaccio* on page 104. But there are some excellent slow-cooked dishes, such as the *Osso bucco* itself (see page 120), which is a mellifluous stew of shin of veal gently simmered with finely chopped onion, carrots and celery, white wine, sage and lemon. Classicists aver that a proper osso bucco should never contain tomato but I like a little fresh pulp for a touch of acidity. There's also the *Moussaka* (see page 101), which I think is as good a recipe as you will get for this very well known Greek dish. Lastly the *Rabbit cacciatora with grilled polenta* (see page 124) is a great favourite. I thoroughly enjoy the Italian way of sautéing rabbit or chicken with whole cloves of garlic, pungent herbs such as sage or rosemary, and a splash of white wine.

Wild mushroom risotto

I recently stayed at an agriturismo hotel, high up in the hills just outside Assisi in Umbria. I asked the waitress what was in the risotto for dinner that night, and she just said it was made with some very good stock; brodo was the word she used. And it was just that: rice, shallots, a very good broth, some parmesan and butter, and maybe there was a sprinkling of parsley. But that was it. It was soft, with a little residual hardness left in the rice, moist, almost runny, and satisfying, with a great depth of flavour and definitely not needing anything else. So the important point to remember when making this recipe is to use the best-flavoured beef stock you can get – preferably home-made. And if using ceps, they should be young and firmly fresh. They are fried separately in butter, then scattered over the top of the risotto rather than mixed into it. This risotto is almost as good made with mixed wild mushrooms or even chestnut or the larger portabello mushrooms.

SERVES 4

About 1 litre (1¾ pints) light *beef stock* (page 278)
225 g (8 oz) ceps, mixed wild or chestnut mushrooms, wiped clean
60 g (2½ oz) unsalted butter
2 large shallots, finely chopped
1 garlic clove, finely chopped
250 g (9 oz) risotto rice, such as Carnaroli or Arborio
15 g (½ oz) parmesan cheese, freshly grated, plus extra to serve (optional)
Sea salt and freshly ground black pepper

Bring the beef stock to the boil and keep it hot over a low heat.

Trim away half the stalks of the ceps, mixed wild or chestnut mushrooms and finely chop them. Thinly slice the remainder and set aside.

Melt 40 g (1½ oz) of the butter in a pan, add the chopped mushroom stalks, shallots and garlic and cook gently for 3–4 minutes, until soft but not browned. Add the rice and turn it over for a couple of minutes until all the grains are coated in the butter. Add a ladleful of the hot stock and stir over a medium heat until it has all been absorbed before adding another. Continue like this for about 20 minutes, stirring constantly, until you have added most or all of the stock and the rice is tender but still a little *al dente*. The risotto should still be quite moist.

About 5 minutes before the risotto is ready, heat another 15 g (½ oz) of the butter in a large frying pan, add the sliced mushrooms and some salt and pepper and fry quickly until soft and lightly browned.

To serve, stir the rest of the butter and the parmesan into the risotto and season to taste with salt and pepper. Spoon on to 4 warmed plates – it should run out to cover the base of the plate in an even layer – and then spread the mushrooms out over the top. Grind over a little black pepper and serve with extra parmesan, if you wish.

Monkfish with saffron and roasted red pepper dressing

The idea of mixing what is basically a vinaigrette with a wine and fish stock reduction and some butter to make it lighter came to me in what I thought was a flash of inspiration. Then I noticed that everyone else was doing exactly the same thing. That always seems to be the case with cooking, but never the less it's still a really good dressing for fish. As I say, 'It should taste tart but not too tart, salty but not too salty and generally round and pleasing'.

SERVES 4

4 filets of monkfish, each weighing about 200 g (7 oz)
2 tablespoons olive oil
1 tablespoon finely chopped thyme
Salt and freshly ground black pepper
FOR THE ROASTED RED PEPPER DRESSING:
600 ml (1 pint) *fish stock* (page 279)
85 ml (3 fl oz) dry vermouth
A large pinch of saffron
2 *roasted red peppers* (page 280)
85 ml (3 fl oz) extra virgin olive oil
1 tablespoon balsamic vinegar or sherry vinegar
1 teaspoon unsalted butter
1.2 litre (2 pint) measuring jug loosely filled with salad leaves
1 tablespoon *lemon olive oil* (page 280)
Pinch coarse sea salt

For the roasted red pepper dressing, put the fish stock (see page 279), vermouth and saffron into a small pan and simmer until reduced by three-quarters. Meanwhile, peel and de-seed the peppers and finely chop the flesh. Mix together the extra virgin olive oil and vinegar with some salt and pepper.

If you are using a charcoal barbecue, light it 30 minutes before you want to cook. If you are using a gas barbecue, light it 10 minutes beforehand. You could also use a ridged cast iron griddle if you wish.

Mix the olive oil with the thyme and some salt and pepper. Brush it over the monkfish fillets and cook them on the barbecue or griddle for 10 minutes, turning them until cooked through. Lift onto a plate and keep warm.

Return the reduced fish stock to the heat and add the chopped red peppers and the vinegar dressing and bring to a brisk boil. Once it has taken on a concentrated flavour, whisk in the butter to give the sauce a light amalgamation. Remove from the heat.

Mix the salad leaves with the lemon olive oil (see page 280) and some salt and place on 4 plates. Slice each monkfish fillet on the diagonal into four thick pieces so that they fall against each other pleasingly. Place each sliced fillet on top of the leaves and pour the sauce around it. Serve immediately.

Moussaka

The things that make all the difference and transform this dish into something quite special are exceptionally good minced lamb, a tomato sauce flavoured only with cinnamon and preferably Greek oregano, a smooth béchamel sauce with a little cheese, and a thick base of fried aubergines. It needs none of the other bits and bobs that seem to crop up regularly, like green peppers, chilli or raisins.

SERVES 6

150–175 ml (5–6 fl oz) olive oil
1 large onion, finely chopped
3 garlic cloves, crushed
900 g (2 lb) lean minced lamb
50 ml (2 fl oz) white wine (a generous splash)
400 g (14 oz) can of chopped tomatoes
5 cm (2 inch) cinnamon stick
A handful of fresh oregano leaves, preferably wild Greek oregano, chopped
3 large aubergines, cut lengthways into slices 5 mm (¼ inch) thick
Sea salt and freshly ground black pepper

FOR THE TOPPING:

75 g (3 oz) butter
75 g (3 oz) plain flour
600 ml (1 pint) full-cream milk
50 g (2 oz) parmesan cheese, freshly grated
2 eggs, beaten

Heat 2 tablespoons of the oil in a pan, add the onion and garlic and fry until just beginning to brown. Add the minced lamb and fry over a high heat for 3–4 minutes. Add the wine, tomatoes, cinnamon and oregano and leave to simmer gently for 30–40 minutes.

Heat a frying pan until it is very hot, add 1 tablespoon of the oil and a layer of aubergine slices and fry quickly until tender and lightly coloured on both sides. Lift out with tongs and arrange over the base of a deep 2½–2¾ litre (4½–5-pint) ovenproof baking dish. Season lightly with a little salt and pepper. Repeat with the rest of the oil and the aubergines, seasoning each layer as you go.

For the topping, melt the butter in a pan, add the flour and cook, stirring, over a medium heat for 1 minute. Gradually beat in the milk, then bring to the boil, stirring. Simmer very gently for 10 minutes, stirring occasionally. Add the cheese and some salt and pepper to taste. Cool slightly and then beat in the eggs.

Preheat the oven to 200°C/400°F/Gas Mark 6. Remove the cinnamon stick from the lamb sauce, season to taste with some salt and pepper and spread it over the aubergines. Pour the topping over the sauce and bake for 25–30 minutes, until golden and bubbling.

Grilled red mullet with an aubergine and pesto salad

What could be better than fillets of red mullet with some grilled aubergines, pesto and salad? A perfect combination of flavours. This dish has its roots in the cooking of Simon Hopkinson, who used to be the chef at Bibendum *restaurant in London. I'd rate him as about the best cook in the country.*

SERVES 4

½ aubergine
Olive oil, for brushing
4 fillets of red mullet, weighing about 75–100 g (3–4 oz) each
FOR THE PESTO:
15 g (½ oz) fresh basil
2 large garlic cloves
175 ml (6 fl oz) olive oil
15 g (½ oz) parmesan cheese, finely grated
15 g (½ oz) pine nuts
FOR THE SALAD:
75 g (3 oz) mixed salad leaves
1 tomato, skinned, seeded and chopped (page 283)
1 teaspoon *lemon olive oil* (page 280) or olive oil with
    a squeeze of lemon juice
Sea salt and freshly ground black pepper

Put all the pesto ingredients in a liquidiser, blend for about 10 seconds and then remove half the mixture and set aside; it should be fairly coarse at this stage. Blend the remaining pesto until it is smooth.

Preheat the grill to high. Cut the aubergine into four 1 cm (½-inch) thick slices. Brush liberally with olive oil and season with salt. Grill until just cooked through.

Brush the red mullet fillets with olive oil and season with salt and pepper. Grill for about 4 minutes, 2 minutes on each side.

Meanwhile, spread the aubergine slices with the coarse pesto and place under the grill until the pesto has warmed through. Place an aubergine slice on each of 4 warmed plates and arrange the fish alongside them.

Toss the salad leaves with the tomato, lemon olive oil (see page 280), or just add a squeeze of lemon juice with your best olive oil, and salt and put a small pile on each plate. Pour the smooth pesto around each plate, making sure that some, but not all, trickles over the fillets, and serve at once.

Beef carpaccio

The original recipe for beef carpaccio came from Harry's Bar in Venice, and was thinly sliced top rump of beef served ice-cold, with a mustardy mayonnaise-based dressing thinned down with lemon juice, milk and Worcestershire sauce. This was drizzled back and forth across the red beef in Jackson Pollock fashion. Indeed, the dish is so distinctive in appearance that it's become a bit of a 60s' icon. Time has moved on, however, and now you're more likely to find carpaccio served with a sprinkling of good extra virgin olive oil, rocket and shaved parmesan cheese. I like both methods, but these days I prefer the cleaner taste of the rocket and parmesan version.

SERVES 6

675 g (1½ lb) top rump of beef, chilled overnight
Extra virgin olive oil, for drizzling
50 g (2 oz) wild rocket
25 g (1 oz) parmesan shavings
sea salt and freshly ground black pepper

Using a long, razor-sharp, thin-bladed carving knife, cut the beef across into the thinnest possible slices. Arrange the slices over 6 chilled 25 cm (10-inch) plates, so that they cover the entire base, with the edges of the slices just butting up together but not overlapping very much.

Season the beef with some salt and pepper and then drizzle over a little olive oil. Pile the rocket leaves into the centre, scatter over the parmesan shavings and serve straight away.

Warm poached skate with the sunny and aromatic flavours of Morocco

Few fish go together so well with such flavours as saffron, chilli, coriander, garlic and olive oil as skate. Like all members of the shark family, it needs strong flavours to accompany it, being almost overassertive after the first half-a-dozen mouthfuls.

SERVES 4

2 x 450 g (1 lb) prepared skate wings

FOR THE *COURT-BOUILLON*:

1 onion, sliced

2 celery sticks, sliced

1 fresh bay leaf

3 tablespoons white wine vinegar

2 teaspoons salt

6 black peppercorns

1.2 litres (2 pints) water

FOR THE SAUCE:

A pinch of saffron strands

2 plum tomatoes, skinned, seeded and diced (page 283)

¼ teaspoon crushed coriander seeds

A pinch of ground cumin

1 small *roasted red pepper* (page 280), skinned, seeded and cut into thin strips

1 medium-hot red chilli, seeded and finely chopped

2 garlic cloves, finely chopped

150 ml (5 fl oz) extra virgin olive oil

1 tablespoon lemon juice

2 teaspoons each of shredded coriander and mint

Sea salt and freshly ground black pepper

For the *court-bouillon*, put all the ingredients into a large, shallow pan. Bring to the boil and simmer for 20 minutes.

Cut each skate wing in half. Add them to the *court-bouillon* and simmer gently for 10 minutes.

Meanwhile, for the sauce, steep the saffron in a couple of teaspoons of warm water for 5 minutes. Then put the saffron and its water, tomatoes, coriander, cumin, red pepper, chilli, garlic, oil, lemon juice, 1 teaspoon of salt and freshly ground black pepper into a small pan and, just before the skate is ready, warm the sauce through over a very gentle heat.

Lift the pieces of skate out of the *court-bouillon*, drain off the excess liquid and put on to 4 warmed plates. Stir the coriander and mint into the sauce, spoon some over each piece of skate and serve.

Leek cannelloni with lemon thyme and provolone piccante

I came up with this recipe as a celebration of the organic vegetables I had tasted at Coleshill Organics near Swindon. Cultivating vegetables without recourse to chemicals is very hard work, but there does seem to be more flavour in a leek grown organically. I thought that to make a vegetable (which is mostly just added to flavour other ingredients) the star of the dish would do justice to Peter Richardson and Sonya Oliver's hard work. If you can't get provolone piccante, other good cheese for this would be Beaufort or Gruyère.

SERVES 4

50 g (2 oz) butter
900 g (2 lb) leeks, cleaned and thinly sliced
2 garlic cloves, crushed
2 teaspoons lemon thyme leaves
2 tablespoons water
250 g (9 oz) ricotta cheese
12 sheets (250 g/9 oz) of fresh lasagne
Sea salt and freshly ground black pepper

FOR THE TOMATO SAUCE:
2 tablespoons olive oil
1 onion, finely chopped
1 garlic clove, crushed
400 g (14 oz) can of chopped tomatoes
50 ml (2 fl oz) red wine vinegar
2 teaspoons caster sugar

FOR THE CHEESE SAUCE:
1 small onion, halved
3 cloves
450 ml (15 fl oz) full-cream milk
1 bay leaf
½ teaspoon black peppercorns
30 g (1¼ oz) butter
30 g (1¼ oz) plain flour
2 tablespoons double cream
150 g (5 oz) provolone piccante cheese, coarsely grated
1 egg yolk

For the cheese sauce, stud the onion with the cloves and put it into a pan with the milk, bay leaf and black peppercorns. Bring the milk to the boil and set it aside for 20 minutes to infuse.

For the tomato sauce, heat the oil in a medium-sized pan. Add the onion and garlic and cook gently until softened. Add the tomatoes and simmer gently for 15–20 minutes, stirring now and then, until reduced and thickened. Put the vinegar and sugar into a small pan and boil rapidly until reduced to 1 teaspoon. Stir into the tomato sauce with salt and pepper to taste, then spoon the sauce over the base of a large, shallow ovenproof dish.

For the cannelloni filling, melt the butter in a large pan. Add the sliced leeks, garlic, lemon thyme leaves and water and cook gently, uncovered, for 15 minutes, until they are tender and all the excess liquid has evaporated. Transfer to a bowl and leave to cool. Then beat in the ricotta cheese and season to taste with salt and pepper.

Bring a large pan of salted water to the boil. Drop in the sheets of lasagne one at a time, take the pan off the heat and leave them to soak for 5 minutes. Drain well and leave to cool. Spoon some of the leek filling along one short edge of each sheet and roll up. Arrange the cannelloni, seam-side down, on top of the tomato sauce.

Preheat the oven to 200°C/400°F/Gas Mark 6. Strain the milk for the cheese sauce. Melt the butter in a non-stick pan, add the flour and cook over a medium heat for 1 minute to cook out the flour. Gradually beat in the milk, bring to the boil, stirring, and leave to simmer very gently over a low heat for 10 minutes, giving it a stir every now and then. Remove the pan from the heat and stir in the cream, 75 g (3 oz) of the grated provolone, the egg yolk and some seasoning to taste.

Pour the sauce over the cannelloni, sprinkle over the rest of the cheese and bake in the oven for 30 minutes, until golden and bubbling.

Turkish kofta kebabs with minted yoghurt and kohlrabi and carrot salad

If you are using a charcoal barbecue for this recipe, light it 30–40 minutes before you want to start cooking. If using a gas barbecue, light it 10 minutes beforehand.

SERVES 4

900 g (2 lb) minced lamb
2 onions, finely grated
6 garlic cloves, crushed
2 teaspoons dried chilli flakes
1 small bunch of flat-leaf parsley, chopped
Oil, for brushing
2 vine-ripened tomatoes, thinly sliced
Sea salt and freshly ground black pepper

FOR THE MINTED YOGHURT:
200 g (7 oz) Greek natural yoghurt
2 tablespoons chopped mint

FOR THE KOHLRABI AND CARROT SALAD:
2 large carrots, halved
2 kohlrabi, peeled
2 tablespoons sunflower oil
4 teaspoons cumin seeds
4 teaspoons lemon juice

Cover 8 bamboo skewers with cold water and leave them to soak.

Put the minced lamb into a bowl with the onions, garlic, chilli flakes, parsley, 1 teaspoon of salt and some freshly ground black pepper. Mix together well with your hands until the mixture has bound together. Divide the mixture into 8 and then mould it into long sausage shapes around the drained bamboo skewers.

For the minted yoghurt, mix the yoghurt with the mint, ½ teaspoon of salt and some pepper and set aside.

For the salad, finely shred the carrots and kohlrabi, on a mandolin or on the coleslaw setting of your food processor so that you get nice long, thin, crunchy strips. Put them into a bowl with a large pinch of salt and mix together well. Heat the oil in a small pan, add the cumin seeds and, as soon as they start to sizzle, add them to the vegetables with the lemon juice and toss once more.

Brush the kofta generously with oil and lightly oil the bars of a barbecue or griddle. Cook for 5 minutes, turning them now and them, until browned all over and cooked through.

Spread the minted yoghurt over 1 large or 4 individual serving plates. Lay the kofta kebabs on top, garnish with the sliced tomatoes and serve with the kohlrabi and carrot salad.

Fillets of John Dory with olives, capers and rosemary

I've waxed lyrical about this dish in my introduction to the chapter. It's the same sort of assembly as a salad nicoise if, like me, you use warm potatoes in it. It's very much a restaurant dish, where the success is largely based on the quality of the ingredients, the preciseness of the cooking of the fish and, perhaps most importantly, the attractive way the ingredients are put on the plate.

SERVES 4

2 x 350–450 g (12 oz–1 lb) John Dory, filleted
50 ml (2 fl oz) extra virgin olive oil
4 small waxy new potatoes, such as Charlotte
2 anchovy fillets in olive oil, drained
3 pieces sun-dried tomato in olive oil, drained
A small handful of flat-leaf parsley leaves
4 very small, vine-ripened tomatoes, skinned,
    quartered and seeded (page 283)
8 black olives, pitted and cut in half
12 nonpareille capers
The leaves from 1 x 5 cm (2 inch) rosemary sprig
Salt and freshly ground black pepper

Preheat the grill to high. Cut each John Dory fillet diagonally across into 2 similar-sized pieces. Brush each piece with olive oil, season with salt and pepper and place, skin side up, on a baking tray.

Cut each potato lengthways into quarters and cook in a pan of boiling, salted water for a few minutes until tender. Drain, return to the pan, cover and keep warm.

Cut the anchovy fillets lengthways into fine slivers. Cut each piece of sun-dried tomato into thin strips. Very roughly chop the flat-leaf parsley, so that the leaves are still almost intact.

Grill the John Dory fillets for 3–4 minutes until only just cooked. Meanwhile, put the remaining olive oil, potatoes, anchovies, sun-dried tomatoes, parsley, tomatoes, olives, capers and rosemary into a small, shallow pan and warm through over a low heat, but do not overheat the oil. Then season and very gently stir the ingredients around so that they are all coated in the oil and parsley.

Overlap 2 pieces of John Dory onto 4 warmed plates and arrange the contents of the pan over the fish, making it look as attractive as possible and that each plate has roughly the same quantity of ingredients. Serve straight away.

Pizza Margherita

This isn't any old recipe for pizza – this is my recipe, and it's worth making for the following reasons. Firstly, the dough will give you the lightest, crispest, thinnest base. The buffalo mozzarella will give you a very good-tasting cheese on a pizza, and the use of the best vine-ripened tomatoes, peeled and seeded, then concentrated in hot olive oil, will give you a really fresh tomato sauce. I add a bit of garlic and oregano, too, but basically this is just a pizza Margherita, which is finished with fresh basil leaves and said to resemble the Italian flag – i.e. red tomato, white mozzarella and green basil.

I'm extremely conservative about my toppings for pizzas. The only thing that I like to add occasionally is anchovy fillets, and those are the ones salted and preserved in olive oil – definitely not the ones in vinegar! These are 25 cm (10-inch) pizzas and, because they are baked on preheated trays or tiles, you can only cook two at a time. Obviously a pizza 'peel' is the right tool to transfer your pizza to the hot oven, but you can easily use a spare baking sheet, or even a piece of cardboard or hardboard, best sprinkled with a little cornmeal or polenta to help them slide.

MAKES 4

4 tablespoons olive oil, plus extra for drizzling
2 garlic cloves, finely chopped
1½ kg (3½ lb) vine-ripened tomatoes, skinned, seeded
   and roughly chopped (page 283)
1 tablespoon chopped oregano
350 g (12 oz) buffalo mozzarella cheese, thinly sliced
A large handful of basil leaves, torn into pieces
Sea salt and freshly ground black pepper

FOR THE BASE:
550 g (1¼ lb) strong white flour
4 teaspoons easy-blend yeast
2 teaspoons salt
325–350ml (11–12 fl oz) hand-hot water
4 teaspoons olive oil
4 tablespoons polenta or semolina

For the base, sift the flour, yeast and salt into a bowl and make a well in the centre. Add the warm water and olive oil and mix together into a soft dough. Tip the dough out on to a lightly floured surface and knead for 5 minutes, or until smooth and elastic. Then return it to the bowl, cover with cling film and leave in a warm place for approximately 1 hour, or until doubled in size.

Meanwhile, for the topping, heat the oil and garlic in a large, shallow pan. As soon as the garlic starts to sizzle, add the tomatoes and some salt and pepper and simmer quite vigorously for 7–10 minutes, until reduced to a thickish sauce. Adjust the seasoning if necessary.

Put 2 large baking sheets or quarry tiles into the oven and heat it to its highest setting. Knock the air out of the dough and knead it briefly once more on a lightly floured surface. Divide into 4 pieces and keep the spare ones covered with cling film while you shape the first pizza.

Sprinkle a spare baking sheet or a pizza peel with some of the polenta or semolina. Roll the dough out into a disc approximately 25 cm (10 inches) in diameter, lift it on to the baking sheet and reshape it with your fingers into a round. Spread over one quarter of the tomato sauce to within about 2½ cm (1 inch) of the edge. Sprinkle with some of the oregano and then cover with a quarter of the mozzarella cheese slices. Drizzle with a little olive oil, then open the oven door and quickly slide the pizza off the tray (give it a little shake before you open the oven door to make sure it's not stuck anywhere) on to the hot baking sheet on the top shelf. Bake for 10 minutes or until the cheese has melted and the crust is crisp and golden. Meanwhile, prepare another pizza and slide it on to the second hot baking sheet.

Take the first pizza out of the oven and move the second one on to the top shelf to continue cooking. Slide the cooked pizza directly on to wooden chopping boards placed in the centre of the table, scatter with the torn basil leaves and cut into wedges with a pizza wheel. Make sure everybody starts while you make and cook the other 2 pizzas.

Fegato alla Veneziana with parmesan polenta

This dish is really a simple sautéed calves' liver and onion and is another dish from Harry's Bar in Venice. It's wonderful served with a chilled glass of Pinot Grigio.

SERVES 4

600 g (1 lb 5 oz) calves' liver, trimmed and
    any thin membrane removed
5 tablespoons extra virgin olive oil
450 g (1 lb) small onions, very thinly sliced
30 g (1¼ oz) butter
A small bunch of flat-leaf parsley, chopped
Sea salt and freshly ground black pepper

FOR THE PARMESAN POLENTA:

900 ml (1½ pints) water
115 g (4½ oz) polenta
40 g (1½ oz) butter
75 g (3 oz) parmesan cheese, finely grated

For the parmesan polenta, bring the water to boil in a medium-sized pan. Pour in the polenta in a slow, steady stream, stirring all the time, bring to a simmer and leave to cook gently, stirring frequently, for 20 minutes.

Meanwhile, cut the liver lengthways into slices (get your butcher to do this for you if you like) and then cut across each slice, at a slight angle, into thin, short strips which are about 2½ cm (1 inch) wide.

Heat 3 tablespoons of the oil in a large, heavy-based frying pan over a medium-high heat. Add the onions and cook, stirring frequently, until they are soft and a deep golden brown. Transfer to a bowl and keep warm.

Add another 1½ teaspoons of oil to the pan and return it to a high heat. When the oil is sizzling hot, add a quarter of the liver and some seasoning and cook for 30 seconds, stirring constantly, until lightly browned. Tip on to a plate and repeat three more times with the remaining liver.

Return all the liver to the pan with the onions and any juices from the plate and toss over a high heat for another 30 seconds. Spoon on to a warmed serving platter.

Add the butter to the pan and scrape up any browned bits from the base; remove from the heat and stir in the chopped parsley. Spoon over the liver and onions.

Stir the butter, parmesan cheese and a little salt to taste into the polenta. To serve, spoon the polenta on to warmed plates and spoon some of the liver and the buttery juices on top.

Roasted salmon on roasted tomatoes with salsa verde

To make life easy, prepare the salmon in the morning and refrigerate, but remove it from the fridge 30 minutes before roasting to allow it to come back to room temperature.

SERVES 10-12

2½–2¾ kg (5½–6 lb) salmon, scaled and filleted
   or 2 x 1 kg (2¼-lb) salmon fillets
FOR THE TOMATOES AND SALSA VERDE:
15 g (½ oz) flat-leaf parsley leaves
A handful of mint leaves
4 tablespoons capers
6 anchovy fillets in olive oil, drained
3 garlic cloves
4 large vine-ripened tomatoes, each cut into 8 slices
½ teaspoon dried chilli flakes
A large bunch of thyme
About 4 tablespoons olive oil
10 tablespoons water
Sea salt and freshly ground black pepper

Preheat the oven to 220°C/425°F/Gas Mark 7. Chop the parsley and mint leaves, 3 tablespoons of the capers, the anchovy fillets and 1 garlic clove together on a board into a coarse paste and season to taste with a little salt.

Line the base of a large baking tray or roasting tin with a sheet of non-stick baking paper and then lay the tomatoes in rows of 4 down the centre of the paper (diagonally if necessary, so that your salmon will fit). Scatter over the rest of the capers, the remaining garlic, cut into slices, half of the chilli flakes and the leaves of all but 1 sprig of the thyme and sprinkle over 3 tablespoons of the oil, the water and some salt. This will prevent the salmon from sticking and produce a lovely sauce to serve with the salmon.

Brush the skin side of one salmon fillet with a little of the remaining oil, season lightly with salt and place skin side down on top of the tomatoes. Lightly season the flesh side with salt and then cover with the salsa verde mixture. Lightly season the cut face of the second salmon fillet and place skin side up on top. Brush the skin with the rest of the oil and scatter with the remaining chilli flakes and the leaves from the remaining thyme sprig. Season with salt and pepper. Roast the fish for 25 minutes, until the skin is lightly browned and the flesh still slightly pink in the centre. Remove the salmon and leave it to rest briefly.

To serve, cut the salmon across into portion-sized pieces and serve with some of the cooking juices spooned over and a 'line' of the thyme-flavoured tomatoes. Accompany with steamed new potatoes and green beans.

Crab linguine with parsley and chilli

Though the recipe for this is very short, there are a number of nuances that need to be explained. Firstly, it's very important that the pasta is cooked perfectly al dente. *I've suggested a cooking time of 7–8 minutes, but I always test pasta by biting it. Secondly, when I say warm the sauce ingredients through a gentle heat, I really mean it – the temperature should never get much above 60°C. Lastly, try not to break up the crab meat if it's fresh and has been hand-picked, because lumps of crab meat folded through the pasta look very appetising.*

SERVES 4

450 g (1 lb) dried linguine or spaghetti
3 vine-ripened tomatoes, skinned, seeded
   and chopped (page 283)
300 g (10 oz) fresh white crab meat
1 tablespoon chopped parsley
1½ tablespoons lemon juice
50 ml (2 fl oz) extra virgin olive oil
A pinch of dried chilli flakes
1 garlic clove, finely chopped
Sea salt and freshly ground black pepper

Cook the pasta in a large pan of boiling, well-salted water (1 teaspoon per 600 ml/1 pint) for 7–8 minutes or until *al dente*.

Meanwhile, put the tomatoes, crab meat, parsley, lemon juice, olive oil, chilli flakes and garlic into another pan and warm through over a gentle heat.

Drain the pasta, return to the pan with the sauce and briefly toss together. Season to taste. Divide between 4 warmed plates and serve immediately.

Osso buco with risotto Milanese

I don't know if my recipe for osso buco is the same as Bertorelli's, but it's one of those dishes I associate with a certain period of my life in London. I have particular memories of the finish to the dish – gremolata, that exciting mixture of finely chopped lemon zest, garlic and parsley. What I love about osso buco is getting it with the marrow still in the shinbones so that you can pick it out, that silky, unctuous texture adding an immeasurable pleasure to an already memorable dish. It's served with risotto Milanese, but I leave out the traditional extra beef marrow and parmesan, which I would only include if this simple and perfect saffron-flavoured risotto was to be served on its own.

SERVES 4

1½ kg (3-lb) shin of veal, cut into slices 4 cm (1½ inches) thick
4 tablespoons olive oil
25 g (1 oz) plain flour
1 onion, finely chopped
1 small carrot, finely chopped
1 celery stick, finely chopped
Leaves from 1 rosemary sprig
2 sage leaves
150 ml (5 fl oz) dry white wine
2 tomatoes, skinned and chopped (page 283)
600 ml (1 pint) light *beef stock* (page 278)
1 pared strip of lemon zest
Sea salt and freshly ground black pepper

FOR THE RISOTTO MILANESE:
1.2 litres (2 pints) light *beef stock* (page 278)
A small pinch of saffron strands
50 g (2 oz) unsalted butter
2 shallots, finely chopped
225 g (8 oz) risotto rice, such as Carnaroli or Arborio

FOR THE GREMOLATA:
1 garlic clove, peeled
A small handful of flat-leaf parsley leaves
1 pared strip of lemon zest

MEDITERRANEAN & MIDDLE EAST

RICK STEIN

Season the slices of shin with ½ teaspoon of salt and leave for 20 minutes before cooking. Heat the olive oil in a heavy-based flameproof casserole. Coat the pieces of shin economically with the flour, pat off the excess and fry until nicely browned on both sides. Transfer to a plate, taking care not to disturb the marrow.

Add the vegetables, rosemary leaves and sage to the pan and fry until lightly browned. Add the wine and tomatoes and cook until the wine has almost completely evaporated. Return the meat to the pan and add the beef stock, pared lemon zest, ½ teaspoon of salt and some pepper. Bring to the boil, then cover and simmer gently for 1 hour. Uncover and skim off the excess fat from the surface. Increase the heat slightly and simmer more vigorously for 30 minutes to reduce and concentrate the flavour of the sauce.

Meanwhile, make the risotto Milanese. Put the beef stock into a pan and bring to the boil. Reduce the heat, add the saffron and keep hot. Melt half the butter in a pan, add the shallots and cook gently for 3–4 minutes, until soft but not browned. Add the rice and turn it over for a couple of minutes, until all the grains are coated in the butter. Add a ladleful of the hot stock and stir over a medium heat until it has all been absorbed before adding another. Continue like this for about 20 minutes, stirring constantly, until you have added all the stock and the rice is tender and creamy but still a little al dente. Stir in the remaining butter and season to taste with salt and pepper.

For the gremolata, chop the garlic, parsley and lemon together quite finely. Sprinkle it over the top of the stew and then spoon into 4 warmed, deep plates. Spoon the risotto Milanese alongside and serve.

Seafood lasagne

This is the Italian version of fish pie. Unusually for fish dishes, it tastes just as good when reheated. You can, of course, put any type of seafood in a lasagne and add mussels, clams or squid, but I find that, in the baking, the mussels become very fishy-tasting and the squid tough. For me, the perfect combination is a flaky white fish, those sweet, pink North Atlantic prawns and white crab meat. At our deli we've recently discovered the perfect container for baking lasagnes, fish pies and thermidors. I think they always look a bit mass-produced in silver foil trays so we've found a box made from thin woven wood much like the baskets you get oysters in in Brittany that colour up quite nicely in the oven.

SERVES 8

550 g (1¼-lb) ling, coley or pollack fillets, skinned
12 sheets (250 g/9 oz) of fresh lasagne
175 g (6 oz) peeled North Atlantic prawns
225 g (8 oz) fresh white crab meat
Sea salt and freshly ground black pepper

FOR THE TOMATO SAUCE:

4 tablespoons olive oil
2 onions, finely chopped
2 garlic cloves, finely chopped
2 x 400 g (14 oz) cans of chopped tomatoes
100 ml (3½ fl oz) red wine vinegar
4 teaspoons caster sugar
A large handful of basil leaves, thinly shredded

FOR THE BÉCHAMEL SAUCE:

1 large onion, halved
6 cloves
1.2 litres (2 pints) full-cream milk
2 bay leaves
1 teaspoon black peppercorns
65 g (2½ oz) butter
65 g (2½ oz) plain flour
4 tablespoons double cream
50 g (2 oz) parmesan cheese, freshly grated

For the tomato sauce, heat the oil in a pan, add the onions and garlic and cook gently until softened. Add the tomatoes and simmer gently for 15–20 minutes, stirring now and then, until reduced and thickened. Put the vinegar and sugar into a small pan and boil rapidly until reduced to 2 teaspoons. Stir into the tomato sauce and season to taste with salt and pepper. Stir in the basil and set aside.

For the béchamel sauce, stud the onion with the cloves and put it into a pan with the milk, bay leaves and peppercorns. Bring to the boil and then set aside for 20 minutes to infuse.

Bring the milk back to the boil, add the fish fillets and simmer for 8 minutes. Lift the fish on to a plate and strain the milk into a jug. When cool enough to handle, break it into large flakes, discarding any bones.

Bring a large pan of well-salted water to the boil (1 teaspoon salt per 600 ml/1 pint water). Drop in the sheets of lasagne, one at a time, take the pan off the heat and leave them to soak for 5 minutes. Drain well and set aside.

To finish the béchamel sauce, melt the butter in a non-stick pan, add the flour and cook over a medium heat for 1 minute. Lower the heat and gradually beat in the milk, then bring to the boil, stirring. Simmer gently over a low heat for 10 minutes, giving it a stir every now and then. Remove the pan from the heat and stir in the cream, half the parmesan cheese and some seasoning to taste.

Preheat the oven to 200°C/400°F/Gas Mark 6. To assemble the lasagne, arrange a layer of the pasta over the base of a 3½ litre (6-pint) shallow ovenproof dish. Spoon over half the tomato sauce and then scatter over half the flaked white fish, prawns and crab meat. Spoon over one third of the béchamel sauce and then repeat the layers once more. Finish with a final layer of the pasta and the remaining béchamel sauce. The lasagne can be prepared in advance to this stage; cover and chill until needed.

If the lasagne has been chilled for some time, allow it to come back to room temperature before baking. Sprinkle over the remaining parmesan cheese and bake for 40–50 minutes, until golden and bubbling.

Rabbit cacciatora with grilled polenta

This rabbit cacciatora ('hunter's style') is so well known that it is almost impossible to pin down a definitive recipe. I like unpeeled cloves of garlic and lots of sage, rosemary and oregano fried in the olive oil before adding the rabbit and a small quantity of a very concentrated tomato sauce with black olives and a little chilli. It is equally good made with chicken.

SERVES 4

3 tablespoons olive oil
1 head of garlic, cloves separated but unpeeled
10 sage leaves
The leaves from 1 rosemary sprig
2 oregano or thyme sprigs
1 rabbit, jointed into 8 pieces
120 ml (4 fl oz) dry white wine
400 g (14 oz) can of chopped tomatoes
12 small black olives
A pinch of dried chilli flakes
Sea salt and freshly ground black pepper
A small handful of coarsely chopped parsley, to garnish
FOR THE GRILLED POLENTA:
900 ml (1½ pints) water
150 g (5 oz) polenta
25 g (1 oz) parmesan cheese, freshly grated

Bring the water to the boil in a medium-sized pan and then add the polenta in a slow, steady stream, stirring all the time. Lower the heat and leave to simmer gently for 20 minutes, stirring frequently. Stir in the parmesan cheese and ¾ teaspoon of salt and pour the mixture into a lightly oiled 25 x 18 cm (10 x 7 inch) shallow, rectangular tin. Leave for 3–4 hours, until completely cold and set.

For the cacciatora, heat the olive oil and unpeeled garlic cloves in a large, shallow pan and fry for 3–4 minutes, until the garlic is lightly browned. Add the sage, rosemary and oregano or thyme and fry for another minute. Lower the heat slightly, add the rabbit pieces and fry until lightly browned all over.

Add the white wine to the pan and cook until reduced to a couple of tablespoons. Stir in the tomatoes, black olives, chilli flakes and 1 teaspoon of salt and season very well with black pepper. Cover and simmer for 30 minutes or until the rabbit is tender, then uncover, increase the heat slightly and cook until the sauce has reduced, thickened and become concentrated in flavour.

Turn the polenta out on to a board and cut it into 8 pieces. Heat a large, dry, non-stick frying pan over a high heat, add the pieces of polenta and fry for 2–3 minutes on each side, until lightly golden. Overlap 2 pieces of polenta on each of 4 warmed plates, spoon the rabbit alongside and serve.

Risi e bisi (rice with peas)

This dish is designed to exalt the sweet flavour of spring peas from the Venetian island of Sant'Erasmo, which has great market gardens on it. I thought it would be a fitting dish to celebrate the abundance of peas in Norfolk in the early summer; most of them are destined to be frozen but they can be bought fresh locally. It's somewhere between a risotto and a soup, flavoured with good stock and pancetta. My friend Simon Hopkinson, who loves this dish, says he likes to add a bit of fresh mint, but the Italians never would.

SERVES 4

900 g (2 lb) fresh peas in the pod
1½ litres (2½ pints) *chicken stock* (page 278)
3 tablespoons olive oil
50 g (2 oz) pancetta, diced
1 small onion, finely chopped
225 g (8 oz) risotto rice, such as Carnaroli or Arborio
15 g (½ oz) butter
A small handful of parsley leaves, chopped
25 g (1 oz) parmesan cheese, freshly grated
Sea salt and freshly ground black pepper

Shell the peas, reserving the pods. You should be left with about 175 g (6 oz) of shelled peas. Put the stock into a pan with the pea pods, bring to the boil and leave to simmer for 20 minutes. Strain into a clean pan, pressing out all the liquid with the back of a wooden spoon, and keep hot.

Heat the olive oil in a medium-sized pan, add the pancetta and onion and fry gently until the onion is soft but not browned. Add the stock, rice and peas, bring to the boil and simmer very gently for about 15 minutes, stirring once or twice.

Finally stir in the butter, parsley and parmesan and season to taste with salt and pepper. Ladle into warmed soup bowls and eat as you would soup, with a spoon rather than a fork.

Roasted skate wings with chilli beans

Technically, this is a recipe for ray rather than skate. Sadly the latter is now seriously depleted. So why do I call it skate? Because it sounds better and is a name people are familiar with.

SERVES 4

4 x 225 g (8 oz) prepared skate wings
1 teaspoon paprika
1 teaspoon coarsely crushed black pepper
50 g (2 oz) butter
3 tablespoons sherry vinegar
Sea salt and freshly ground black pepper

FOR THE CHILLI BEANS:

350 g (13 oz) dried cannellini beans, soaked in cold water overnight
2 tablespoons extra virgin olive oil
1 garlic clove, finely chopped
2 medium-hot red chillies, seeded and finely chopped
1 small onion, finely chopped
350 ml (12 fl oz) *chicken stock* (page 278)
2 beef tomatoes, skinned, seeded and diced (page 283)
1 teaspoon chopped tarragon

Drain the cannellini beans and put them into a pan with fresh water to cover. Bring to the boil, skimming off any scum as it rises to the surface. Cover and simmer for 1 hour or until just tender. Drain and set aside.

Preheat the oven to 200°C/400°F/Gas Mark 6. Dry the skate wings with kitchen paper and then sprinkle on both sides with the paprika and coarsely crushed black pepper.

For the chilli beans, put the olive oil, garlic and red chillies in a pan over a medium heat. As soon as the garlic and chillies start to sizzle, add the onion and cook for 5 minutes until soft. Add the beans and 300 ml (10 fl oz) of the stock and leave them to simmer for 10 minutes.

To cook the skate wings, melt the butter in a roasting tin on top of the stove. Add the wings and lightly brown them for 1 minute on each side. Sprinkle with a little salt, transfer to the oven and roast for 10 minutes.

Meanwhile, stir the tomatoes into the beans and simmer for a further 10 minutes. Stir in the tarragon and season to taste with salt and pepper.

To serve, spoon some of the beans on to the centres of 4 warmed plates and put one of the roasted skate wings on top. Place the roasting tin over a moderate heat, add the sherry vinegar and the rest of the chicken stock and leave it to boil for a minute or two, scraping up all the crusty bits from the bottom of the tin. Strain the sauce through a fine sieve into a small pan, season to taste and then spoon over the top of the skate.

Linguine with porcini, garlic and truffle oil

The hero of this piece is the pasta. I have no real insider knowledge of the best factory-made pasta, but I do know what I like and that is, above all, De Cecco, particularly the linguine no 7. The most important element in a good pasta is the flour – hard semolina – but almost as important is the length of time it is dried. The longer it takes, the harder the finished pasta and the better it keeps its al dente quality during cooking. De Cecco is amazingly robust in this way and it makes all the difference, even in the way that it falls on the plate, retaining bounce and shape, served with this simple olive oil, parsley and dried porcini sauce clinging to it.

SERVES 4

25 g (1 oz) dried porcini mushrooms
450 g (1 lb) dried linguine
5 tablespoons extra virgin olive oil
4 small garlic cloves, thinly sliced
1 teaspoon minced truffle
8 tablespoons roughly chopped flat-leaf parsley
Sea salt
Truffle oil, to serve

Cover the dried porcini with warm water and leave to soak for 30 minutes.

Drop the linguine into a large pan of well-salted, boiling water (1 teaspoon of salt per 600 ml/1 pint of water), bring back to the boil and cook for 7–8 minutes or until *al dente*.

Meanwhile, drain the mushrooms and slice them thinly.

Put the oil into a large pan with the garlic and leave to sizzle gently for 1 minute. Add the mushrooms and cook them for another minute.

Drain the pasta, add to the garlic, mushroom and oil pan with the minced truffle and chopped parsley. Toss together.

Spoon the pasta into 4 warmed bowls, sprinkle each one with a little truffle oil and serve immediately.

Light fig tarts with crème fraîche

This is one of the most pleasing ways I know to serve seasonal fruit as a hot sweet. The same technique also works with thinly sliced apple or pears. It's an incredibly easy dish to produce and I often make a bigger tart if I've got a lot of people round for dinner. When I first wrote a recipe for these tarts, 25 years ago, I picked up the idea from a smart Michelin-starred restaurant in France – I can't remember which one – and back then not only did I have to include a recipe for puff pastry but also for crème fraîche, which you couldn't get in the UK. I used to mix double cream and yoghurt and leave it in the fridge overnight to produce an approximation of crème fraîche.

SERVES 8

1 kg (2¼ lb) puff pastry
12 fresh figs
4 teaspoons granulated sugar
3 tablespoons redcurrant jelly
Crème fraîche, to serve

Preheat the oven to 220°C/425°F/Gas Mark 7.

Divide the pastry into 8, roll out each piece thinly on a lightly floured surface and cut into a 15 cm (6-inch) disc. Put them well spaced apart on 2 lightly greased baking trays.

Cut each fig across into 4–5 slices and arrange them slightly overlapping on the pastry discs, leaving a 1 cm (½-inch) border. Sprinkle each tart with ½ teaspoon of granulated sugar and bake for about 12 minutes, until the pastry is puffed up and golden and the sugar has lightly caramelised.

Meanwhile, put the redcurrant jelly into a pan with 2 teaspoons of water and leave over a gentle heat until melted. Set aside to cool slightly but do not let it set.

Remove the tarts from the oven and brush the fruit with the redcurrant glaze. Slide each tart on to a warmed plate and serve with the crème fraîche.

White wine, olive oil and polenta cake with poached peaches

This is a really unusual dessert cake, which has a lovely crunchy texture, and where you can really taste white wine and fragrant olive oil after it's baked.

SERVES 8

FOR THE CAKE:
2 large eggs
250 g (8 oz) caster sugar
150 ml (5 fl oz) white wine, such as a Sauvignon or Riesling
150 ml (5 fl oz) olive oil
1 teaspoon vanilla extract
Finely grated zest 1 large lemon
175 g (6 oz) plain flour
1½ teaspoon baking powder
90 g (3 oz) instant polenta
Icing sugar, for dusting
FOR THE POACHED PEACHES:
600 ml (20 fl oz) water
350 g (12 oz) granulated sugar
Pared zest 4 lemons
1 vanilla pod, split open lengthways
8 firm, ripe peaches
Vanilla ice cream, to serve

For the poached peaches, put the water, sugar, lemon zest and vanilla pod into a medium-sized pan. Place over a low heat and leave until the sugar has dissolved, then bring to the boil, remove from the heat and set aside for 30 minutes to allow the flavours to infuse the syrup. Remove and discard the strips of zest and vanilla pod. Make a small, shallow cross into the top of each peach. Bring the syrup back to the boil, add the peaches, 4 at a time if necessary, and simmer for 3–4 minutes or until just tender. Lift the peaches out of the syrup and peel off the skins. Cover and set aside. Leave the syrup to cool. Return the peaches to the syrup, cover and chill until needed.

For the cake, preheat the oven to 160°C/325°F/Gas Mark 3. Butter a 24 cm (9½-inch) clip-sided tin and line with baking paper. Put the eggs and sugar into a large bowl and whisk with an electric hand whisk for 10 minutes until they are thick and moussey and have reached the trail stage. Gently beat in the wine, olive oil, vanilla and lemon zest. Sift over the flour and baking powder and fold in gently, followed by the polenta.

Pour the cake mixture into the tin and bake for 1–1¼ hours or until a skewer inserted into the centre of the cake comes out cleanly. Leave to cool in its tin for 15 minutes. Then run a knife around the outside of the cake, transfer to a serving plate and dust lightly with icing sugar. While the cake is still warm, cut it into wedges and serve with the peaches and a scoop of vanilla ice cream.

Panna cotta with stewed rhubarb

A great thing about panna cotta is that it is set with only a tiny amount of gelatine, and in this particular recipe the cream only just holds its shape. For the television series for which I developed this recipe, we filmed me instructing a dozen or so chefs on a four-course menu at Blenheim Palace for 100 guests. I demonstrated the dishes and then we all prepared them together. However, disaster loomed when it looked extremely doubtful whether the tiny amount of gelatine I had allowed for the 100 portions of panna cotta would, in fact, set the cream. In the end, I reluctantly decided that we would have to tip the mixture out into a big bowl and add more gelatine, which would firm it up more than I wanted. Just as we were about to do that, Paul Ripley, our head chef, came in bearing a plate of panna cotta that had just set in the softest, most melting way. At some stage in any 'away match', as I like to call it, things start to go wrong and you think it is all going to collapse. It just takes a little moment like that to make you think, 'Oh, it's going to be all right after all.' And it was – everybody said the panna cotta tasted so fresh.

SERVES 6

1 vanilla pod
300 ml (10 fl oz) double cream
300 ml (10 fl oz) milk
6 tablespoons caster sugar
2 teaspoons powdered gelatine
2 tablespoons water

FOR THE STEWED RHUBARB:
350–400 g (12 oz–14 oz) young, pink, thin-stemmed rhubarb
100 g (4 oz) light muscovado sugar
Pared zest and juice ½ small orange
50 ml (2 fl oz) water
7½ cm (3-inch) cinnamon stick

For the panna cotta, split open the vanilla pod and scrape out the seeds. Put both the pod and seeds into a pan with the cream, milk and sugar and simmer gently for 5 minutes, then remove from the heat. Meanwhile, put the 2 tablespoons of cold water in a small pan and sprinkle the gelatine over it. Set aside for 5 minutes, then heat gently until clear.

Remove the vanilla pod from the cream and stir in the dissolved gelatine. Pour into 6 dariole moulds or 6 cm (2½-inch) ramekins, cover and chill for 3 hours or until set.

Cut the rhubarb into 2½ cm (1 inch) lengths. Put the sugar, orange zest, orange juice, water and cinnamon stick into a pan and leave over a low heat until the sugar has completely dissolved. Bring to the boil and boil for 3 minutes. Lift out the orange zest and cinnamon stick, add the rhubarb and simmer for 2–3 minutes or until the rhubarb is just tender and starting to collapse. Transfer to a bowl, and leave to cool.

To serve, dip the moulds briefly into tepid water, unmould the panna cotta on to 6 serving plates and spoon some of the rhubarb alongside.

India

Imagine a world that didn't have Indian food in it; unthinkable I think. It's so important to us, particularly in Britain with so much contact over the last 400 years. Where would we be without kedgeree, HP Sauce, tea, chutneys, and even something as mundane as curry sauce with fish and chips? Curries are right at the top of the list our favourite food. Interestingly, when I'm away abroad with a film crew, we all secretly crave lamb chops with broccoli and mint sauce, however lovely the food is where we are, but when we're travelling in the UK it's always a good Indian we hope to find in the next small town we're staying at.

Every time I go to India, I'm delighted by the infinite variety of the food. There's far more going on than what we see back home. The reason for that is partly that most of the Indian sub-continent restaurants were originally run by Bangladeshis and thus many of the dishes were their interpretations of regional food designed to approximate the real thing for a public that didn't know the difference. Recently, however, not just in the UK, but in countries like Australia and the US, Indian restaurants increasingly specialise in authentic cooking from a particular area. I wouldn't mind guessing that that trend started in Britain. I recall going to a very good Keralan restaurant in the capital some years ago, ages before London was taken seriously for really good food, and being amazed that, seated at the table next to me, was a French family of 8 or 10 from Paris, over just to enjoy a really good regional Indian meal, in this case from Kerala. An example of one of these regional dishes would be the *Lamb and spinach karahi* on page 157. It came from a Pakistani restaurant in Bradford. Like some recipes in this book they've appeared in earlier books of mine, such as *Food Heroes*. I've repeated it because it has turned out to be the most popular recipe from the book and one which my friends cook all the time.

As I mentioned in the introduction, the fish curries of southern India were a bit of a watershed for me because after that I stopped worrying about putting really foreign food on my menus. I remember thinking at the time that we had to have spicy dishes on that made fish taste so very good. Take the *Sardine and potato curry puffs* on page 146. It's really hard to find sauces that compliment oily fish like mackerel, sardines and herrings, but curry sauces like that used in *Mackerel recheado* on page 140 make oily fish taste positively better. Other really good curries are the *Keralan curry with prawns and kokum* (see page 150) and the *Goan fish curry with coconut milk and okra* (see page 151). Thinking of them, I'm aware I haven't been back for a while. I miss the reassuring sound of cockrels crowing in the early morning; the smell of bonfires and sweet, cheap Indian perfume; the deep reds and blues of the saris; the sandy dusty roads down to the beach; the bamboo huts; and grilling prawns and Kingfish as the sun sets over the Arabian sea.

Mackerel recheado with katchumber salad

I often wonder whether this is the best way to serve mackerel. It's a bit like when you're enjoying some really excellent fish and chips and think that cod never tastes better than when in a light and crispy batter. Mind you, the Grilled salted cod with beer, bacon and cabbage *on page 44 is pretty excellent too, as is the* Red chilli mackerel *on page 147, but there is something about the way the oily fish and the flavours of the garlic, ginger, Kashmiri chilli, onion, tamarind and spices blend together which is endlessly pleasing.*

SERVES 4

4 x 225 g (8 oz) mackerel
1 quantity of *Goan masala paste* (page 280)
FOR THE KATCHUMBER SALAD:
450 g (1 lb) vine-ripened tomatoes, thinly sliced
1 red onion, quartered and thinly sliced
2 tablespoons roughly chopped coriander leaves
¼ teaspoon ground cumin
A pinch of cayenne pepper
1 tablespoon white wine vinegar
¼ teaspoon salt
1 quantity of *pilau rice* with crispy shallots (page 280), to serve

If you are cooking the mackerel on the barbecue, light it 40 minutes before you are ready to cook.

Prepare the mackerel. Cut the heads off the mackerel. Start to cut away the top fillet until you can get the whole blade of the knife underneath. Rest a hand on top of the fish and cut the fillet away from the bones until you are about 2½ cm (1 inch) away from the tail. Turn the fish over and repeat on the other side. Pull back the top fillet and snip out the backbone, close to the tail, with scissors. The fillets will still be attached at the tail. Spread the cut face of one fillet with a tablespoon of the masala paste. Push the fish back into shape and tie in two places with string. If you are grilling the mackerel, preheat the grill to high.

For the katchumber salad, layer all the ingredients in a shallow dish.

Barbecue or grill the mackerel for 3–4 minutes on each side until crisp and lightly golden. Lift them on to 4 warmed plates. Serve with some of the katchumber salad and pilau rice.

Coconut chilli prawns with cumin puris

The combination of chilli, coconut and coriander is what I would call the holy trinity of Indian fish cookery. These are the flavours that everybody goes wild about. Even though this dish appears to be pretty exotic, I designed it to use ingredients that I could get in the high street. The real pleasure here is the cumin puris, which are freshly made using wholemeal flour flavoured with cumin seeds.

SERVES 4

3 tablespoons sunflower oil
2½ cm (1-inch) piece of fresh ginger, finely grated
3 garlic cloves, crushed
2 tablespoons ready-made rogan josh or *Goan masala paste* (page 280)
450 g (1 lb) peeled, large, raw prawns
50 g (2 oz) creamed coconut, roughly chopped
150 ml (5 fl oz) hot water
2 tablespoons chopped coriander
2 red bird's eye chillies, seeded and very finely chopped
2 spring onions, thinly sliced

FOR THE CUMIN PURIS:

100 g (4 oz) wholemeal flour
100 g (4 oz) plain flour
½ teaspoon salt
2 tablespoons sunflower oil, plus extra for brushing
1 teaspoon cumin seeds
150 ml (5 fl oz) water

First make the puris: sift the flours and salt into a large bowl, add the oil and rub it into the flour with your fingertips until well mixed in. Stir in the cumin seeds. Gradually mix in the water to make a soft, slightly sticky dough, then turn out on to a well-floured work surface and knead for 5 minutes. Rub the ball of dough with a little more oil, put it in a clean bowl, cover and leave for 30 minutes.

Preheat the grill to high.

Knead the dough again for about 3 minutes, until smooth. Divide into 12 balls, dust each one quite heavily with flour and then roll out into a 12½ cm (5-inch) disc. Brush them on both sides with oil and grill the puris for 1 minute on each side.

Heat the 3 tablespoons of oil in a large pan, add the ginger and garlic and fry for 30 seconds. Add the curry paste and fry for 2 minutes, until it looks as if it is splitting away from the oil. Add the prawns to the pan and stir-fry over a high heat for 3 minutes, until firm and pink. Add the creamed coconut and hot water and stir occasionally until the coconut has melted. Simmer for 1 minute.

Mix the coriander with the chillies and spring onions. Stir into the prawns and serve immediately, with the cumin puris.

Lamb and potato curry with coconut milk and black mustard seeds

Make this the day before, as curries always taste better after they have been allowed to stand. But don't leave it where it can be found by any hungry chefs. Debbie Major, my home economist, made this for a photoshoot in Padstow not so long ago and left it in the fridge for the next day. It came in very handy that night when I returned from the Golden Lion with the lads.

SERVES 6

100 g (4 oz) butter
500 g (1 lb 2 oz) onions, chopped
50 g (2-oz) piece of fresh ginger, finely chopped
50 g (2 oz) garlic cloves, chopped
4 medium-hot red chillies, stalks discarded, chopped
1 tablespoon crushed pasilla chillies (page 283)
400 g (14 oz) can of chopped tomatoes
1 tablespoon ground turmeric
1 tablespoon ground cumin
1 tablespoon ground coriander
2 tablespoons paprika
1 kg (2¼ lb) lean lamb, such as leg, cut into 4 cm (1¾-inch) pieces
150 ml (¼ pint) water
200 ml (7 fl oz) canned coconut milk
500 g (1 lb 2 oz) small waxy potatoes, such as Charlotte, peeled and cut into 2–3 cm (about 1-inch) pieces
2 tablespoons sunflower oil
1 tablespoon black mustard seeds
A bunch (about 40 g/1½ oz) of coriander, roughly chopped
Sea salt

Melt the butter in one large or two smaller heavy-based pans. Add the onions, ginger, garlic, red chillies and crushed pasilla chillies and cook over a medium heat, stirring now and then, for 20–30 minutes, until everything is very soft and the onions are light brown.

Spoon the onion mixture into a liquidiser and blend to a smooth paste. Return to the pan and add the tomatoes, spices, lamb, water, coconut milk and 4 teaspoons of salt. Simmer for 1¼ hours.

Stir in the potatoes, cover and continue to cook for 20–30 minutes or until the potatoes are tender. (You can now chill it overnight if you wish.)

Shortly before serving, heat the sunflower oil in a small pan. Add the black mustard seeds and leave them to sizzle vigorously for a few seconds. Tip them into the curry and stir in, with the coriander and a little more seasoning if necessary.

Matar paneer

Paneer is a firm Indian cheese, made by curdling hot milk with lemon juice or vinegar, then straining through muslin, rinsing off in water and pressing into rectangular blocks. It has the unusual properties of being suitable for frying and it does not melt when cooked, but stays in soft, neat little chunks.

SERVES 4

275–350 g (10–12 oz) paneer
3 tablespoons sunflower oil
1 small onion, finely chopped
1 garlic clove, crushed
2½ cm (1-inch) piece of fresh ginger, peeled and grated
2 medium-hot green chillies, seeded and chopped
1 teaspoon cumin seeds
1 teaspoon ground coriander
½ teaspoon turmeric powder
½ teaspoon cayenne pepper
2 vine-ripened tomatoes, skinned and roughly chopped (page 283)
350 g (12 oz) fresh or frozen peas, 900 g (2 lb) in the pod
1 small bunch coriander, roughly chopped
Salt and freshly ground black pepper
Pilau rice (page 280) or naan bread, to serve

Break the paneer roughly into 2½ cm (1-inch) pieces. Heat half of the oil in a large shallow pan, add the paneer and fry gently until lightly golden on all sides. Lift onto a plate and set aside.

Add the rest of the oil and the onion, garlic, ginger, chillies, cumin seeds, coriander, turmeric and cayenne pepper to the pan and fry gently until the onion is soft but not browned.

Add the tomatoes, peas, ¾ teaspoon salt and 2 tablespoons of water and simmer for 5 minutes. Stir in the paneer and cook gently for another 5 minutes.

Stir in the coriander and sprinkle with a little black pepper to garnish. Serve with pilau rice (see page 280) or some warm naan bread.

Sardine and potato curry puffs

Oily fish such as sardines and herrings are only great grilled whole if they are extremely fresh – 'stiff fresh', as they say in the fishmongering trade. Some of the previously frozen sardines sold at supermarket counters and optimistically labelled 'suitable for barbecuing' are, in my opinion, only suitable for adding to the barbecue as fuel. But the same sardines, or even mackerel, trout and herrings, that aren't tip-top for grilling are ideal for a hot, robustly flavoured dish like this. The point is that the oil in the fish will develop more flavour as the fish ages. These would also work well with mackerel, pilchards, sprats, herrings and any other oily fish with lots of flavour.

MAKES 12

100 g (4 oz) potato, cut into 1 cm (½-inch) cubes
1 tablespoon groundnut or sunflower oil, plus extra for deep-frying
2 garlic cloves, crushed
1 cm (½-inch) piece of fresh ginger, finely grated
½ onion, thinly sliced
1 tablespoon good-quality garam masala paste or *Goan masala paste* (page 280)
225 g (8 oz) sardines, cleaned, filleted and cut across into strips 2½ cm (1 inch) wide
1 medium-hot red chilli, seeded and finely chopped
1 tablespoon lemon juice
¼ teaspoon salt
2–3 spring onions, sliced
2 tablespoons chopped coriander
450 g (1 lb) puff pastry
Lemon wedges and coriander sprigs, to garnish

Boil the potato in salted water until just tender, then drain. Heat the oil in a large frying pan and fry the garlic, ginger and onion for 1 minute. Add the *Goan masala paste* (see page 280) and fry for 1 minute, then add the pieces of sardine and fry for another minute. Finally put in the potato, chilli, lemon juice and salt and cook for 1 minute. Take the pan off the heat, stir in the spring onions and coriander and leave to cool.

Roll out the pastry on a lightly floured surface and cut out twelve 10 cm (4-inch) circles. Spoon a heaped teaspoon of the filling mixture on to each circle. Brush half of the pastry edge with a little water, then fold it over the filling and press together well to seal the edge. Mark along the edge with a fork to make an even tighter seal.

Heat some oil for deep-frying to 190°C/375°F or until a cube of day-old bread rises to the surface and browns in about a minute. Deep-fry the puffs 3 or 4 at a time for 7–8 minutes, turning them over every now and then until they are golden brown. Drain on kitchen paper. Keep warm in a low oven while you cook the rest. Pile them on to a plate and serve warm, garnished with some lemon wedges and coriander.

INDIA

RICK STEIN

Red chilli mackerel
with fresh onion chutney

This dish is part of my continuing obsession with oily fish and the curry pastes of southern India. They go together so well that I just don't think it's true that all that spice ruins the taste of a perfectly fresh fish. Pilau rice is a great accompaniment (see page 280).

SERVES 4

8 x 225–275 g (8–10 oz) mackerel, cleaned and fins trimmed
6–8 tablespoons sunflower oil
Sea salt
Lime wedges, to garnish

FOR THE MASALA PASTE:
20 g (¾ oz) dried guajillo (little gourd) chillies or Kashmiri
    chillies (page 283)
1 teaspoon black peppercorns
1 teaspoon cloves
1 tablespoon light muscovado sugar
6 garlic cloves, roughly chopped
4 cm (1½ inch) piece of fresh ginger, roughly chopped
4 tablespoons red wine vinegar

FOR THE FRESH ONION CHUTNEY:
1 medium-hot red chilli, seeded and thinly sliced
4 tablespoons red wine vinegar
1 red onion, quartered and sliced
Juice of ½ a lime
A handful of coriander, roughly chopped

For the masala paste, slit open the dried chillies and remove the stalks and seeds. Cover with hot water and leave to soak for 20 minutes.

For the onion chutney, cover the red chilli with the vinegar and set aside.

Drain the soaked dried chillies, reserving the soaking liquor. Grind the peppercorns and cloves and put them into a food processor with the soaked chillies, sugar, garlic, ginger, vinegar and ½ teaspoon of salt. Blend, adding a little of the chilli-soaking liquor if necessary, to make a smooth paste.

Make 3 deep, diagonal slashes on each side of the mackerel. Season inside the cuts and the gut cavities with salt and then spread plenty of the masala paste inside the cavities and into the cuts with a palette knife.

When cooking 8 mackerel for 4 people, I would use 2 frying pans rather than cook them in batches. Heat 3–4 tablespoons of sunflower oil in each large frying pan over a medium heat. Add the fish and fry them for 6–7 minutes on each side until cooked through. Meanwhile, drain the vinegar off the red chilli and mix with the rest of the ingredients for the fresh onion chutney, with some salt to taste. Serve the fish with the chutney, garnished with a wedge or two of lime.

Keralan curry with prawns and kokum

I serve this dish as an entrée and offer a small soup bowl of the curry to each guest and some pilau rice in a small dish served separately. Kokum is a dried fruit that looks very much like passion-fruit when fresh. The slightly sweet and sour flavour is not quite the same, but very similar to tamarind. You will find it in some Asian grocers.

SERVES 4

15 g (½ oz) kokum rind or 4 tablespoons tamarind water (page 281)
3 tablespoons sunflower oil
½ small aubergine, about 150 g (5 oz), cut into 2 cm (1-inch) dice
1 teaspoon garam masala
3 garlic cloves, finely chopped
2½ cm (1-inch) piece of fresh ginger, finely chopped
1 medium-hot red chilli, deseeded and finely chopped
350 g (12 oz) raw, peeled, large prawns
400 ml (14 fl oz) can coconut milk
¼ teaspoon ground turmeric
1 large handful of coriander leaves, finely chopped
Sea salt
Pilau rice (page 280), to serve

Heat 2 tablespoons of the oil in a small pan over a medium heat. Add the aubergine and fry until golden brown. Remove from the pan with a slotted spoon to a plate lined with kitchen paper.

Add the remaining oil to the pan and add the garam masala, garlic, ginger and chilli. Cook gently for a couple of minutes. Add the kokum or tamarind water (see page 281), coconut milk and turmeric. Bring gently to the boil and simmer for a few minutes until the sauce has slightly thickened. Add the prawns to the sauce and simmer for 3 minutes, until just cooked through. Stir in the coriander and season to taste with salt. Serve with pilau rice (see page 280).

Goan fish curry with coconut milk and okra

The seafood curries from southern India are so delightful. Generally in Indian restaurants in England, unless they are Goan or Keralan, the fish curries are a disappointment, but when one makes a fresh curry paste, simmers the fish with the coconut milk and finishes the dish with something like okra and coriander, it's a different matter altogether.

SERVES 4

4 x 175 g (6 oz) fillets of fish such as sea bass, bream or John Dory
65 g (2½ oz) piece of tamarind pulp
150 ml (¼ pint) warm water
3 tablespoons groundnut or sunflower oil
½ teaspoon black mustard seeds
½ teaspoon cumin seeds
½ teaspoon fennel seeds
¼ teaspoon fenugreek seeds
1 onion, thinly sliced
1 quantity of *Goan masala paste* (page 280)
1 teaspoon ground turmeric
6 curry leaves
2 small medium-hot red chillies, seeded and sliced across diagonally
12 small okra, topped and tailed
3 tomatoes, skinned and quartered (page 283)
400 ml (14 fl oz) coconut milk
Sea salt
Coriander sprigs, to garnish

Lightly salt the fish fillets and set to one side. For the tamarind water, put the tamarind pulp into a small bowl with the warm water. With your fingers, work the paste into the water until it has broken down and all the seeds have been released. Now strain the slightly syrupy mixture through a sieve into another bowl and discard the fibrous material left in the sieve.

Heat the oil in a pan just large enough to take the fish in one layer. Add the whole spices and fry them for about 30 seconds.

Add the sliced onion and fry until golden. Add the Goan masala paste and turmeric and fry for 3–4 minutes until it starts to smell aromatic. Add the curry leaves, chillies, okra, tomatoes, coconut milk, 4 tablespoons of tamarind water, another 150 ml (¼ pint) of water and some salt to taste; simmer for 5 minutes. Add the fish fillets and simmer for another 5 minutes or until the fish is just cooked. Serve with some steamed basmati rice, garnished with sprigs of fresh coriander.

Mussel, cockle and clam masala

The sauce for this dish shouldn't be too wet; it's much better if it is quite thick and clinging to the shells. I use three different molluscs here because we get plenty of all of them at my restaurant, but it's nearly as good made with only one. Unusually for curry sauces from southern India, the spices are roasted before being blended and this gives a slightly spicier and less aromatic flavour.

SERVES 4

1¾ kg (4 lb) mixed live mussels, cockles and small
    clams, cleaned (page 283)
2 tablespoons sunflower oil
2 tablespoons roughly chopped coriander

FOR THE MASALA PASTE:

1 tablespoon coriander seeds
1 teaspoon cloves
2 tablespoons cumin seeds
2 onions, quartered
8 large garlic cloves
50 g (2 oz) fresh ginger, chopped
A walnut-sized piece of seedless tamarind pulp
1 teaspoon ground turmeric
3 medium-hot red chillies, chopped
2 tablespoons red wine vinegar
40 g (1½ oz) creamed coconut

For the masala paste, heat a dry heavy-based frying pan over a medium-high heat. Add the coriander seeds, cloves and cumin seeds and cook until they darken slightly and start to smell aromatic. Tip into a spice grinder and grind to a powder. Put this mixture and all the other paste ingredients into a food processor and blend until smooth.

Heat the oil in a large pan, add the masala paste and fry for a few minutes until it starts to separate from the oil.

Add the mussels, cockles and clams, cover and cook over a high heat for 3–4 minutes, shaking the pan now and then, until they have all opened.

Add a little water if there is not quite enough sauce, season with a little salt if necessary, then add the chopped coriander. Spoon into warmed bowls and serve.

Rui's turmeric fish with masala dhal

My friend Rui, from Goa, cooked this dish one summer many years ago when he came to Cornwall. We went wild about it, but Rui, who is very modest, couldn't understand what all the fuss was about – he said that he'd just cooked it up from the spices he'd found in the kitchen cupboards. But no one in England would have done it quite like this. So we asked him to cook it once more when we filmed in Goa, in the back garden of a beautiful old blue and white Portuguese house. I was worried that he might lose it a bit in front of the camera, but he was a natural and the dish was as good then as it was back in Padstow. Rui stirs some quickly fried mustard seeds, ginger, onions, tomatoes and green chilli into the dhal right at the end of cooking. Now that's real fun.

You can get pomfret pretty easily now in the UK, but any firm-flesh fish, such as John Dory, would work equally well; in fact, Rui used thick lemon sole fillets when he cooked it in Padstow, which were very good. You could also use large fillets of plaice or thin fillets of small cod and haddock.

SERVES 4

1 teaspoon salt
Juice of 1 lime
1 teaspoon ground turmeric
4 x 175–225 g (6–8 oz) skinned pomfret or sea bass fillets
3 tablespoons vegetable oil

FOR THE MASALA DHAL:

250 g (9 oz) red lentils
600 ml (1 pint) water
225 g (8 oz) onions
225 g (8 oz) tomatoes, skinned (page 283)
175 g (6 oz) ghee or *clarified butter* (page 279)
2 garlic cloves, finely chopped
1 tablespoon ground turmeric
1 teaspoon chilli powder
150 ml (5 fl oz) coconut milk
15 g (½ oz) black mustard seeds
2½ cm (1-inch) piece of fresh ginger, finely chopped
2 medium-hot green chillies, seeded and finely chopped
A pinch of asafoetida powder (optional)
3 tablespoons roughly chopped coriander
Sea salt

For the dhal, cover the lentils with the water and leave them to soak. Coarsely chop half the onions and finely chop the rest. Cut half the tomatoes into small chunks and finely dice the rest. Heat half the ghee or clarified butter in a heavy-based pan. Fry the garlic, coarsely chopped onions and tomato chunks for 5 minutes, until the mixture has cooked to a golden-brown paste. Pour in the lentils and their soaking water and bring to the boil. Add the turmeric, chilli powder and coconut milk and simmer until the lentils have broken down and the mixture has thickened (about 30 minutes). Season to taste with some salt and remove from the heat.

To finish the dhal, heat the rest of the ghee or butter in a large, deep frying pan. Add the mustard seeds, cover the pan with a lid and fry until the seeds begin to pop. Add the ginger, the rest of the onions and tomatoes, the green chillies and the asafoetida, if using. Cook for 5 minutes and then pour everything into the lentil mixture and stir well. Keep warm while you fry the fish.

Mix the salt, lime juice and turmeric together and rub well into the fish fillets. Heat the oil in a large, non-stick frying pan, add the fillets and fry for 2–3 minutes on each side. Stir the coriander into the dhal and serve with the fish. This would be great served with the kachumber salad from the recipe for *Mackerel recheado with kachumber salad* (see page 140) and pilau rice (see page 280).

Mumrez Khan's lamb and spinach karahi curry, from the *Karachi Restaurant*

My brother-in-law, Shaun, rang me one day from the Yorkshire Dales, where he now lives and which he enthuses greatly about after years in London working as a TV director. He'd been to the Karachi Restaurant *in Bradford and was somewhat surprised to have seen a letter from me on the table by the kitchen asking Mumrez for his recipe for the karahi curry. It's not the most exclusive restaurant, with Formica tables, a kitchen area on view in an entirely unforced sort of way, a tandoor oven in the back turning out sublime naan bread, and local customers; they probably think curries are always like this, but they're not. The lamb and spinach karahi was sensational, alive with coriander and cumin and fresh green chillies, and I drank far too much salted lassi, it was so good. It's the sort of place you hesitate to write about for fear of changing a place of great style. Shaun loved it, too; he was brought up in Sri Lanka.*

SERVES 6

250 g (9 oz) ghee or *clarified butter* (page 279)
550 g (1¼ lb) onions, chopped
400 g (14 oz) can of chopped tomatoes
120 ml (4 fl oz) water
50 g (2 oz) fresh ginger, roughly chopped
65 g (2½ oz) garlic
900 g (2 lb) boneless leg or shoulder of lamb,
    cut into 4 cm (1½-inch) pieces
1 tablespoon salt
1 tablespoon ground turmeric
1 tablespoon red chilli powder
1 tablespoon ground cumin
1 tablespoon paprika
1 tablespoon ground coriander
350 g (12 oz) fresh spinach, washed and large stalks removed
4 medium-hot green chillies, roughly chopped
2–3 tablespoons water
3 tablespoons coriander, chopped
½ tablespoon garam masala
A pinch of ground cumin and freshly ground black
    pepper, to garnish
Pilau rice (page 280), to serve

Heat the ghee in a large, heavy-based pan. Add the onions and cook over a medium heat, stirring now and then, for 20–30 minutes until they are very soft and a light brown.

Put the tomatoes, water, ginger and garlic into a liquidiser and blend until smooth. Remove the fried onions with a slotted spoon, add them to the paste and blend briefly until smooth.

Return the purée to the ghee left in the pan and add the lamb and salt. Simmer for 30 minutes, by which time the lamb will be half cooked and the sauce will be well reduced. Stir in the turmeric, chilli powder, cumin, paprika and coriander and continue to cook for 30–45 minutes for shoulder, or 45 minutes–1 hour for leg, until the lamb is tender, adding a little water now and then if the sauce starts to stick.

Meanwhile, put 175 g (6 oz) of the spinach into a large pan and cook until it has wilted to the bottom of the pan. Cook for 1 minute, then transfer to the rinsed out liquidiser and blend to a smooth purée. Set aside. Rinse out the liquidiser again and add the green chillies and water and blend until smooth. Set aside.

When the lamb is cooked, there should be a layer of ghee floating on the top of the curry. You can either skim it off or leave it there, whichever you prefer. Then stir in the spinach purée and the remaining leaf spinach and cook for 2 minutes.

Now taste the curry and add as much green chilli purée as you wish, according to how hot you like your curries. Simmer for 2 minutes. Stir in the fresh coriander and garam masala. Transfer the curry to a serving dish and sprinkle with a little more ground cumin and some freshly ground black pepper just before you take it to the table. Serve with pilau rice (see page 280).

Prawn-stuffed papads

Like so many of my Goan recipes, this comes from Rui Madre de Deus, at the Ronil Beach Resort Hotel in Baga. It makes the most delightful appetiser and is ideal as a nicely spicy canapé for a drinks party. You have to be a bit careful with the papads, or poppadoms, though. When we were making them in India, we found that it's easy enough to buy freshly made poppadoms there that are quite flexible, but in the UK you need to buy a good brand. Try to get them from an Indian grocer because they will be slightly bendy (and far cheaper than the supermarket boxed ones). Liberally brush them with water, then leave them for a couple of minutes until they are moist enough to fold. This recipe can make as many as 48 pieces, depending on the number of poppadoms you use.

MAKES 42

2 tablespoons groundnut or sunflower oil, plus extra for shallow-frying
225 g (8 oz) onions, finely chopped
225 g (8 oz) tomatoes, skinned and chopped (page 283)
275 g (10 oz) peeled, raw prawns, finely chopped
3–4 medium-hot green chillies, seeded and finely chopped
2 garlic cloves, crushed
2½ cm (1-inch) piece of fresh ginger, finely grated
1 teaspoon ground turmeric
1 teaspoon chilli powder
Juice of ½ lime
Sea salt
14–16 x 15 cm (6-inch) uncooked plain poppadoms
1 small egg, beaten

Heat the oil in a frying pan, add the onions and fry over a high heat, stirring now and then, until they are richly golden. Add the tomatoes and continue to fry until everything has reduced to a golden-coloured paste. Add the chopped prawns, green chillies, garlic, ginger, turmeric, chilli powder, lime juice and salt. Fry for about 1 minute, until the prawns are cooked, then take off the heat.

Pour about 5 mm (¼ inch) of oil into another frying pan and heat it to 200°C/400°F or until a cube of day-old bread rises to the surface and browns in less than a minute. Taking 2–3 poppadoms at a time, brush them generously with water on both sides and leave to soften for 2 minutes. Place 2 good tablespoons of the prawn filling down the centre of each one and brush the edge with a little beaten egg. Roll them up and press the open ends together to seal.

Once you have filled all the poppadoms, shallow-fry them 3 or 4 at a time for 1–1½ minutes, turning them frequently, until crisp and golden. Place on kitchen paper to remove any greasiness, then slice off the ends and cut each one into 3 pieces. Spear each piece with a cocktail stick and serve hot.

Monkfish vindaloo

I originally used shark in this recipe – specifically the Cornish porbeagle shark – but of late, sadly, stocks have diminished alarmingly, so we changed to monkfish, which is possibly even better. I suppose I should be happy with the longevity of my TV programmes, but I get a bit disconcerted when I get an email criticising me for using shark in a recipe I came up with 15 years ago.

SERVES 4

3–4 tablespoons groundnut or sunflower oil
1 onion, chopped
2 tomatoes, roughly chopped
300 ml (10 fl oz) water
4 medium-hot green chillies
900 g (2 lb) skinned monkfish tail, sliced across
    into 2½ cm (1-inch) thick steaks
Coconut or white wine vinegar, to taste
Sea salt
FOR THE VINDALOO CURRY PASTE:
40 g (1½ oz) dried Kashmiri chillies
1 small onion, unpeeled
1 teaspoon black peppercorns
1½ teaspoons cloves
7½ cm (3-inch) cinnamon stick
1 teaspoon cumin seeds
2½ cm (1-inch) piece of fresh ginger
4 tablespoons roughly chopped garlic
A walnut-sized piece of tamarind pulp, without seeds
1 teaspoon light soft brown sugar
2 tablespoons coconut or white wine vinegar
Pilau rice with crispy shallots (page 280), to serve

For the vindaloo paste, cover the chillies with plenty of hot water and leave them to soak overnight.

The next day, preheat the oven to 230°C/450°F/Gas Mark 8. Place the unpeeled onion on the middle shelf and roast for 1 hour until the centre is soft and the skin is nicely caramelised. Remove and leave to cool, then peel off the skin. Drain the chillies, squeeze out the excess water and then roughly chop. Put the peppercorns, cloves, cinnamon and cumin seeds into a mortar or spice grinder and grind to a fine powder. Tip the powder into a mini food processor and add the roasted onion, chillies, ginger, garlic, tamarind pulp, sugar and vinegar. Blend to a smooth paste.

Heat the oil in a large, deep frying pan. Add the onion and fry until richly browned. Add the tomatoes and cook until they form a deep-golden paste. Stir in 4 tablespoons of the vindaloo paste and fry gently for 5 minutes, stirring, until it has slightly caramelised. Add the water and leave the sauce to simmer for 10 minutes, giving it a stir every now and then.

Meanwhile, slit the green chillies open along their length and scrape out the seeds but leave them whole. Add the monkfish steaks and the chillies to the sauce and simmer for 10 minutes, carefully turning the fish halfway through if necessary. Then lift the steaks out on to a plate and boil the sauce rapidly until reduced to a good consistency. Add some vinegar and salt to taste, return the steaks to the sauce and reheat.

Spoon on to 4 warmed plates and serve with pilau rice (see page 280).

Dry-spiced potatoes and cauliflower with fennel seeds

I originally developed this recipe for our deli about 20 years ago, and we called it dry veg curry, which doesn't sound quite as attractive. Basically, the idea is to produce a dish of firm vegetables like potatoes and cauliflower with not much more than a coating of well-flavoured spice. You can use other vegetables like broccoli, green beans, mange tout or peas, but it should always contain potato.

SERVES 4

450 g (1 lb) waxy maincrop potatoes, such as Desirée
1 cauliflower (you need about 450 g/1 lb of florets)
½ teaspoon each cumin seeds, coriander seeds and black peppercorns
6 tablespoons sunflower oil
½ teaspoon fennel seeds
½ small onion, finely chopped
2 garlic cloves, finely chopped
2½ cm (1-inch) piece of fresh ginger, finely chopped
1 medium-hot green chilli, finely chopped
1 teaspoon ground turmeric
½ teaspoon cayenne pepper
A handful of roughly chopped coriander leaves
½ teaspoon sea salt

Peel the potatoes and cut them into 2 cm (¾-inch) pieces. Put them into a pan of well-salted water, bring to the boil and cook for 6–7 minutes, until just tender. Drain and set aside. Meanwhile, break the cauliflower into small florets, measuring about 4 cm (1½ inches) across.

Heat a dry, heavy-based frying pan over a high heat. Add the cumin seeds, coriander seeds and black peppercorns and shake them around for a few seconds, until they darken slightly and start to smell aromatic. Tip them into a spice grinder and grind them to a fine powder.

Heat the oil in a large, deep frying pan, add the cauliflower and fennel seeds and shake around for 2–3 minutes, until the cauliflower is coloured with brown spots. Add the onion, garlic, ginger and green chilli, cover and fry gently for another 4–6 minutes until the cauliflower is just tender, but still with a little bit of crunch.

Add the potatoes, roasted spices, turmeric, cayenne pepper and salt to the pan and stir gently to mix. Continue to cook over a low heat for 3–4 minutes, until the potatoes are heated through. Add the coriander, toss together briefly and serve. This is very nice served with tandoori chicken.

Mussels in pilau rice with a coconut, cucumber and tomato relish

I like to gently sauté the rice in this recipe in flavoured oil or butter and then cook with liquid for only about 15 minutes so that the grains remain firm and separate.

SERVES 4

1½ kg (3 lb) live mussels, cleaned (page 283)
300 ml (10 fl oz) water
1 teaspoon cumin seeds
1 teaspoon black mustard seeds
1 large leek, cleaned
50 g (2 oz) butter
½ teaspoon ground turmeric
½ teaspoon dried chilli flakes
350 g (12 oz) basmati rice
½ teaspoon sea salt

FOR THE COCONUT, CUCUMBER AND TOMATO RELISH:
½ cucumber, peeled, seeded and diced
2 vine-ripened tomatoes, seeded and diced (page 283)
50 g (2 oz) fresh coconut, peeled and finely grated
1 medium-hot green or red chilli, seeded and chopped
A small bunch of coriander, roughly chopped
4 teaspoons lime juice

Put the mussels and water into a large pan, cover and cook over a high heat for 3–4 minutes, shaking the pan every now and then until the mussels have all just opened. Tip them into a colander set over a bowl to collect the cooking liquor. Pour all but the last tablespoon or two of the liquor into a measuring jug and make up to 600 ml (1 pint) with water, if necessary.

Heat a dry, heavy-based frying pan. Add the cumin seeds and mustard seeds and shake them around for a few seconds until they darken slightly and start to smell aromatic. Remove from the heat.

Cut the leek lengthways into long, thin strips, then bunch the strips together and slice them across quite finely. Melt the butter in a 20 cm (8-inch) heavy-based saucepan, add the leeks and spices and cook over a medium heat for 2–3 minutes, until the leeks have softened. Add the rice and fry briefly until all the grains are well coated in the butter.

Add the mussel cooking liquor and salt and bring quickly to the boil. Stir once, cover with a tight-fitting lid, reduce the heat to low and cook for 15 minutes. Meanwhile, remove all but 12 of the mussel meats from their shells and season them with a little salt.

Mix the relish ingredients together with a large pinch of salt.

Uncover the rice and gently fork in the mussel meats. Garnish with the mussels in their shells and serve with the relish.

Far East

The food of South-east Asia, Japan and China is fascinating. The markets are a cornucopia of strange and exciting sounds and smells. I love wandering down the aisles of somewhere like the Russian market in Phnom Penn, throbbing with pungent heat and noise. There's freshly cooked, plump omelettes filled with bean sprouts, prawns and minced pork with some sort of accompaniment made with fish sauce, chilli, palm sugar and lime. Smoke rises from a score of wood fires in little clay barbecues blackening the tin roof above. I stop at a fresh orange juice store where the girl presses each half of a sliced orange twice to extract every drop of juice. It costs about five pence.

Everywhere you go in Phnom Penh, Hanoi, Bangkok, Denpasar, Kuala Lumpur, Hong Kong or Tokyo, everyone lives and breathes food. We think of the food as being healthy. It's low in fat and the cooking, particularly stir-frying, is quick and flavours and nutrients are preserved. Most of us like spicy food and much of the cooking is built on a vivid balance of the basic flavours: salty, sweet, sour and spicy. It's immediately attractive to us. A famous Chinese chef who lived and worked in England, Kenneth Lo, thought that many of our casseroles and stews would be improved a great deal by a tablespoon or two of soy sauce. The cooking of the Far East seems to me to be immensely practical in its perfect understanding of our taste processes and appealing to them rapidly and economically. An example of this in these recipes would be the famous *Hot and sour fish soup* from Thailand (see page 178). Incidentally, the savouriness found in fish and soy sauce has been identified as a basic flavour by the Japanese, which they call *umami,* from whence comes our word 'yummy'.

One of the things that travels in South-east Asia, China and Japan have really brought home to me is the extreme importance of texture in Far Eastern food. The Chinese have an enormous spectrum of textures, for example, ranging from something like tofu, which is very soft, to chicken feet or sea cucumber, which are very chewy, or from our perspective rubbery. As an example of the enjoyment of a texture in a dish, I would recommend the *Green papaya salad* on page 170. Here, under-ripe papayas, in my opinion a far better flavour than ripe ones, are finely shredded and mixed with peanuts, dried shrimps and green beans, and the whole is flavoured with fish sauce, lime juice, palm sugar, garlic and chilli. It's a lovely dish, but the thing that really appeals is the crispiness of the papaya and beans, the soft but slightly rubbery texture of the dried shrimps and the crunchiness of the peanuts – and, of course, it contains all the basic elements of taste.

Green papaya salad

This really is one of the world's great dishes – green papaya, lightly crushed with some chilli, peanuts, tomatoes, green beans, garlic, lime juice and fish sauce. You may find it difficult to get hold of the under-ripe papaya needed here, but you should be able to find it in Asian or Thai grocers. If you really can't get it, the same dish can be made with very under-ripe mango. In Thailand, they serve the green mango salad with horseshoe crabs. You only eat the roes, and in fact you only eat the roes of one species – eat those of any other and you die. You can also die from the roes of the edible one too if you are allergic to them, a fact conveyed to me just before I tried them. I've written this recipe for only one serving because that's how they do it in Thailand, simply because it is impossible to bruise and mix all the ingredients for more than one salad at a time.

SERVES 1

1 small green (under-ripe) papaya
1 teaspoon palm sugar or light muscovado sugar
A pinch of chopped garlic
A pinch of chopped red bird's eye chilli
5 x 10 cm (4-inch) pieces of snake bean or 5 French
    beans, halved lengthways
A few roasted, unsalted peanuts
A pinch of chopped dried shrimps
1 tablespoon Thai fish sauce (nam pla)
1 tablespoon *tamarind water* (page 281)
4 cherry plum tomatoes, halved
Juice of 1 lime

Peel the papaya and finely shred it on a mandolin into long, thin shreds. Work your way around the fruit until you get to the core and seeds, which you discard.

Moisten the palm sugar (which is always very hard) with a little cold water.

Put the garlic, red chilli and green beans into a mortar or mixing bowl and lightly bruise with the pestle or the end of a rolling pin. Add the sugar, peanuts, dried shrimps, fish sauce, tamarind water, tomatoes and lime juice and bruise everything once more, turning the mixture over with a fork as you do so. Add a good handful of the shredded papaya (about 50 g/2 oz) and turn over and bruise one last time. Serve straight away.

Nigiri sushi

I really enjoy making, serving and eating nori sushi (also often called maki sushi), where
a small core of fish and such things as avocado, Japanese pickles and cucumber are rolled in
a sushi mat and sliced to form sushi rolls, but the serious side of sushi is nigiri, where sticky
rice flavoured with rice vinegar and a little sugar is made into finger shapes and topped with
slices of fish, shellfish or sometimes meat. For this recipe, I've chosen seafood which will be easy
to get hold of, but you can make it with slices of almost any fish or shellfish. I recently made a
programme in Japan. The highlight of it for me was visiting the sushi bars around the central
Tsukiji fish market in Tokyo. Rather fortunately, as I later realised, the first morning of filming
there had to be repeated, as there was something wrong with the camera. I say fortunately
because the first impression was rather oppressively overwhelming, since it is so enormous and
so busy that you feel, as yet another porter's truck tries to run you over, that you are definitely
not wanted there. On the second day, a familiarity with what was really going on and a
realisation that the locals were not interested in whether we were there or not led me to start
really enjoying it and even revel in nimbly jumping out of the way of the trucks. I formed
a lasting impression of the incredible freshness of the fish for sushi and sashimi, much of
it still alive before it is filleted and sliced.

SERVES 6

6 small, raw, unpeeled prawns
40–50g (1½–2 oz) piece of thick tuna loin
40–50g (1½–2 oz) thick piece of skinned salmon fillet
40–50g (1½–2 oz) skinned lemon sole fillet
A little wasabi paste
6 teaspoons keta (salmon roe)

FOR THE STICKY RICE:

375 g (13 oz) Japanese sticky rice
600 ml (1 pint) cold water
6 tablespoons rice vinegar
2 tablespoons caster sugar
1 teaspoon salt

TO SERVE:

4 tablespoons Japanese dark soy sauce
1 tablespoon mirin (Japanese rice wine)
25 g (1 oz) Japanese pickled ginger

For the sticky rice, put the rice into a large bowl, pour over cold water and run the grains through your fingers, changing the water now and then, until the water stays relatively clear. Drain the rice and put it into a pan with the 600 ml (1 pint) cold water. Bring to the boil, boil for 1 minute and then reduce the heat to low and simmer, uncovered, for 10 minutes. Remove from the heat, cover with a lid and leave undisturbed for 10 minutes. Meanwhile, put 4 tablespoons of the rice vinegar, the sugar and salt into a small pan and heat gently until the sugar has dissolved. Pour into a bowl and leave to cool.

Turn the cooked rice out into a large shallow tray and gradually add the vinegar mixture, gently lifting and folding the rice, so that as it cools it takes on a nice sheen. Transfer to a bowl and cover with cling film, but do not refrigerate.

To stop the prawns from curling when you cook them, push a cocktail stick or fine bamboo skewer just under the shell, from the head, along the under-belly, down to the tail. Drop them into lightly salted, boiling water and simmer for 3 minutes. Drain, drop them into cold water and leave to cool. Pull out the sticks, peel the prawns and then make a cut along the under-belly down to the tail, part-way into the flesh, so that you can open them out flat.

Cut the tuna and salmon into thin slices and then cut all the fish into small rectangles, measuring about 6 x 3 cm (2½ x 1¼ inches).

Mix the remaining 2 tablespoons of rice vinegar with 225 ml (8 fl oz) cold water. Wet your hands with the vinegared water and mould a 20 g (¾ oz) ball of the rice into a small block, slightly smaller than the piece of fish. Do not squash the rice together too hard.

Smear one side of the tuna, lemon sole and salmon slices and the cut face of the prawns with a very small dot of wasabi paste. Lay each piece of fish and the prawns, wasabi-side down, on top of each block of rice and press down lightly. Spread the top of the last remaining blocks of rice with wasabi and spoon 1 teaspoon of keta on to each.

To serve, mix the soy sauce and mirin together and divide between 6 dipping saucers. Arrange the sushi in the centre of each plate. Put a little pile of pickled ginger and a small dipping saucer of the sauce to the side and serve.

Seafood tempura

This is the recipe from the Japanese ambassador's residence in London where we filmed his chefs. The two most important tips I picked up were firstly to make the batter at the very last minute and hardly whisk it at all, and second to fry everything in small batches.

SERVES 8

250 g (9 oz) medium-sized squid (pouches and tentacles), cleaned (page 283)
20 raw tiger prawns
250 g (9 oz) skinned lemon sole fillet
Lots of sunflower oil, for deep-frying

FOR THE TEMPURA BATTER:
115 g (4½ oz) plain flour
115 g (4½ oz) cornflour
300 ml (10 fl oz) ice-cold soda water, from a new bottle
Sea salt

FOR THE SOY AND GINGER DIPPING SAUCE:
90 ml (3 fl oz) dark soy sauce
2 thin slices of peeled fresh ginger, very finely chopped
½ bunch of thin spring onions, very thinly sliced

FOR THE SWEET CHILLI AND FIVE-SPICE DIPPING SAUCE:
150 ml (5 fl oz) sweet chilli sauce, such as Lingham's
1 tablespoon light soy sauce
¼ teaspoon Chinese five-spice powder
1½ tablespoons cold water

Mix together the ingredients for each dipping sauce and divide between 4 shallow dipping saucers or bowls.

Cut the cleaned squid pouches across into thin rings and separate the tentacles into pairs. Remove the heads from the prawns and then peel them, leaving the last tail segment in place. Cut the lemon sole fillets diagonally across into strips about the thickness of your little finger.

Heat some oil for deep-frying to 190°C/375°F or until a cube of day-old bread rises to the surface and browns in about a minute. To make the batter, sift half of the flour, half the cornflour and a pinch of salt into 2 large bowls. Just before you start cooking, stir 150 ml (5 fl oz) of the ice-cold soda water into one lot of flour/cornflour until only just mixed; the batter should still be a little bit lumpy and, if it seems a bit thick, add a drop more water. When it's cooked, you want it to coat the food in a very thin, almost transparent layer.

Drop 8 pieces of mixed seafood into the batter, lift out one at a time and drop straight away into the hot oil. Fry for just 1 minute until crisp and lightly golden, then lift out and drain on lots of kitchen paper. Repeat once more, transfer the seafood to a warmed platter, together with a bowl of each dipping sauce, and eat right away, while it's still crisp and hot. Continue to cook the seafood in the same way and make a second batch of batter when you need it.

Osuimono (clear soup with prawns)

This soup is incredibly simple and quick to make and relies for its fascinating taste on a good-quality dashi. Dashi is the standard Japanese stock made with water, kombu seaweed, bonito flakes and soy sauce, and it's really the quality of the bonito flakes that makes the difference. You can buy it as a powder, but if you go to a good oriental supermarket you'll find packets of what look like wood shavings, which are in fact shaved from a lump of dried bonito and always have a better flavour. When you drop them into the hot stock they disappear like snowflakes.

SERVES 4

8 raw, unpeeled prawns
15 cm (6-inch) long thin piece of dried
    wakame seaweed
750 ml (1½ pints) *dashi* (page 279)
½ teaspoon salt
1 tablespoon dark soy sauce
1 tablespoon cornflour
24 enoki mushrooms, trimmed
1 pared strip of lemon zest, cut lengthways
    into very fine julienne

Peel the prawns, leaving the last tail segment of the shell in place.

Drop the wakame seaweed into a pan of boiling water and stir it around for 30 seconds. Lift it out of the hot water, plunge into a bowl of cold water and leave it to soak for 20 minutes. Then lift it out on to a board, cut out and discard any hard parts and cut the rest into 2½ cm (1-inch) lengths.

Pour the dashi into a clean pan and bring almost to the boil. Add the salt and soy sauce and keep hot.

Bring a small pan of lightly salted water to the boil. Sprinkle the prawns with a little salt, lightly dredge with cornflour and drop into the water. Cook for 1 minute then lift out on to a plate.

Fill 4 soup bowls (lacquered Japanese ones if you can) with hot water, leave to get warm, then drain and wipe dry. Put 2 prawns and 4–5 small pieces of the wakame seaweed into each one. Carefully ladle over the hot stock, taking care not to splash the sides of the bowl and only fill to three-quarters full. Garnish each bowl with 6 enoki mushrooms and 1 fine shred of lemon zest and serve immediately.

Crab and sweetcorn soup

My reason for including this in the book is that – apart from the fact that it is the first oriental dish I ever ate at a Chinese restaurant, in Peterborough, England, in 1964 as it happens – it is also a world classic and is so often ruined by sickly-sweet cans of creamed corn, tasteless crab and gloopy cornflour. I thought it would be interesting to restore the dish to its simplicity and reliance on good, fresh ingredients. Paradoxically, when you first taste it you'll probably find it a bit under-flavoured, unencumbered as it is with MSG and too much soy. But then the subtlety will grow on you.

SERVES 4

1.2 litres (2 pints) *chicken stock* (page 278)
2 fresh sweetcorn cobs
225 g (8 oz) fresh white crab meat
5 teaspoons cornflour
1 teaspoon very finely chopped fresh ginger
2 spring onions, cut into 2½ cm (1-inch) pieces
    and finely shredded lengthways
1 tablespoon light soy sauce
1 tablespoon Chinese rice wine or dry sherry
1 teaspoon salt
1 egg white, lightly beaten
Freshly ground black pepper

Bring the chicken stock to the boil in a pan. Meanwhile, stand the sweetcorn cobs up on a board and slice away the kernels with a large sharp knife. Add the sweetcorn to the stock and simmer for 5 minutes.

Check over the crab meat for any little pieces of shell, keeping the meat in the largest pieces possible.

Mix the cornflour to a smooth paste with a little cold water, stir it into the soup and simmer for 2 minutes. Stir in the crab meat, ginger, spring onions, soy sauce, rice wine or sherry, salt and some pepper to taste. Simmer for 1 minute.

Now give the soup a good stir, remove the spoon and slowly trickle in the beaten egg white so that it forms long, thin strands in the soup. Simmer for about 30 seconds and then serve at once.

Hot and sour fish soup

One of the endearing things about life in Thailand is that all the houses are open to the street, so you can walk past somebody's front room and see a whole family watching the telly and eating. It's as if one wall has been entirely removed. I was wandering through the streets of a town a few years back and found a family sitting on a terrace in front of their house eating breakfast. I suppose I was quite rude because I watched them a little bit too long, but they asked me if I'd like to try some of their meal – and this was it! I couldn't even begin to describe how the vegetables were cooked, but I've since found this recipe for the soup and it's very good. You can use any fillets of small fish, such as lemon sole, plaice, flounder, prawns, scallops and even cooked mussels dropped in at the end and brought back to the boil.

SERVES 4

4 red bird's eye chillies, roughly chopped

2½ cm (1-inch) piece of fresh galangal or ginger, roughly chopped

1 teaspoon blachan (dried shrimp paste)

3 garlic cloves, roughly chopped

6 shallots, roughly chopped

½ teaspoon palm sugar or light muscovado sugar

3–4 tablespoons *tamarind water* (page 281) or lemon juice

100 g (4 oz) prepared squid (page 283)

1 litre (1¾ pints) *chicken stock* (see page 278)

3 tablespoons Thai fish sauce (nam pla)

75 g (3 oz) snake beans or French beans, topped, tailed and cut into small pieces

100 g (4 oz) monkfish fillet, cut into thin slices

150g of baby bok choi, cut into 2½ cm (1-inch) pieces, or 50 g (2 oz) baby leaf spinach

TO GARNISH:

A small handful of coriander leaves

1 medium-hot red chilli, seeded and thinly sliced

Put the chillies, galangal or ginger, blachan, garlic, shallots and sugar into a mortar or a food processor and work to a coarse paste, adding a little of the tamarind water if necessary.

Cut the body pouch of the squid open along one side and score the inner side with the tip of a small, sharp knife into a fine diamond pattern. Cut the squid into approximately 3 cm (1¼-inch) squares.

Bring the chicken stock and the rest of the tamarind water to the boil in a pan. Add the spice paste and simmer for 10 minutes. Strain through a muslin-lined or very fine sieve and add the Thai fish sauce and the beans. Simmer for 1 minute. Add the monkfish and squid and simmer for 1 minute. Add the bok choi or spinach and simmer for a further minute. Ladle the soup into warmed bowls and serve sprinkled with the coriander leaves and red chilli.

Thai Red Seafood

This is an expensive dish to make, but well worth it, as it has so much of interest in it: pieces of lobster, crab, prawns, a delicious sauce, and accompaniments of deep-fried garlic, shallots and nuts, chilli-flavoured vinegar and fresh basil.

SERVES 6

1 cooked lobster weighing about 450 g (1 lb)

1 cooked crab, weighing about 750 g (1½ lb)

225 g (8 oz) prepared squid (page 283)

1 red mullet, weighing about 250 g (12 oz), filleted

3 tablespoons sunflower oil

1 quantity of *Thai red curry paste* (page 281)

1.2 litres (2 pints) *chicken stock* (page 278)

100 g (4 oz) creamed coconut

3 tablespoons of Thai fish sauce (nam pla)

2 limes

3 fresh or dried kaffir lime leaves (optional)

12 large, raw, unshelled prawns

24 large live mussels, cleaned (page 283)

1 small bunch of fresh basil, finely shredded

FOR THE GARNISHES:

4 red bird's eye chillies, thinly sliced

85 ml (3 fl oz) rice vinegar or white wine vinegar

300 ml (10 fl oz) sunflower oil

4 shallots, thinly sliced

6 garlic cloves, thinly sliced

50 g (2 oz) cashew nuts, split in half

Pull the claws off the lobster, break each one into three and lightly crack the shells with a rolling pin. Detach the head and legs from the tail section and discard. Cut the tail section through the shell into 3 even-sized pieces. Detach the legs and claws from the crab, break them into 3 and lightly crack the shell. Remove the body from the back shell, scoop the brown meat out of the back shell and set aside. Discard the back shell. Remove and discard the dead man's fingers from the body, then cut the body into quarters.

Slice the squid across into rings and each red mullet fillet into 3 pieces.

For the garnishes, mix the chillies with the vinegar in a small bowl. Heat the oil in a frying pan, add the shallots, garlic and cashew nuts and fry for about 3 minutes, until crisp and golden. Lift out with a slotted spoon, drain on kitchen paper and then spoon into another small bowl. Set aside.

Heat the oil in a large pan, add the red curry paste and fry for 2 minutes, until the paste starts to separate from the oil. Add the stock, creamed coconut and fish sauce and heat gently until the coconut dissolves.

Meanwhile, pare 2 strips of zest from 1 lime and cut them across into very fine shreds. Squeeze out the juice from both limes. Add the zest and juice to the pan with the dried kaffir lime leaves, if using, and simmer everything together for 2 minutes.

Add the lobster and crab pieces to the pan and simmer for 2 minutes. Add the prawns and simmer for 1 minute. Add the squid and red mullet and simmer for 2 minutes. Add the mussels, cover and simmer for 2 minutes until they have opened. Discard any that remain closed.

Stir in the basil and the fresh kaffir lime leaves, if using, then transfer everything to a large shallow serving platter and serve with the little bowls of prepared garnishes and Thai jasmine rice.

Nasi goreng with mackerel

The secret of a good nasi goreng is rice that has been cooked well so that the grains are separate, and which has been left to cool but not refrigerated. Leftover rice that has been stored in the fridge overnight does not taste as good. Like so many rice or noodle street dishes from South-east Asia, nasi goreng is a bit of a 'put whatever you like into it' sort of dish. However, it should always include a good curry paste, some thinly sliced omelette and plenty of crisp fried-onion flakes. I always put prawns in my nasi goreng and I love some broken-up well-flavoured fish such as mackerel in it too; grilled and flaked sea trout, fresh sardines, red mullet, snapper or bream are equally good.

SERVES 4

225 g (8 oz) long-grain rice
2 x 175–225 g (6–8 oz) mackerel, cleaned
2 large eggs
Sunflower oil, for frying
6 large shallots, thinly sliced
175 g (6 oz) peeled, cooked North Atlantic prawns
1 tablespoon light soy sauce
5 cm (2-inch) piece of cucumber, quartered lengthways and sliced
4 spring onions, chopped
Sea salt and freshly ground black pepper

FOR THE NASI GORENG PASTE:

3 tablespoons groundnut oil
4 large garlic cloves, roughly chopped
2 large shallots, roughly chopped
15 g (½ oz) roasted salted peanuts
6 medium-hot red chillies, roughly chopped
1 tablespoon tomato purée
½ teaspoon blachan (dried shrimp paste)
1 tablespoon ketjap manis (sweet soy sauce)

First make the nasi goreng paste: put the paste ingredients into a food processor and blend until smooth.

Cook the rice in boiling, salted water for 15 minutes, until just tender. Drain, rinse well and then spread it out on a tray and leave until cold.

Preheat the grill to high. Season the mackerel on both sides with salt and pepper. Lay them on a lightly oiled baking tray or the rack of a grill pan and grill for 4 minutes on each side. Leave them to cool and then flake the flesh into large pieces, discarding the bones.

Next, beat the eggs with salt and pepper and then heat a little oil in a frying pan and make three omelettes. The object is to get them as thin as possible. Cook each one till the egg has lightly set on top, then flip over and cook a few seconds on the other side. Roll the omelettes up and leave them to cool. Then thinly slice the omelettes into strips.

Pour 1 cm (½ inch) of sunflower oil into a frying pan. Add the shallots and fry over a medium heat until crisp and golden brown. Lift them out with a slotted spoon and leave to drain on kitchen paper.

Spoon 2 tablespoons of the oil from frying the shallots into a large wok and get it smoking hot. Add 2 tablespoons of the nasi goreng paste and stir-fry for 2 minutes. Add the cooked rice and stir-fry over a high heat for another 2 minutes, until it has heated through. Add the prawns, the strips of omelette, the fried shallots and the flaked mackerel and stir-fry for another minute. Add the soy sauce, cucumber and most of the spring onions, toss together well and then spoon on to a large, warmed plate. Sprinkle with the remaining spring onions and serve straight away.

Grilled red snapper with portabello mushrooms and spinach

I'm afraid that this recipe is a little wasteful, but the Japanese would use the trimmings from the fish and mushrooms for another dish, such as the recipe for Japanese fishcakes with ginger and spring onions *(page 189).*

SERVES 4

450 g (1-lb) piece of red snapper fillet, taken from
    a fish weighing about 2–2½kg (4½–5 lb)
4 large portabello mushrooms, cleaned and trimmed
    but stalks left in place
Sunflower oil, for brushing
100 g (4 oz) English spinach, washed and dried
200 ml (7 fl oz) *dashi* (page 279)
A few drops of dark soy sauce
Finely grated lemon zest (done on a Microplane
    grater would be perfect), to garnish
Sea salt
FOR THE DIPPING SAUCE:
3 tablespoons *dashi* (page 279)
3 tablespoons mirin (Japanese rice wine)
3 tablespoons light soy sauce

Soak eight 18 cm (7½-inch) bamboo skewers in cold water for 30 minutes. Preheat the grill to high.

Mix together the ingredients for the dipping sauce and set aside.

Trim the belly flap away from the fillet of fish and trim the remaining loin very neatly, so that you have one long, evenly shaped piece of fish. Cut it across into eight 40 g (1½-oz) pieces, about 2 cm (¾ inch) thick. Slice each mushroom through the stalk into slices about 5 mm (¼ inch) thick – you should get 3 perfect slices from each mushroom. Discard the remainder.

Working with 2 slices of fish at a time, lay them flat on a board and thread them through the skin, on to 2 parallel skewers. Brush them on both sides with oil, season generously with salt and lay on the rack of a grill pan. Put the mushroom slices on a lightly oiled baking tray and sprinkle with salt. Grill the fish for 2 minutes on each side and the mushrooms for 1 minute only.

Bring the dashi to the boil in a small saucepan. Add the spinach and, as soon as it has wilted into the stock, drain well and season lightly with salt.

Lift two of the skewers on to each of 4 warmed plates and overlap 3 of the mushroom slices alongside. Add a small pile of spinach to each plate, sprinkle a few drops of dark soy sauce on to the mushrooms and scatter the fish with a little of the lemon zest. Serve straight away.

Stir-fried eel in black bean sauce

It's quite difficult to get hold of fresh eel unless you know of a fishmonger that does a lot of business with Chinese restaurants. It's a shame because it has a fabulous taste, well loved by both Chinese and Japanese and, of course, the original locals of the East End of London and Kent and Essex. I don't know why, but many people have an aversion to fatty flavours and yet there is nothing quite so appetising as the fat on a really good joint of roast pork, lamb or beef. To the Japanese, the fat belly of tuna is the best part and nowhere is the fine quality of good fat in fish better to be found than in eel. I hope you will note the picture that accompanies this recipe – it's important for the best flavour to use these dried, fermented and salted black beans, not the jars of black bean sauce, which are more easy to get hold of.

SERVES 2

225–275 g (8–10 oz) skinned eel fillet
1½ teaspoons cornflour
1½ tablespoons Chinese fermented salted black beans
½ teaspoon caster sugar
2 tablespoons sesame oil
2 garlic cloves, cut into fine shreds
2½ cm (1-inch) piece of fresh ginger, cut into very thin shreds
1 medium-hot red chilli, seeded and thinly sliced
3 tablespoons Chinese rice wine or dry sherry
1 teaspoon dark soy sauce
4 spring onions, cut on the diagonal into long, thin slices
Sea salt

Cut the eel fillet diagonally into pieces 2½ cm (1 inch) wide. Toss with a little salt and then with the cornflour.

Put the black beans, sugar and 2 tablespoons of cold water into a small bowl and crush to a coarse paste.

Heat a wok over a high heat until it is smoking hot. Add the sesame oil and garlic, quickly followed by the ginger, red chilli and black-bean paste. Stir-fry for a few seconds, then add the eel pieces and stir-fry for 1 minute.

Add the rice wine or sherry, soy sauce and 3–4 tablespoons of water and cook for 2 minutes, until the eel is cooked through.

Add the spring onions to the wok and stir-fry for about a minute. Serve immediately, with steamed rice (see page 281).

Singapore seafood noodles

The essence of this dish is the dried shiitake mushrooms and smoked bacon with noodles and some seafood, such as prawns, scallops and squid. Chinese-style scallops with bacon, if you like. Cooked, peeled North Atlantic prawns, cooked, shelled mussels, white crab meat, lobster and firm fish such as monkfish or Dover sole fillet are also delicious in this recipe.

SERVES 4

25 g (1 oz) dried shiitake mushrooms
15 g (½ oz) dried shrimps (optional)
120 ml (4 fl oz) hot water
175 g (6 oz) vermicelli noodles (also known as stir-fry noodles)
2 tablespoons sunflower oil
2 fat garlic cloves, finely chopped
2½ cm (1-inch) piece of fresh ginger, finely grated
100 g (4 oz) rindless smoked back bacon, cut into thin strips
1 tablespoon good-quality garam masala paste
100 g (4 oz) squid, prepared (see page 283) and thinly sliced
100 g (4 oz) prepared queen scallops, also known as 'queenies'
175 g (6 oz) peeled cooked tiger prawns
3 tablespoons dark soy sauce
1 tablespoon Chinese rice wine or dry sherry
4 spring onions, thinly sliced

Soak the dried mushrooms and the dried shrimps, if using, in the hot water for 30 minutes, until soft. Drain, reserving the soaking liquid, and thinly slice the mushrooms.

Drop the noodles into a pan of boiling water, cover and take off the heat. Leave to soak for 1 minute, then drain. Toss with a little of the oil, to separate the strands.

Heat the rest of the oil in a large wok. Add the garlic and ginger and stir-fry for a few seconds. Add the bacon, curry paste and squid and stir-fry for 2 minutes. Add the mushrooms, dried shrimps and scallops and stir-fry for another minute. Add the prawns, reserved soaking water, soy sauce and rice wine or sherry, followed by the noodles, and toss together gently over a high heat, using 2 forks, for about 1 minute, until everything is hot and well mixed. Toss in the spring onions and serve at once.

Japanese fishcakes with ginger and spring onions

I picked this recipe idea up from a magazine I read called The Week. *It's rather good; a potted digest of all the week's news, with a pick of food journalists' recipes and restaurant reviews, too. This refreshing recipe works equally well with all types of oily fish, such as herring, mackerel and salmon.*

SERVES 4

3 rainbow trout, filleted (you need about 500 g/1¼ lb fillets in total)
4 cm (1½-inch) piece of fresh ginger, very finely chopped
3 fat spring onions, finely chopped
4 chestnut mushrooms, finely chopped
A little oil, for frying
Sea salt and freshly ground black pepper

FOR THE SALAD:
100 g (4 oz) rocket
2 teaspoons dark soy sauce
1 teaspoon roasted sesame oil
1 teaspoon cold water
A pinch of caster sugar

Skin and then pin-bone the trout fillets and then cut them lengthways into long, thin strips. Now bunch these strips together and cut them across into very small pieces – you should not work the fish into a very fine paste, but neither should it be too coarse, or it won't hold together.

Put the fish into a mixing bowl with the ginger, spring onions, mushrooms and some salt and pepper. Mix together well and then divide the mixture into 8 and, with slightly wet hands, shape into patties about 7½ cm (3 inches) in diameter.

Heat a lightly oiled non-stick frying pan over a medium heat. Add the fishcakes, and fry for about 1½ minutes on each side, until golden brown and cooked through. Put on to warmed plates and pile some of the rocket alongside. Whisk together the remaining ingredients to make a dressing and drizzle some over the rocket and a little around the outside edge of the plate.

Crisp Chinese roast pork

These days, most roasting joints of pork don't produce crackling. There's just not enough fat between the flesh and the skin to make the skin go crisp. Such is our apparent desire to eat ever-leaner meat, we seem to have foregone the delights of such things as crackling and really marbled steak. The Chinese, however, esteem belly pork. I imagine this is because of its high fat content, from which comes succulent meat and crisp, crackly skin. Here, a square of belly pork is dry-marinated with Chinese spices and then slow-roasted, to produce crisp and tender roast pork. Serve with some steamed Chinese greens in oyster sauce and steamed rice and, only my opinion of course, you can forget endless stir-fries; this is Chinese food at its best.

SERVES 4-6

1½ kg (3-lb) piece of thick belly pork with skin, bones removed
1 tablespoon Sichuan peppercorns
1 teaspoon black peppercorns
2 tablespoons sea-salt flakes
2 teaspoons Chinese five-spice powder
2 teaspoons caster sugar
1 quantity of steamed rice (page 281), to serve

Spike the skin of the pork with a fine skewer or a larding needle as many times as you can, going through into the fat but not so deep that you go into the flesh. Then pour a kettle full of hot water over the skin, leave it to drain and then dry it off well.

Heat a dry, heavy-based frying pan over a high heat. Add the Sichuan and black peppercorns and shake them around for a few seconds until they darken slightly and start to smell aromatic. Transfer them to a spice grinder and grind to a fine powder. Tip them into a bowl and stir in the sea salt, five-spice powder and sugar.

Turn the pork flesh side up on a tray and rub the flesh all over with the spice mixture. Set it aside somewhere cool for 8 hours or overnight.

Preheat the oven to 200°C/400°F/Gas Mark 6. Turn the pork skin side up and place it on a rack resting on top of a roasting tin of water. Roast the pork for 15 minutes. Then lower the oven temperature to 180°C/350°F/Gas Mark 4 and roast it for a further 2 hours, topping up the water in the roasting tin now and then when necessary.

Increase the oven temperature once more to 230°C/450°F/Gas Mark 8 and continue to roast the pork for a further 15 minutes. Then remove it from the oven and leave it to cool. It is best served warm.

Cut the pork into bite-sized pieces and arrange them on a warmed platter. Serve with steamed Chinese greens in oyster sauce and steamed rice (see page 281).

Beef rendang with cucumber sambal

There is no other hot and aromatic beef stew like a rendang. It has a sweet and intensely spicy flavour and is unique in that the liquid ingredient, coconut milk, is cooked down to such an extent that it disappears with the spices into a pleasing sticky, brown coating for the beef, so that it becomes a truly 'dry' curry.

I find it much more satisfactory to make my own spice paste for this sort of dish, using whole spices. For this you will need either a very good mortar and pestle – there's a green granite one from Thailand, which is easy to get hold of here now and is by far the best – or a small electric grinder, where you grind the dry spices first and then mix them with the wet ones. There are also one or two liquidisers on the market now, notably the Breville, which has six blades, two pointing down, two horizontal, and two pointing up, which can grind wet and dry spices together in one go. These are in fact commonly available in India, too.

SERVES 4-6

1½ kg (3 lb) blade or chuck steak, cut into 2½–4 cm
    (1–1½-inch) pieces
85 ml (3 fl oz) *tamarind water* (page 281)
2 x 400 ml (14 fl oz) cans of coconut milk
1 tablespoon light soft brown sugar
Sea salt

FOR THE SPICE PASTE:

1 tablespoon coriander seeds
1 teaspoon cumin seeds
2½ cm (1-inch) cinnamon stick
4 cloves
6 dried Kashmiri chillies, stalks removed
2½ cm (1-inch) piece of fresh ginger, peeled
6 garlic cloves, finely chopped
1 lemongrass stalk, outer layers removed and reserved
    and the rest roughly chopped
1 onion, roughly chopped
1 teaspoon turmeric
1 tablespoon chopped galangal (optional)
2 tablespoons water

FOR THE CUCUMBER SAMBAL:

1 cucumber
3 tablespoons coconut cream (from a carton)
1 medium-hot red chilli, halved, seeded and thinly sliced
1 medium-hot green chilli, halved, seeded and thinly sliced
1 small red onion, very thinly sliced
2 tablespoons lime juice

...he coriander seeds, cumin seeds, cinnamon, ...into a spice grinder and grind to a fine powder. ...hopped lemongrass, onion, turmeric and galangal, ...ssor, with the ground spices and 2 tablespoons of ...a smooth paste.

...rge, heavy-based pan and add the reserved ...the beef, tamarind water (see page 281), coconut ...on of salt. Bring to a simmer and cook, uncovered, ...ring now and then. Stir more frequently towards ...e sauce becomes concentrated, to stop it from ...oil from the coconut milk will start to separate ...nue to cook for a minute or two longer, to allow ...to fry lightly in the oil. Remove and discard the ...he seasoning if necessary.

...bal, peel the cucumber, cut it in half lengthways ...with a teaspoon. Cut across into thin, half-moon- ...a colander with 1 teaspoon of salt. Leave for 15 ...cold water and dry on a tea towel. Mix with all ...gredients.

...h the cucumber sambal and some steamed rice

Steamed monkfish
with wild garlic and ginger

Chinese seafood cooking is some of the best in the world. It never ceases to amaze me how rarely one comes into contact with it. Most Chinese restaurants seem to adopt a policy of one menu for Westerners and one for them. I've been into restaurants in Soho, London, with chef friends who have explained patiently to the staff, 'No, we don't want what's on the menu, we want proper Chinese food,' and mysteriously, lovely dishes of clams fragrant with coriander, aromatic stews with star anise and tangerine peel, and beautiful, delicately steamed fish appear. The problem is not unique to this country. I recall seeing a message printed in Chinese in an Australian food magazine designed to be torn out and taken with you, which ran something like, 'I'm not one of your ignorant Westerners. Please give me some proper Chinese food.' Occasionally though, with restaurants like the Mandarin Kitchen *in London, or the restaurant where I had this in Glasgow,* Ho Wong, *they do give you the real thing, and those places are always packed with grateful gweilos.*

SERVES 2

350–400 g (12–14 oz) monkfish fillet
½ tablespoon very finely shredded fresh ginger
A small bunch of wild garlic (about 4 leaves), or a small bunch
    of garlic chives, or 1 garlic clove, cut into fine shreds
1 teaspoon sesame oil
1 tablespoon dark soy sauce
2 spring onions, thinly sliced on the diagonal
Sea salt

Lightly season the monkfish fillet with salt and then cut it across into thin slices. Arrange the slices in a single layer over a heatproof serving plate and scatter over the ginger.

Put some sort of trivet in a wide, shallow pan, add 1 cm (½ inch) of water and bring to the boil. Rest the plate on the trivet, cover the pan with a well fitting lid and steam for 2–3 minutes, until the fish is almost cooked.

Scatter the wild garlic, garlic chives or shredded fresh garlic over the fish and steam, covered, for a further minute. Meanwhile, put the sesame oil and soy sauce into a small pan and heat briefly.

Remove the fish from the steamer and pour away about half the cooking juices. Scatter over the spring onions, pour over the hot sesame oil and soy mixture and serve with some steamed rice (see page 281).

Chinese white-cooked chicken with ginger, spring onion and coriander

This recipe really brings out the best in a free-range chicken. It really is the most satisfying of dishes. I first had it in Singapore where my then very young sons sat entranced by the number of lizards running across the walls in the restaurant. I love hot and cold food – here, the cold chicken and the hot rice. The secret of the success of this dish is in the cutting of the chicken. The pieces need to be on the bone and you can only cut it up cleanly when the chicken is quite cold and firm. The three dips and the crisp lettuce with coriander go towards making a fascinatingly complex combination of flavours – the best food ever, especially if you're on a diet!

SERVES 4

2¾ litres (5 pints) water
5 cm (2-inch) piece of fresh ginger, sliced
1½ kg (3½ lb) chicken

FOR THE SEASONINGS:
1 teaspoon Sichuan peppercorns
1 teaspoon black peppercorns
1 teaspoon sea salt flakes
4 spring onions, trimmed
1 slice of fresh ginger, finely chopped
3 tablespoons dark soy sauce
1 medium-hot red chilli, seeded and thinly sliced
1 teaspoon caster sugar
2 tablespoons rice wine or white wine vinegar

FOR THE SALAD:
½ iceberg lettuce
1 small bunch fresh coriander

Put the water into a pan just large enough to take the chicken. Add the ginger and bring to the boil. Add the chicken, bring back to the boil and boil rapidly for 10 minutes. Then turn the heat right down and simmer very gently for 20 minutes. Remove from the heat and leave the chicken to go cold in the liquid. You can do this the day before if you wish and keep it cold, but don't refrigerate it.

Remove the chicken from the pan and cut it into 5 cm (2-inch) pieces. You will need a large kitchen knife that is sharp enough to cut through chicken bones (and some poultry shears are also quite useful). Cut off the legs, cut them in 2 at the joint and then cut each thigh section in half. Now remove the breasts still on the bone from the carcass; cut horizontally just under the breasts from the cavity end of the chicken, through all the rib bones and down towards the wings. Separate the 2 breasts by cutting through the breast bone and then cut each breast into 3 pieces. Finally, cut off the wing bones. Arrange all the pieces attractively on a cold serving platter.

For the seasonings, heat a dry, heavy-based frying pan, add the Sichuan and black peppercorns and shake them around until they start to smell aromatic. Transfer to a mortar and coarsely grind with the pestle. Stir in the sea salt and transfer to one small dish. Thinly slice the spring onions and mix with the ginger and soy sauce in a second dish. Mix the chilli, sugar and vinegar together in a third dish.

Tear the iceberg lettuce into 5–7½ cm (2–3-inch) pieces. Pick small sprigs from the bunch of coriander and mix with the lettuce in a salad bowl. Take the chicken and salad to the table with the seasonings and serve with a bowl of steamed rice (see page 281).

Sashimi of salmon, tuna, sea bass and scallops

The size and shape of the fish fillets are quite crucial to the finished look of this dish. The salmon and sea bass should both come from reasonable sized fish where the fillets are between 2.5 cm (1 inch) and 4 cm (1½ inch) thick. The tuna is a little more difficult to achieve. You need to buy a piece of loin that is about 10 cm (4 inch) long, cut from the thicker end of the fillet and then cut it lengthways into about 3 long narrow pieces which are each about 5 cm (2 inch) across.

SERVES 4

THE FISH:
90 g (3 oz) piece skinned salmon fillet,
    pin bones removed
90 g (3 oz) piece sea bass fillet, skinned
    and pin bones removed
90 g (3 oz) piece tuna fillet
4 scallops, out of the shell, corals removed

FOR THE DIPPING SAUCE:
3 tablespoons *dashi* (page 279)
3 tablespoons mirin
3 tablespoons light soy sauce

FOR THE GARNISH:
1 x 7.5 cm (3 inch) piece daikon radish (mooli),
    peeled and then finely shredded lengthways
    into long thin shreds on a mandolin
Wasabi paste
Japanese pickled ginger

Carefully trim away the brown meat from the skinned side of the salmon fillet. Then using a super-sharp knife, neatly trim up all the fish fillets to remove any thin pieces of fish, then cut each one across into 5 mm (¼-inch) thick slices. Cut each scallop horizontally into 3 slices.

Mix the ingredients for the dipping sauce together and divide between 4 small dipping saucers.

To serve, arrange each type of fish, overlapping the slices very slightly, attractively on each plate and put the daikon, a hazelnut-sized amount of wasabi and a little saucer of dipping sauce alongside. Serve with chopsticks.

Vietnamese pho (aromatic beef broth with fillet steak, spring onions and rice noodles)

This is one of those brilliant Asian dishes, that you can get for breakfast or indeed any time of day and is packed full of amazing flavours. It's also very satisfying in that it is the best dish I know for those on a diet – lovely, comforting flavours and you're losing weight too.

SERVES 6

175 g (6 oz) dried rice noodles
75 g (3 oz) fresh beansprouts
6 large spring onions, thinly sliced
A small handful of mint leaves
A small handful of coriander leaves
1 medium-hot red chilli, seeded and thinly sliced
2 limes, cut into wedges
275 g (10 oz) fillet steak, very thinly sliced
Sea salt

FOR THE BROTH:

1¾ litres (3 pints) light *beef stock* (page 278)
900 g (2 lb) beef marrow bones
225 g (8 oz) shin of beef
6 cloves
1 teaspoon black peppercorns
2½ cm (1-inch) piece of fresh ginger, sliced but not peeled
7½ cm (3-inch) cinnamon stick
3 star anise
5 green cardamom pods
2 tablespoons Thai fish sauce (nam pla), plus extra to serve

Bring the stock to a boil in a large pan and add the bones, shin of beef, spices and fish sauce to the pan. Bring to the boil, then simmer for an hour, skimming any scum and fat from the surface every now and then. Strain the broth, reserving the shin, into a clean pan and remove any fat from the surface. Thinly slice the shin and return it to the pan, with 1 teaspoon of salt.

Put the rice noodles into a large bowl, cover with lots of boiling water and leave to soak for 15 minutes. Drain the noodles and divide between 6 warmed, deep bowls. Top with the beansprouts and spring onions.

Put the mint and coriander leaves, chilli, lime wedges and some fish sauce into separate small bowls and arrange them on 1 large or 6 dinner plates.

Bring the broth back to a vigorous simmer. Take a large soup ladle and fill it with some of the fillet steak slices. Dip the ladle into the boiling stock and leave for 5–10 seconds, until the beef has changed to pale pink; then pour into one of the bowls and top up with extra broth to cover the noodles. Repeat for each of the bowls. Serve immediately, with the plate of garnishes, which can be added to the soup as wished.

Mussels with lemongrass, chilli, and kaffir lime leaves

It is important to use coconut cream and not coconut milk for this recipe, because the juices from the mussels would dilute the milk too much and make the dish less intense in flavour. I originally wrote this recipe to be cooked on the barbecue, but it can just as easily be done on the top of the stove, in a wok or a large, deep saucepan.

SERVES 4

2 kg (4½ lb) live mussels, cleaned (page 283)
2 lemongrass stalks
1 tablespoon sunflower oil
2 red bird's eye chillies, seeded and finely chopped
2 garlic cloves, finely chopped
3 cm (1½-inch) piece of fresh ginger, finely grated
2 x 200 ml (7 fl oz) cartons of coconut cream
2 fresh kaffir lime leaves
1 tablespoon Thai fish sauce (nam pla)
2 tablespoons lime juice, or to taste
A handful of Thai basil leaves
Lime wedges, to serve

Remove the outer layers from each lemongrass stalk, cut them in half and set to one side. Chop the core very finely.

Place a flat-bottomed wok directly on the bars of the barbecue or on the side burner and, when hot, add the oil and the chopped lemongrass, chilli, garlic and ginger and cook briefly for about 30 seconds.

Add the mussels, coconut cream, kaffir lime leaves and lemongrass leaves, cover with any large lid you have to hand and cook for 3–4 minutes, giving the mussels a quick stir halfway through, until they have all opened.

Uncover and stir in the Thai fish sauce, lime juice and Thai basil leaves. Divide between warmed, deep bowls and serve garnished with the lime wedges, with plenty of crusty bread.

Sri Lankan fish curry

I got this recipe from a Sri Lankan living in Cumbria. Manel Trepte used to run a company called Demel's Chutneys in Ulverston and although she retired in 2003, the company still produces the chutneys. Using recipes from her home country, she made chutneys and fresh pickles that had an astounding clarity and purity of taste. One of the reasons for this, she said, was that she didn't use onion in any of her products, as she believed it would overpower them. You feel as if you are tasting every element of the chutneys. While I was filming there, she knocked up this little dish for lunch. Fragrant and fresh, it's a perfect recipe to use for farmed salmon. Interestingly, she said that in southern India and Sri Lanka spices are not roasted for fish curries, giving a more delicate flavour to the dish. Rampe or screwpine is a plant of the genus Pandanus whose leaves, or an essence extracted from them, are a popular flavouring in South-east Asian cooking, especially desserts and rice dishes. It should be available from Asian food stores.

SERVES 4

85 ml (3 fl oz) *tamarind water* (page 281)
4 x 225 g (8 oz) salmon steaks
2 tablespoons sunflower oil
1 large onion, chopped
4 garlic cloves, finely chopped
8 fresh curry leaves
2 small pieces rampe (screwpine, optional, see above)
½ teaspoon ground turmeric
1 teaspoon chilli powder
2 tomatoes, skinned and chopped (page 283)
400 ml (14 fl oz) can of coconut milk
Sea salt
1 quantity of *Sri Lankan curry powder* (page 281)

Rinse the fish steaks under cold water and dry on kitchen paper.

Heat the oil in a large, shallow pan, add the onion, garlic, curry leaves and rampe, if using, and fry gently for 7–10 minutes, until the onion is soft and lightly golden.

Add the turmeric, chilli powder and 2 tablespoons of the Sri Lankan curry powder (see page 281) and fry for 1–2 minutes. Add the tomatoes, tamarind water (see page 281), coconut milk and 1 teaspoon of salt and simmer gently for 15 minutes.

Add the salmon steaks to the pan and spoon some of the sauce over them. Simmer gently for 5 minutes, then cover the pan and set aside for 30 minutes. By this time the fish should be cooked through – but if not, just return it to the heat for a few minutes. Serve with some steamed rice (see page 281) and mango, lime, aubergine or tamarind chutney.

Australia & New Zealand

In my book *Seafood Odyssey*, first published in 1999, I described Australia as a cook's heaven and indeed I would now add New Zealand to that, having been there quite a few times since. The reason, quite simply, is that it's so easy to buy good food. Australia is such a big country that food from every region of the world can be grown locally, whether it is apples and pears and English summer berries from cool Tasmania right through to pineapples, papaya, coconuts and some of the best mangoes in tropical Northern Queensland. The meat is excellent too. They seem to supply most of South-east Asia with their quality red meat and, like Britain, there's a sort of 'Food Heroes' movement producing excellent free-range poultry, pork and organic vegetables and fruit. I recall a visit to a farmers' market in Sydney, going to a free-range eggs stall in front of which was a chicken in a (large) cage and a note saying 'We've invited one of our producers along for the day'! It's much easier there to get good seafood in the cities than in the UK. The cheeses are not bad, and getting better all the time, and what I love about Australia and New Zealand are the wine regions, which always seem to have good small artisan food producers too, so that the symbiosis of wine and food in places like Margaret River, the Barossa Valley or the Mornington Peninsula are great regions to eat in as well as drink in. There are fascinating food markets too – places like Flemington in Sydney, Prahran in Melbourne and the Central Market in Adelaide, where you can buy the sort of special ingredients that make cooking ethnic food come alive. I mean things like Vietnamese mint, galangal, ginger buds and morning glory leaves for South-east Asian cooking, Zahtar, dried broad beans and Aleppo pepper for Turkish dishes or a really good selection of Japanese soy sauces, pickled vegetables and sushi rice for Japanese food. It's not that you can't get similar products on the internet in the UK, you can, and there are one or two very good markets and some of the bigger supermarkets are now stocking ingredients from everywhere, but there is nothing to beat walking through a market teaming with stalls and all the atmosphere to really get your enthusiasm for cooking going.

I would suggest that either the Australians or Californians invented fusion food. It's not always my favourite type of cooking, but I do think there is a greater ease and informality about Australian cooks, use of Mediterranean and Asian ingredients than anywhere else, and a lot of those dishes appear now as part of the local cuisine. I'm thinking of recipes like the *Oyster soup with ginger, soy and chilli* on page 210 or the *Prawns with the split tomato sauce* on page 236. I love the place; I've got a house with my partner Sarah in Neutral Bay and, as I said during the first filming I did in Australia way back in 1996, every time I get off the plane at Kingsford Smith Airport I feel 10 years younger.

Crab with rocket, basil and lemon olive oil

This is based on the memory of a dish from Assaggi, a modern Italian restaurant above a pub in Notting Hill. It is light, lively and perfectly composed for bringing the best out of fresh white crab meat.

SERVES 4

350 g (12 oz) fresh hand-picked white crab meat
2 teaspoons lemon juice
4 teaspoons extra virgin olive oil, preferably *lemon olive oil* (page 280), plus extra for drizzling
8 basil leaves, finely shredded
A handful of wild rocket leaves
Sea salt and freshly ground black pepper,
    and cracked black pepper to garnish

Put the crab meat into a bowl and gently stir in the lemon juice, olive oil, basil and some seasoning to taste.

Make a small, tall pile of the crab mixture on 4 plates, placing them slightly off centre. Put a small pile of rocket leaves alongside. Drizzle a little more olive oil over the rocket and around the outside edge of the plate, sprinkle the oil with a little sea salt and cracked black pepper and serve.

Oyster soup with ginger, soy and chilli

This soup really celebrates the subtle flavours of oysters. The flavours are clean but restrained, allowing for the oyster meats, just slipped in at the last minute, to sing out loud. It's almost good enough to warrant using the native oysters from West Mersea near Colchester but, in the end, I think that natives should be served au naturel, and this dish is better made with the much cheaper Pacific oysters, which, incidentally, are also grown in that pretty part of Essex. For perfect results with this soup, the stock that you use needs to be chilled until the fat sets on the top and can be strained off, otherwise there will always be disappointing droplets on the top of your otherwise beautifully clear soup.

SERVES 4

12 Pacific oysters
1½ litres (2½ pints) cold *chicken stock* (page 278)
2 teaspoons Thai fish sauce (nam pla)
1 teaspoon light soy sauce
1 medium-hot green chilli, seeded and roughly chopped
1 cm (½-inch) piece of fresh ginger, sliced
100 g (4 oz) cheap white fish fillet, finely chopped
50 g (2 oz) leeks, cleaned and thinly sliced
1 egg white
1 teaspoon salt
A few tarragon, chervil and young flat-leaf parsley
    leaves, to garnish

Open the oysters and pour off the juices into a bowl. Release the oyster meats from their shells and keep them chilled until needed.

Put the cold chicken stock, oyster juice, Thai fish sauce, soy sauce, green chilli, ginger, chopped fish, leeks, egg white and salt into a large pan. Place over a medium heat and slowly bring to the boil, giving the mixture a stir every now and then. Allow the stock to boil vigorously for 5–10 seconds, then lower the heat and leave it to simmer undisturbed for 30 minutes.

Pass the soup into a clean pan through a fine sieve lined with a double thickness of muslin.

Slice the oyster meats lengthways into 2 or 3 slices, depending on their size. Bring the soup back to the boil, add the oyster slices and leave them to cook gently for just 5 seconds. Then ladle the soup into warmed bowls and scatter each one generously with the herb leaves. Serve immediately.

Seared escalopes of wild salmon with a warm olive oil, basil and caramelised vinegar dressing

This dish is designed for making the most of wild salmon. It is very much a last-minute affair, so make sure everything is ready before you start. If using farmed salmon, pay a little extra and go for the best. In Australia and New Zealand the quality of farmed salmon is consistently good – firm flesh with not too much fat and, as there is no wild Atlantic salmon, Tasmanian salmon would be ideal for this.

SERVES 4

1 tablespoon caster sugar
4 tablespoons Cabernet Sauvignon vinegar
5 tablespoons extra virgin olive oil
4 teaspoons lemon juice
550 g (1¼-lb) piece of unskinned wild (or best-quality farmed) salmon fillet, taken from a large fish
A small bunch of basil
Sea salt and freshly ground black pepper

Put the sugar into a small saucepan and leave over a low heat until it has turned into a light brown caramel – about the colour of golden syrup. Immediately remove from the heat, add the vinegar, then return to a low heat and stir with a wooden spoon until all the caramel has dissolved. Bring to the boil and reduce to 1½ tablespoons, leave to cool a little and then stir in 4 tablespoons of the oil, the lemon juice and ½ teaspoon of salt; season with black pepper. Keep warm.

Put the salmon skin side down on a board and, using a long, thin-bladed knife, cut at a 45-degree angle down towards the skin into twelve 5 mm (¼-inch) thick slices. Brush them on both sides with the remaining oil and season lightly with salt and quite generously with black pepper.

Heat a ridged cast-iron griddle until smoking hot. Cook the escalopes, no more than 2 at a time, for 15 seconds on each side, turning them with a palette knife, then quickly lifting them on to a warmed baking tray.

Slightly overlap 3 of the salmon slices on each warmed plate. Very finely shred the basil leaves and sprinkle them around the outside edge of the plate. Spoon the warm dressing over the shredded basil. You can, if you like, garnish the salmon with some deep-fried basil leaves – just drop them into hot oil for a few seconds and then drain.

211

Cured duck breasts with melon, soy and pickled ginger

I first ate this in the 1980s at the legendary restaurant Berowra Waters, on the Hawkesbury River, north of Sydney. You could only get to the restaurant by boat or seaplane from Rose Bay or Palm Beach, so even the arrival was memorable, as was the food. Gay Bilson, who ran the restaurant with her husband Tony, and latterly with another fantastic cook, Yanny Kyritsis, had a restaurant which, with one or two others, created modern Australian cookery, and this combination of salt duck, sweet melon, pickled ginger and soy is a perfect example.

SERVES 4

2 large duck breasts
300 ml (10 fl oz) water
½ a melon, preferably Charentais or Canteloupe
Sea salt

FOR THE SALT CURE:
½ teaspoon black peppercorns
½ teaspoon coriander seeds
1 tablespoon thyme leaves
2 bay leaves
50 g (2 oz) salt
40 g (1½ oz) sugar

FOR THE PICKLED GINGER:
75 g (3 oz) fresh ginger
1 medium-hot red chilli, seeded and thinly sliced
1 teaspoon salt
25 g (1 oz) sugar
200 ml (7 fl oz) white wine vinegar
6 allspice berries
2½ cm (1-inch) cinnamon stick

FOR THE SOY SAUCE DRESSING:
2 teaspoons red wine vinegar
2 teaspoons dark soy sauce
3 tablespoons groundnut oil
A pinch of Sichuan peppercorns, crushed

For the salt cure, put the peppercorns, coriander seeds, thyme leaves, bay leaves and salt into a spice grinder and grind to a powder. Mix with the sugar. Put half the cure into a shallow dish and lay the duck breasts, flesh side down, on top. Cover with the rest of the cure and refrigerate for at least 12 hours.

For the pickled ginger, peel the ginger and slice it thinly. Pile up a few slices at a time and cut them into fine matchsticks. Mix the ginger and chilli with 1 teaspoon of salt and then transfer them to a glass jar or small bowl. Put the rest of the ingredients into a small pan, bring to the boil and simmer for 5 minutes. Pour over the ginger and chillies, leave to cool, then cover and leave for at least 24 hours.

Preheat the oven to 160°C/325°F/Gas Mark 3. Rinse the salt cure off the duck breasts, put them into a small ovenproof casserole and add the water. Cover and cook for 25 minutes (or until the internal temperature of the duck reaches 60–65°C, if you have a meat probe). Remove them from the casserole to a plate and leave them to cool.

Just before serving, whisk together the ingredients for the soy sauce dressing. Remove the seeds from the melon with a spoon and cut it into 4 wedges. Slice the flesh neatly away from the skin and then cut it diagonally into thin slices. Slice the duck breasts lengthways, slightly on the diagonal, into long, very thin slices. Arrange the duck and melon slices on 4 plates and put about 1 tablespoon of the pickled ginger alongside. Sprinkle the dressing around the edge of the plate and serve.

Grilled spatchcock and sautéed shiitake, oyster and chestnut mushrooms with lemon thyme

This is a nice café-style dish – just the sort of thing you might find in one of those interesting restaurant-lined lanes off Collins or Flanders St in Melbourne.

SERVES 4

4 poussins, each weighing about 500 g (1 lb 2 oz)
4 tablespoons olive oil
2 tablespoons balsamic vinegar
2 garlic cloves, finely chopped
1 teaspoon salt
Extra virgin olive oil, balsamic vinegar and lemon
    thyme leaves, to garnish

FOR THE MUSHROOMS:

50 g (2 oz) butter
350 g (12 oz) mixed shiitake, chestnut and oyster
    mushrooms, wiped clean and thickly sliced
1 teaspoon lemon thyme or common thyme leaves
Sea salt and freshly ground black pepper

To spatchcock each poussin, put it on a chopping board, back side down, and make a horizontal cut from the cavity end, just under the point of the breastbone, through the ribs on either side, over the top of the legs and stopping at the neck, just before you cut the whole breast away from the body. Lift the breast up, over and down on to the chopping board, still hinged at the neck. Spread-eagle the legs apart on the board. Turn it over skin side down and flatten the chicken.

Take a large roasting tin and add the olive oil, the balsamic vinegar, garlic, salt and pepper. Add the poussins and rub the marinade into both sides of each one and leave for 30 minutes.

Preheat the grill to high. Lift the poussins out of the marinade on to a lightly oiled baking tray or the rack of the grill pan. Grill them for 8 minutes, basting with a little of the leftover marinade now and then, until they are a good colour and the skin is crisp. Then turn them over and cook for another 10 minutes or until cooked through – they will need about 15–20 minutes cooking time in all. Turn off the grill and keep them warm.

Heat the butter in a large frying pan. Add the mushrooms, thyme leaves and some salt and pepper and stir-fry over a high heat for 2–3 minutes.

Lift the poussins on to 4 warmed plates and scatter over the mushrooms. Drizzle a little extra virgin olive oil over and around the birds, and sprinkle with a few drops of balsamic vinegar and a few more lemon thyme leaves.

Trout with a soy, ginger and chilli glaze with steamed bok choi

At the centre of this dish is a very simple process: the reduction of soy sauce and balsamic vinegar, which is then used to coat a just-seared fillet of fish with a deliciously sticky and aromatic glaze. This was not my idea, I hasten to add, but that of a good chef friend of mine living in Sydney called Leigh Stone-Herbert. He gave me the recipe 12 years ago, and I've been using it ever since with oily fish, particularly tuna, which I will always serve up seriously undercooked in the centre.

SERVES 4

4 x 350 g (12 oz) rainbow trout, filleted
2 tablespoons sunflower oil
6 tablespoons dark soy sauce
4 tablespoons balsamic vinegar
1 garlic clove, finely chopped
2½ cm (1-inch) piece of fresh ginger, very finely chopped
1 medium-hot red chilli, seeded and finely chopped
4 fresh coriander sprigs, to garnish

FOR THE STEAMED BOK CHOI:

450 g (1 lb) small heads of bok choi, halved lengthways
½ teaspoon roasted sesame oil
2½ cm (1-inch) piece of fresh ginger, finely shredded
1 teaspoon cornflour
Sea salt
1 quantity of *steamed rice* (page 281), to serve

Blanch the bok choi in lightly salted, boiling water for 3 minutes. Spoon 150 ml (5 fl oz) of the cooking liquor into a small pan; then drain the bok choi, cover and set aside to keep warm.

Season the trout fillets lightly on both sides with some salt and pepper. Heat the oil in a large frying pan over a high heat. Add the trout fillets and sear them for 30 seconds on each side.

Take the pan off the heat and add the soy sauce, balsamic vinegar, garlic, ginger and chilli. Reduce the heat to medium, return the pan to the heat and cook for 3 minutes, until the trout is just cooked through.

Meanwhile, add the sesame oil, shredded ginger and ¼ teaspoon of salt to the reserved bok choi cooking liquor and slake the cornflour with a tablespoon of cold water. Bring the liquor to the boil, add the cornflour and simmer for 1 minute.

Divide the bok choi between 4 warmed plates and spoon over some of the sesame- and ginger-flavoured sauce. Rest 2 of the glazed trout fillets on top and serve garnished with the coriander sprigs, accompanied by steamed rice (see page 281).

Mildly spiced potato curry with cumin, black mustard seeds and coriander, topped with a poached egg

I always think of this as a breakfast dish and, though I originally found the recipe in India, it's the sort of thing you might easily find in one of those delightful places that do breakfast in Sydney or Melbourne. It never ceases to amaze me how breakfasts have improved back in the UK thanks to what we have learnt from Australia and New Zealand. Somerset Maugham said, 'To eat well in England, you should have a breakfast three times a day.' I still love our full English breakfast, but I enjoy the variety of dishes from down under. When I originally wrote this recipe for the Australian magazine Delicious, *I remarked that black coffee is the perfect accompaniment.*

I've specified a waxy potato because I think it's important for the look of the dish that the cubes of potato are well defined when cooked and not a bit mushy.

SERVES 4

500 g (1 lb 2 oz) waxy main-crop potatoes, such as Desirée, peeled and cut into 1 cm (½-inch) pieces
4 tablespoons sunflower oil
1½ teaspoons black mustard seeds
1 teaspoon cumin seeds
1 large onion, finely chopped
1 tablespoon grated fresh ginger
A good pinch of dried chilli flakes
¾ teaspoon ground turmeric
½ teaspoon freshly ground cumin
½ teaspoon freshly ground coriander
The seeds from 2 green cardamom pods, lightly crushed
225 ml (7 fl oz) water
1 teaspoon salt
2 vine-ripened tomatoes, skinned, seeded and roughly chopped (page 283)
1 teaspoon lemon juice
4 large, very fresh, free-range eggs
White wine vinegar
2 tablespoons chopped fresh coriander
Sea salt and freshly ground black pepper

Drop the potatoes into a pan of boiling, salted water and cook for 5–6 minutes, until almost tender; then drain and set aside.

Heat the oil in a deep frying pan over a medium heat. Add the mustard seeds and cumin seeds and cover the pan with a lid until the popping of the mustard seeds subsides. Uncover the pan, add the onion, ginger and dried chilli flakes and cook for 6–7 minutes, until soft but not browned. Stir in the turmeric, ground cumin and coriander and cardamom seeds and cook for 1 minute. Stir in the potatoes, water and salt and leave to simmer gently for 10 minutes, until the potatoes are tender, the liquid has reduced and the flavours have blended together. Stir in the tomatoes and lemon juice and cook for 2 minutes more. Stir in almost all the coriander, cover and keep warm over a low heat.

For the eggs, bring 5 cm (2 inches) of water to the boil in a wide, shallow pan. Add 1½ teaspoons of vinegar and ½ teaspoon salt per 1.2 litres (2 pints) of water and reduce the heat so that just a few small bubbles are rising from the base of the pan. Break in the eggs and leave them to poach gently for 3 minutes. Lift out with a slotted spoon and leave to drain briefly on kitchen paper.

Spoon the potato curry into the centre of 4 warmed plates and put a poached egg on top of each. Season the eggs lightly with a little salt, scatter over the remaining coriander and serve.

Sliced seared fillet steak salad with pickled chicory

In this recipe, I have made the most of the melt-in-the-mouth quality of the best fillet steak, by serving it extremely underdone but with a highly seared crust, flavoured with sea salt, black pepper and Sichuan pepper. I serve it cold and thinly sliced, with pickled chicory and a dressing of lemon and Thai fish sauce. If you can get the red-tinged chicory which seems to be widely available now, it looks really good. The point of the chicory is the contrast between its bitterness and the heat of the chilli in the pickle.

SERVES 4

10 g (¼ oz) Sichuan peppercorns

10 g (¼ oz) black peppercorns

10 g (¼ oz) sea salt flakes

350 g (12 oz) piece of thick beef fillet

2–3 tablespoons sunflower oil

25 g (1 oz) wild rocket leaves

FOR THE SALAD DRESSING:

1½ tablespoons Thai fish sauce (nam pla)

3 tablespoons water

½ teaspoon granulated sugar

½ teaspoon freshly squeezed lemon juice

¼ teaspoon arrowroot

5 cm (2-inch) piece of spring onion, very thinly sliced

FOR THE PICKLED CHICORY:

15 g (½ oz) fresh ginger, peeled

¼ medium-hot red chilli, halved lengthways and seeded

40 g (1½ oz) granulated sugar

150 ml (5 fl oz) white wine vinegar

1 head of red or green chicory

1 teaspoon salt

For the pickled chicory, cut the ginger and red chilli into 2½ cm (1-inch) long, thin matchsticks. Put them in a pan with the sugar and vinegar, bring to the boil and simmer for 5 minutes. Tip into a shallow plastic container and leave to cool.

Meanwhile, break the chicory into leaves, then cut each leaf in half and thinly slice the core. Place in a colander set over a bowl and toss with the salt. Leave for 2 hours to soften. Stir the salted chicory into the cold spiced vinegar, stir well, cover and set aside in the refrigerator for 24 hours. Discard the salty liquor left behind in the bowl.

For the beef, put the Sichuan peppercorns and black peppercorns into a mortar and grind to a coarse powder. Add the salt and grind a little more. Set aside ½ a teaspoon of the mixture for the salad dressing and sprinkle the rest over the base of a large baking tray.

Brush the piece of beef fillet all over with the oil, then roll it in the salt and pepper mixture so that it takes on an even coating. Heat a ridged cast-iron skillet or heavy-based frying pan until hot. Brush with a little more oil, then add the beef and sear it on one side for about 2 minutes. Give it a quarter turn and sear for another 2 minutes. Continue like this, turning maybe once or twice more, until it is richly browned all over but still very rare in the centre. Set aside to cool.

For the dressing, put the fish sauce, water, sugar, reserved salt and pepper mixture and lemon juice into a small pan and bring to the boil. Slake the arrowroot with a tiny amount of water, stir in and simmer for 1 minute. Pour into a small bowl and leave to cool.

To serve, carve the beef across into thin slices and arrange it on 4 large plates. Drain the pickling liquid from the chicory and place a small pile alongside the beef, together with a small pile of rocket leaves. Stir the spring onions into the dressing, spoon a little over the beef and a little more around the outside edge of each plate.

Salad of griddled mackerel with sun-dried tomatoes and fennel seeds

Another warm fish salad – I'm inordinately fond of them. I'm also very keen on the flavour of fennel with fish, in this case fennel seeds, especially when mixed with a dressing made with sherry vinegar and chilli. I've included chervil in this salad, although it's still very hard to get hold of, which is such a shame because its mild aniseed flavour compliments fish dishes very well. If you can't get it, leave it out, or you can substitute it with about half as much tarragon, which is much stronger but again goes very well with fish.

SERVES 4

4 small mackerel, filleted
3 tablespoons olive oil
2 teaspoons lemon juice
1 teaspoon chopped thyme
1 teaspoon fennel seeds, lightly crushed
A pinch of dried chilli flakes
25 g (1 oz) rocket
25 g (1 oz) prepared curly endive
15 g (½ oz) flat-leaf parsley leaves
15 g (½ oz) chervil sprigs
4–6 sun-dried tomatoes in olive oil, drained and thinly sliced
1 tablespoon sherry vinegar
Sea salt and freshly ground black pepper

Place each mackerel fillet in turn on a board and cut out a narrow strip from down the length of each one – this will remove all the pin bones in one go.

Mix together the olive oil, lemon juice, thyme, fennel seeds, chilli flakes, ½ teaspoon of salt and a some black pepper. Brush a little of this mixture over both sides of the fish pieces and set aside for 5 minutes.

Toss the rocket, curly endive, parsley and chervil together and set aside.

Heat a ridged cast-iron griddle until really hot. Reduce the heat slightly, add the strips of mackerel, skin side down, and cook for 1–1½ minutes, turning them over half-way through. Transfer them to a plate to stop them from cooking further.

Arrange the fish, strips of sun-dried tomato and salad leaves on 4 plates, taking care not to flatten the leaves too much.

Add the remaining marinade and the sherry vinegar to the pan and swirl it around briefly. Spoon a little over the salad and the rest around the outside of the plate; serve straight away.

Clams or pipis *a la plancha* tossed with a garlic and *fines herbes* mayonnaise

The method of cooking shellfish a la plancha is, of course, Spanish. You can achieve the same results as the griddles they use there by using the solid plate of your barbeque, or you could use a really hot, dry frying pan. The point of cooking like this is that the shellfish open rapidly on the searing heat and the liquid from inside the shells partially evaporates. As long as you stir the shells while cooking, enough of the concentrated flavour coats the meat and shells of the shellfish and the remaining liquid will thin down the garlic and fine herb mayonnaise to make a really well-flavoured sauce. This is a dish for eating with your fingers, with lots of good bread.

SERVES 4

1 kg (2¼ lb) carpetshell clams or pipis
2 tablespoon *fines herbes* (finely chopped parsley, chervil, tarragon and chives)

FOR THE MAYONNAISE
2 small garlic cloves, peeled
¼ teaspoon salt
1 egg yolk
1 teaspoon white wine vinegar
150 ml (5 fl oz) sunflower oil

For the mayonnaise, make sure that all the ingredients are at room temperature before you start. Put the garlic gloves onto a chopping board and crush them under the blade of a large knife. Sprinkle them with the salt and work them with the blade of the knife into a smooth paste. Scrape the garlic paste into a small bowl and add the egg yolk and vinegar. Rest the bowl on a cloth to stop it slipping. Lightly whisk the egg yolks, then using a wire whisk, beat the oil into the egg mixture a few drops at a time until you have incorporated it all. Set to one side.

Heat the flat grilling plate of your barbecue or preheat the barbecue to high and then place a flat cast-iron griddle plate on the bars and leave it to get really hot.

Give the clams a good wash under cold water and discard any that won't close when given a sharp tap on the work surface. Drain them well and then tip them on to the hot griddle plate and spread them out in an even layer. Turn them over as they open and are just cooked – about 4–5 minutes. Remove them with tongs and drop them into a large bowl.

When all the clams are cooked, drain off the excess clam juice into a small bowl and then stir 1½ tablespoons back into the mayonnaise with the *fines herbes*. Add this mixture to the clams and stir together well. Spoon on to plates and serve with some crusty French bread.

Barbecued butterflied lamb with lemon, garlic and thyme

This is one of those recipes that I have to limit myself to cooking occasionally, otherwise I'd overdose on it, it's that good. But not only is it good, it seems to be the sort of food that everyone else likes, too: rough slices of pink lamb tinged with the flavour of the fire. The best time to eat new season's lamb is June and July, which is also the nicest time for barbecuing. The new season's lamb bred for Easter tends to be tender yet disappointingly bland but, by June, it is full of the taste of summer pastures. There's something immensely satisfying about boning out a leg and cooking it with extreme care, on an early summer's evening, with the odd glass of Beaujolais nearby.

SERVES 6

2½ kg (5½-lb) leg of lamb, butterflied (page 283)

FOR THE MARINADE:

2 large garlic cloves, chopped
1 medium-hot red chilli, seeded and finely chopped
1 teaspoon chopped rosemary
The leaves from 6 thyme sprigs
1 fresh bay leaf, finely chopped
3 strips of pared lemon zest
Juice of ½ a lemon
1 teaspoon sea salt
½ teaspoon black pepper, coarsely crushed
6 tablespoons olive oil

Butterfly the leg of lamb (see page 283).

Mix the marinade ingredients together in a shallow roasting tin. Add the lamb, turn it a few times until well coated, then turn skin side up, cover and leave in the fridge for at least an hour.

If you are using a charcoal barbecue, light it 40 minutes before you want to start cooking. If you are using a gas barbecue, light it 10 minutes beforehand.

Because a leg of lamb contains a good deal of fat, you will need to be careful when barbecuing it, to avoid excessive flare-ups, which would cause the meat to burn. Place it on the bars of the barbecue grill and keep turning and moving it to different parts of the grill. Cook for 10–12 minutes on each side. Alternatively, just barbecue or griddle the leg for 5–7 minutes on each side until well-coloured and then transfer it to an oven set at 200°C/400°F/Gas Mark 6 for 20–25 minutes or until it registers 60°C on a meat thermometer at its thickest part.

Lift the lamb on to a board, cover with foil and leave to rest for 5 minutes. Then carve across into thick slices and serve with chips cooked in olive oil and a tomato, shallot and basil salad.

Jack's mud crab omelette

Jack was a customer at Two Small Rooms, a delightful restaurant in Brisbane. He visited the restaurant every Saturday night and ordered this omelette every time, followed by a steak. There's not much more to the story really, except to say he was one of those much-loved customers who don't complain and keep coming back; then one day they don't. The longer you run a restaurant the more of those there are. It's a great way of writing a dish up on a menu so that Jack's memory lives on.

Mud crabs come from the mangrove swamps of the northern part of Australia. They look a bit like European brown crabs, with equally powerful and dangerous claws. The meat, however, is more like the blue crabs of Australia and Asia – more fibrous and easier to extract. A mud crab salad and a glass or two of Mad Fish Bay white – just perfect.

SERVES 4

FOR THE NAM PRIK SAUCE:
Juice of 1 lime
1 large garlic clove
1 tablespoon nam prik (Thai sweet chilli and dried shrimp sauce)
½ teaspoon sambal oelek (Indonesian red chilli paste)
25 ml (1 fl oz) ketjap manis (sweet soy sauce)
100 g (4 oz) palm sugar or light muscovado sugar
2 tablespoons chopped coriander
1 teaspoon chopped mint

FOR THE VEGETABLE STIR-FRY:
1 tablespoon sunflower oil
40 g (1½ oz) fresh beansprouts
40 g (1½ oz) mangetout peas, thinly shredded
½ red pepper, cut into fine strips
½ medium carrot, cut into fine strips
½ small red onion, thinly sliced
4 fresh shiitake mushrooms, thinly sliced
4 oyster mushrooms, torn into fine strips
15 g (½ oz) Japanese pickled ginger, finely shredded

FOR THE OMELETTES:
4 tablespoons sunflower oil
12 large eggs, beaten
225 g (8 oz) fresh white crab meat
Sea salt and freshly ground black pepper

For the sauce, put the lime juice and garlic into a liquidiser and whizz until smooth. Add all the other ingredients and blend well. Add enough water to make a smooth, sauce-like consistency, then pass through a fine sieve.

For the vegetable stir-fry, heat the oil in a frying pan or wok, add all the vegetables and stir-fry for 1–2 minutes until just cooked but still crunchy. Add the pickled ginger and toss for a few seconds to heat through.

Drizzle some of the nam prik sauce over each serving plate in a zigzag pattern and then put the stir-fried vegetables in the centre of each one.

For the omelettes, heat a 20–23 cm (8–9 inch) omelette pan over a medium heat, add 1 tablespoon of the oil and, when it is hot, a quarter of the beaten eggs. Move the mixture over the base of the pan with the back of a fork until it begins to set, then stop stirring and cook until it is just a little moist on top – about 2 minutes in all. Put a quarter of the crab meat down the centre of the omelette and season to taste with salt and pepper. Fold the omelette over twice and place on the stir-fried vegetables. Serve straight away and cook the remaining omelettes in the same way.

Grilled cod with laksa noodles and sambal blachan

The idea behind this dish is very straightforward: take a lovely thick fillet of grilled cod and set it on top of a spice and coconut laksa with egg noodles, so the soft delicate cod flakes taste sweet against the fiery fragrance of coconut and chilli. This is also excellent made with a thick fillet of snapper, a halibut steak or a thick fillet of haddock.

SERVES 4

120 ml (4 fl oz) sunflower oil, plus extra for brushing
450 ml (15 fl oz) *chicken stock* or *fish stock* (page 278 or 279)
4 x 175–225 g (6–8 oz) pieces of unskinned cod fillet
50 g (2 oz) dried medium egg noodles
400 ml (14 fl oz) coconut milk
100 g (4 oz) fresh beansprouts
4 spring onions, thinly sliced on the diagonal
A handful of chopped mixed mint, basil and coriander
1 lime, cut into 4 wedges
Sea salt and freshly ground black pepper

FOR THE SAMBAL BLACHAN:
2 kaffir lime leaves (optional)
8 medium-hot red chillies, seeded and sliced
1 teaspoon salt
1 teaspoon blachan (dried shrimp paste)
Grated zest and juice of 1 lime

FOR THE LAKSA PASTE:
25g (1 oz) dried shrimps
3 medium-hot red chillies, roughly chopped
2 lemongrass stalks, outer leaves removed and core roughly chopped
25g (1 oz) unroasted cashew nuts
2 garlic cloves
2½ cm (1-inch) piece fresh root ginger, peeled and roughly chopped
1 teaspoon turmeric powder
1 small onion, roughly chopped
1 teaspoon ground coriander
Juice 1 lime

For the sambal blachan, if using lime leaves, remove the spines and shred the leaves very finely. Put them in a mini food processor with the chillies, salt, shrimp paste, lime zest and juice and blend to a coarse paste. Spoon into a small serving bowl.

For the laksa paste, cover the dried shrimps with warm water and leave to soak for 15 minutes. Drain and put into a mini food processor with the rest of the ingredients and 2 tablespoons of cold water.

Blend to a smooth paste.

Heat the oil in a large pan, add the laksa paste and fry for 10 minutes, stirring constantly, until it smells very fragrant. Add the stock and simmer for 10 minutes.

Preheat the grill to high. Brush both sides of the cod with a little sunflower oil and season with some salt and pepper. Place on a lightly oiled baking tray, skin side up, and grill for 8 minutes.

Meanwhile, drop the noodles into a pan of boiling, salted water, cover and remove from the heat. Leave to soak for 4 minutes, then drain.

Add the coconut milk to the soup and simmer for 3 minutes. Add the noodles, beansprouts, spring onions and 1 teaspoon of salt.

To serve, spoon the laksa into 4 large, warmed soup plates and place a piece of cod in the centre of each. Scatter the chopped mint, basil and coriander around the edge and then spoon a little of the sambal blachan over the cod. Serve the rest separately, with the lime wedges.

Seared scallops with noodles, chilli, garlic and coriander

What I like about this dish is the combination of cooked thin egg noodles with seared, caramelised scallops. I find a lot of scallop dishes are over-complicated, but they are expensive and it's nice to bulk them out with plenty of noodles. I flavour this dish simply, with some common Chinese things like garlic, ginger, chilli and soy, and finish it with some coriander and sesame oil. It's the sort of thing they do so well in Australia and New Zealand, being close to Asia – an ease with Asian ingredients is part of the new Australian cooking.

SERVES 4

2 tablespoons sunflower oil
4 garlic cloves, thinly sliced
2 medium-hot red chillies, seeded and sliced
1 cm (½-inch) piece of fresh ginger, cut into slithers
12 large, prepared scallops, halved horizontally
100 g (4 oz) fine dried egg noodles
1 teaspoon dark soy sauce
A handful of coriander leaves, chopped
A few drops of toasted sesame oil

Bring a pan of lightly salted water to the boil. Add the noodles, turn off the heat and leave the noodles for 4 minutes until cooked. Drain and set aside. Add 1 tablespoon of the oil to a frying pan and heat over a medium-low heat. Add the garlic, chilli and ginger and cook for 3–4 minutes, stirring frequently, until they soften. Remove from the pan and keep to one side.

Heat the frying pan again until hot and add the rest of the oil. Fry the scallop slices on both sides until lightly browned – no more than 20 seconds per side. You need to do this in two batches, making sure the pan is hot between each batch.

Return the garlic, chilli and ginger to the pan, with the noodles and soy sauce, and stir until the noodles are well coated. Add the coriander and sesame oil, toss together and serve.

Marinated tuna with passion-fruit, lime and coriander

I developed this recipe in Australia. I like marinating oily fish like salmon and tuna in oil and lime juice, but I thought the addition of passion-fruit juice, which is also quite sour, would give the whole thing a very local flavour. It turned out to be the combination of lime, passion-fruit and sunflower oil with chilli and coriander that made this dish very popular indeed. This is a very good dish to start quite an elaborate meal for a number of people, because you can slice the tuna and have it arranged on plates in the fridge and just add the dressing at the last minute. It's a good idea to leave the dressing on the fish for 10 minutes, just to start the acid in the lime and passion-fruit 'cooking' the fish, but don't leave it for longer because it then becomes less fresh-tasting.

SERVES 4

3 cm (1½-inch) thick piece of tuna loin fillet,
weighing about 400 g (14 oz)
2 small, ripe and wrinkly passion-fruit,
each weighing about 35 g (1¼ oz)
1 tablespoon lime juice
3 tablespoons sunflower oil
1 medium-hot green chilli, seeded and finely chopped
1 teaspoon caster sugar
1½ tablespoons finely chopped coriander
½ teaspoon salt and freshly ground black pepper

Put the piece of tuna loin fillet on to a board and slice it across, in very thin slices. Lay the slices, side by side but butted close up together, over the base of four 25 cm (10-inch) plates. Cover each one with cling film and set aside in the fridge for at least 1 hour, or until you are ready to serve.

Shortly before serving, make the dressing. Cut the passion-fruit in half and scoop the pulp into a sieve set over a bowl. Rub the pulp through the sieve to extract the juice and discard the seeds. You should be left with about a tablespoon of juice. Stir in the lime juice, sunflower oil, green chilli, sugar, coriander, salt and pepper.

To serve, uncover the plates, spoon over the dressing and spread it over the surface of the fish with the back of the spoon. Leave for 10 minutes before serving.

Prawns in the shell, cooked on skewers with a split tomato, saffron and currant sauce

As a regular visitor to Australia, I'm often asked whether their seafood is better than ours, or vice versa, and the answer is simply that some is and some isn't. I feel sorry for any country that doesn't have Dover sole or a slice of turbot available for special occasions, but, on the other hand, I marvel at the quality and universal availability of Australian prawns. In the 60s, Barry Humphries, aka Dame Edna Everage, produced a strip cartoon about a rather uncouth character called Barry McKenzie, whose chief pastimes were drinking vast quantities of beer and chundering (vomiting) and eating prawns by the bucketload, so when I first got there in 1966, I not unnaturally expected to find plenty of prawns. I was not disappointed – perhaps my fondest memory of those distant but magic times.

SERVES 6

36 large, raw, shell-on prawns
4 tablespoons extra virgin olive oil
Juice of ½ lemon
1 teaspoon dried oregano
1 teaspoon dried chilli flakes
Sea salt and freshly ground black pepper

FOR THE TOMATO, SAFFRON AND CURRANT SAUCE:
1 tablespoon extra virgin olive oil
1 small onion, finely chopped
2 garlic cloves, finely chopped
200 g can of good-quality plum tomatoes
A pinch of saffron strands
A pinch of dried chilli flakes
1 teaspoon sugar
2 tablespoons red wine vinegar
15 g (½ oz) currants

FOR THE DRESSING:
125 ml (4 fl oz) extra virgin olive oil
2 tablespoons red wine vinegar
½ teaspoon sea salt

Put the prawns into a shallow dish. Whisk the olive oil, lemon juice, oregano and dried chillies together with ½ teaspoon of salt and some black pepper, pour over the prawns and mix together well. Cover and leave to marinate in the fridge for 1–2 hours.

Meanwhile, make the tomato, saffron and currant sauce. Heat the olive oil in a medium-sized pan. Add the onion and garlic and fry gently for 5 minutes until softened. Add the tomatoes, saffron, dried chilli and some salt and pepper and simmer gently for 15–20 minutes, stirring now and then. Meanwhile, put the sugar and vinegar into a small pan and boil until reduced to 1 teaspoon. Stir into the tomato sauce and adjust the seasoning to taste.

Blend the sauce briefly until smooth and then pass through a sieve into a clean pan, add the currants and leave to simmer gently until it is thick enough to coat the back of a spoon. Set aside.

Preheat your barbecue to high. Thread 6 of the prawns on to pairs of parallel skewers (fine metal or soaked bamboo ones) – this will stop them from spinning around when you come to turn them.

Reheat the tomato sauce. Put the ingredients for the dressing into a bowl with ½ teaspoon of salt and some black pepper and whisk together. Stir into the tomato sauce and keep warm.

Barbecue the prawns for 1½ minutes on each side or until cooked through.

To serve, spoon some of the split tomato, saffron and currant sauce haphazardly over the base of 4 warmed plates. Pull the prawns off each set of skewers, arrange on top of the sauce and serve straight away with finger bowls. Alternatively, to serve, spoon the sauce into small bowls and put on to plates, with the prawns piled alongside.

Steamed mussels with almonds and parsley

One of the reasons why I think Australia is called the lucky country is the local availability of produce from almost any climate, and nowhere is that more obvious than in the availability and the cheapness of really good nuts: cashews, pecan, macadamia and almonds, to name but a few. I wrote this recipe as a celebration of good almonds, not fresh but still with a lingering moistness. It's a very simple dish, but the texture and taste of the chopped almonds with the parsley, olive oil, garlic and lemon make it something quite special.

SERVES 4

2¾ kg (6 lb) live mussels, cleaned (page 283)
100 g (4 oz) unsalted butter
2 fat garlic cloves, finely chopped
50 ml (2 fl oz) dry white wine
Juice of ½ lemon
25 g (1 oz) almonds, lightly toasted and finely chopped
3–4 tablespoons chopped flat-leaf parsley

Melt the butter in a very large saucepan. Add the garlic and cook very gently for 3–4 minutes.

Add the mussels, white wine, lemon juice and chopped almonds. Cover and cook over a high heat, giving the pan a good shake every now and then, until all the mussels have opened. Add half the chopped parsley and stir well.

Scoop the mussels out into 4 large, warmed bowls, discarding any that have remained closed. Divide the juices between each bowl, leaving behind the last tablespoon or two because it might be a bit gritty. Sprinkle over the remaining parsley and serve with plenty of crusty French or sourdough bread.

Pavlova with cream and passion-fruit

This is an Australian dish named after the Russian ballerina Anna Pavlova, who danced there in the late 1920s. Though it's long been associated with strawberries, it is far nicer when made with this more appropriate local fruit. The meringue is marshmallow-like in the centre and the whole thing is a triumph of fragility, created by the addition of cornflour and vinegar to the egg white. The recipe comes from the home economist who works with me on all my books, Debbie Major. She's a bit of a food hero to me, mostly for helping me translate my wild restaurant ideas into servings for two or four people, but also because she feels the same as me about trying to locate the best produce. She's also a very good cook. Here's to all those unsung heroes, the home economists, who quietly make the disorganised work of chefs like me possible.

SERVES 8

6 egg whites
350 g (12 oz) caster sugar
2 teaspoons cornflour
1 teaspoon white wine vinegar
A pinch of salt
600 ml (1 pint) double cream, to serve
8 passion-fruit, to serve

Preheat the oven to 140°C/275°F/Gas Mark 1. Lightly grease 1 large or 2 smaller baking trays and line with non-stick baking paper.

In a large bowl, whisk the egg whites with a pinch of salt into stiff peaks. Gradually whisk in the sugar to make a very stiff and shiny meringue. Whisk in the cornflour and vinegar.

Drop 8 large spoonfuls of the mixture on to the baking sheet(s) and spread each one into a 10 cm (4-inch) round. Bake for 45 minutes until pale in colour and marshmallow-like in the centre. Turn off the oven, leave the door ajar and leave them to cool.

To serve, whip the cream into soft peaks. Spoon some into the centre of each pavlova and spread it out very slightly. Halve the passion-fruit and spoon the pulp over the cream. Serve within 5 minutes.

Black-rice pudding with mango sorbet and coconut milk

Black rice is much used in Asia for sweet dishes and has recently swept through smart restaurants in Australia, whence this recipe came, via our ex-pastry chef from Queensland, Anita Pearce. You can buy it in this country from Asian food stores or any good deli. It has a pleasing al dente quality, even when long cooked. This is a great favourite of mine at The Seafood Restaurant; it's not at all filling and I'm very fond of the combination of mango and coconut.

SERVES 6–8

300 g (11 oz) black rice
A small pinch of salt
750 ml (1¼ pints) full-cream milk
1¼ litres (2¼ pints) water
2 slices of peeled fresh ginger
225 g (8 oz) light muscovado sugar
400 ml (14 oz) can of coconut milk, chilled, to serve
FOR THE MANGO SORBET:
Juice of 2 lemons
200 g (7 oz) caster sugar
75 g (3 oz) liquid glucose
3 ripe mangoes, weighing about 450 g (1 lb) each
    (or 600 ml/1 pint canned mango pulp)

For the mango sorbet, make the lemon juice up to 300 ml (10 fl oz) with cold water. Put the juice, sugar and liquid glucose into a pan and bring slowly to the boil, stirring occasionally to dissolve the sugar. Remove from the heat and leave to cool.

Peel the mangoes and slice the flesh away from the stone. Put the flesh into a food processor and blend to a smooth purée. Stir in the lemon syrup, pass through a sieve and then churn in an ice cream maker. Transfer to a shallow plastic container, cover and freeze until required.

For the black-rice pudding, put the rice into a pan with the salt, milk, water and ginger. Bring to the boil, then reduce the heat and simmer gently, stirring now and then, for 1½ hours. Add the sugar 10 minutes before the end of cooking, by which time the rice should be tender and suspended in a thick, dark purple liquid. Remove and discard the slices of ginger, transfer the rice pudding to a glass serving bowl and leave to cool.

Remove the mango sorbet from the freezer 10–15 minutes before you want to serve it, to allow it to soften slightly. Spoon the rice pudding into shallow serving bowls and top with a scoop of the sorbet. Pour over a little of the ice-cold coconut milk and serve straight away.

Fresh raspberry tart with coconut and hazelnut pastry

While hotter climates produce more succulent fruit than Britain's damp islands, not everything is better. Tayside, in Scotland, produces the best raspberries in the world. The long northern summer day, which is not too hot, leads to exactly the right degree of delicate, sweet acidity in the fruit. Anita Pearce, who used to work for us as our pastry chef, came up with this recipe for me a few years ago, for a TV programme in which we were trying to match beer to food. This was to go with one of those fruit beers from Belgium but, ultimately, I don't think it worked; it was too bitter. I would far sooner go for something like a sweet white Jurançon wine, such as Domaine Cauhapé.

SERVES 8

FOR THE HAZELNUT AND COCONUT PASTRY:
25 g (1 oz) toasted hazelnuts
25 g (1 oz) desiccated coconut
175 g (6 oz) plain flour
A pinch of salt
175 g (6 oz) unsalted butter, softened
65 g (2½ oz) caster sugar
1 medium egg, beaten

FOR THE FILLING:
2 egg yolks
50 g (2 oz) caster sugar
20 g (¾ oz) cornflour
20 g (¾ oz) plain flour
300 ml (10 fl oz) milk
1 teaspoon vanilla extract
15 g (½ oz) unsalted butter
50 ml (2 fl oz) double cream
225 g (8 oz) fresh raspberries
Icing sugar, for dusting

For the hazelnut and coconut pastry, put the toasted hazelnuts and desiccated coconut into a food processor and grind, using the pulse button, until finely chopped. Then add 25 g (1 oz) of the flour and grind to a fine mixture, but don't process it for too long or it will start to go oily. Mix with the rest of the plain flour and salt and set to one side. Cream the butter and sugar together briefly, until smooth. Beat in half of the beaten egg, followed by the flour mixture and enough of the remaining beaten egg to bind the mixture together. Knead briefly until smooth, wrap in cling film and chill for 20 minutes.

Carefully roll out the pastry between 2 sheets of greaseproof paper or cling film and use to line a greased 20 cm (8-inch) loose-bottomed flan tin. Prick the base here and there with a fork and chill for 30 minutes. Preheat the oven to 190°C/375°F/Gas Mark 5.

Line the pastry case with greaseproof paper and baking beans and bake blind for 15 minutes. Then remove the paper and beans and bake for a further 5–7 minutes, until crisp and golden. Remove and leave to cool.

For the filling, mix the egg yolks with the sugar, cornflour, plain flour and 2 tablespoons of the milk in a mixing bowl until smooth. Bring the rest of the milk to the boil in a non-stick pan. Gradually beat the hot milk into the creamed egg yolks, return the mixture to the pan and cook over a medium heat, stirring, until thick and smooth. Simmer gently for 2 minutes, to cook out the flour, and then stir in the vanilla extract and butter, transfer to a bowl and press a sheet of cling film on to the surface to prevent a skin from forming. Leave to cool and then chill until needed.

Shortly before serving, whip the cream into soft peaks and fold it into the pastry cream. Spread the mixture into the base of the pastry case and cover with a single layer of the raspberries. Sprinkle with a light dusting of icing sugar and serve cut into wedges.

I've got a book in my rather disorganised library of cookery books called *It's all American Food* by David Rosengarten. This has been really quite influential to me because, as I've mentioned in the introduction, I think the same has happened with British food: like us, the Americans have taken on so many dishes from the waves of immigration that have happened all through their history that there's not so much of what one would call American cuisine anymore. Nevertheless, the States does boast some regional cooking: the chowders of New England, the Tex-Mex food from the border, dishes like *Huevos rancheros* on page 262 and something which I found in South Carolina and have raved about ever since – Succotash (see *Broiled haddock fillets with succotash* on page 260).

Keith Floyd once said to me that you can eat very well in the States expensively and very cheaply, but the middle ground isn't quite so good! One of the delights of American food to me is street food and, dare I say it, fast food and no dish would better typify this than *Po' boys*, which is prawns (or shrimp as they call them) deep fried in breadcrumbs and served with lots of mayonnaise and iceberg lettuce in a bun, (see page 254). As this chapter is about the Americas generally, and for me that just means North America and Mexico, because I haven't been anywhere further south, I would earnestly draw to your attention the fish tacos on page 272 which came from Baja, California, and the *Char-grilled beef tortillas* which came from Oaxaca on page 252. The *Grilled scallops with pumpkin seed, serrano chilli and coriander sauce* on page 259 were also inspired by a recent trip to Mexico, since they use these seeds a lot to thicken sauces and dressings. Warming to the subject of American fast food, I recall the Reading Terminal market in Philadelphia a couple of years ago. I was there to promote an American edition of my book *Seafood*, but since no one had heard of me, I didn't have much to do in the three or four days I was there, so I wandered around the city and became very attached to it. As a lover of the film *West Side Story*, the rather run-down concrete jungle look of somewhere like south Philadelphia is particularly exciting. Then there's the famous oyster bar *Pearl's* and Rick's Philly Steak Sandwiches. I kept going back for those. They are not exactly good for you – fried onions, provolone cheese and lots of char-grilled steak in a big bun – but, oh gosh, they were good! Edgar Allan Poe lived there for a while and wrote *The Tell-tale Heart* – you can go down into the creepy cellar which gave him so many scary ideas. Rick's Philly sandwiches, Edgar Allan Poe and Bruce Springsteen's 'Streets of Philadelphia', plus a great art museum – worth returning to I'd say and, like so many cities in the USA, layers to be peeled away with almost gastronomic pleasure.

Cod and lobster chowder

I can't resist slipping a chowder or two into each of my books – I love that subtle combination of salt pork, seafood and cream so much. Try this with clams, mussels and any flaky white fish.

SERVES 4

450–550 g (1–1¼ lb) lobster, freshly cooked
4 water biscuits
50 g (2 oz) butter, softened
100 g (4 oz) salt pork or rindless streaky bacon, in one piece
1 small onion, finely chopped
15 g (½ oz) plain flour
1.2 litres (2 pints) milk
2 potatoes (about 225 g/8 oz), peeled and diced
1 bay leaf
450 g (1-lb) thick cod fillet, skinned
120 ml (4 fl oz) double cream
A pinch of cayenne pepper
Sea salt and freshly ground black pepper
2 tablespoons chopped parsley, to garnish

First remove the meat from the cooked lobster. Put the lobster belly side down on to a board and make sure none of the legs is tucked underneath. Cut it in half, first through the middle of the head between the eyes. Then turn either the knife or the lobster around and finish cutting it in half through the tail.

Open it up and lift out the tail meat from each half. Remove the intestinal tract from the tail meat. Break off the claws and then break them into pieces at the joints. Crack the shells with a knife. Remove the meat from each of the claw sections in as large pieces as possible.

Remove the soft greenish tomalley (liver) and any red roe from the head of the shell with a teaspoon and save. Pull out the stomach sac and discard.

Put 2 of the water biscuits into a plastic bag and crush to very fine crumbs with a rolling pin. Then mix with the tomalley, other soft material from the head and half the butter; or blend everything in a small food processor.

Cut the piece of salt pork or bacon into small dice. Heat the rest of the butter in a medium-sized pan, add the pork or bacon and fry over a medium heat until lightly golden. Add the onion and cook gently until softened. Stir in the flour and cook for 1 minute. Gradually stir in the milk, then the potatoes and bay leaf and simmer for 10 minutes or until the potatoes are just tender. Add the cod and simmer for 4–5 minutes. Then lift the fish out of the milk and break the flesh into large flakes with a wooden spoon.

Stir in the water-biscuit paste, lobster meat and cream and simmer for 1 minute. Season with the cayenne pepper, 1 teaspoon of salt and some black pepper. To serve, coarsely crush the 2 remaining biscuits and sprinkle them over the soup with the chopped parsley.

Char-grilled beef tortillas
(Tasajo con guacamole y salsa cruda)

There is an avenue right in the middle of the Mercado de 20th Novembre in Oaxaca, Mexico that is wreathed in smoke right up to the vaulted corrugated iron roofs. There must be twenty charcoal grills creating an inferno of smoke. Each stall displays sheets of thin, lightly salted beef and they sell little pork sausages and escalopes of pork too, orange-hued and rubbed with dried, powdered chilli. At other stalls you buy the corn tortillas, guacamole, large spring onions, coriander and fresh salsa cruda (tomato salsa). You get the onions grilled along with the beef or pork, and then you sit at long, white, Formica tables with a pile of tortillas to make ever-varying combinations of the chewy but well flavoured beef that tastes of the fire, the guacamole, onion and chilli. You rub shoulders with cheerful, reassuringly well-fed Mexicans and drink Corona or Victoria beer. This recipe is based on that whole experience.

SERVES 8

900 g (2 lb) rump of beef, very thinly sliced by your
    butcher (this should give you about 12 large slices)
Oil, for brushing
15 large salad onions, halved lengthways, or 30
    spring onions, trimmed but left whole
2 limes, cut into wedges
Sea salt
FOR THE GUACAMOLE:
1 large, ripe avocado
1 jalapeño chilli or other medium-hot green chilli,
    seeded and chopped
Juice of ½ lime
2 fat spring onions, chopped
1 small handful of coriander leaves, roughly chopped
2 tablespoons sunflower oil
FOR THE SALSA CRUDA:
350 g (12 oz) vine-ripened tomatoes, skinned (page 283)
3 serrano chillies or other medium-hot green
    chillies, roughly chopped
1 small onion, roughly chopped
A handful of coriander leaves
Corn tortillas (page 279)

For the guacamole, peel and stone the avocado and put the flesh into a mortar or a food processor. Add the chilli, lime juice, spring onions, coriander, oil and ½ teaspoon of salt and mash or blend briefly, so it's still a little lumpy. Transfer to a serving bowl.

For the salsa cruda, put the tomatoes, chillies, onion and coriander into the cleaned bowl of the food processor and, using the pulse button, blend into a coarsely chopped sauce. Transfer to a serving bowl.

Make the corn tortillas (see page 279).

Lightly sprinkle each slice of beef (on both sides) with ¼ teaspoon of salt and set aside for 10 minutes. Meanwhile, heat a ridged cast-iron griddle over a high heat until smoking hot. Brush very lightly with oil and cook the onions for 2–3 minutes, turning them once or twice, until tender. Transfer to a large, warmed serving plate and keep warm.

Brush the griddle lightly with oil once more, add one of the beef slices and cook for 20 seconds on each side. Transfer to the serving plate with the onions and cook another 3 slices.

Garnish the plate of beef and onions with the lime wedges and take it to the table with the warm tortillas, guacamole and salsa cruda, so people can start eating while you cook the rest of the beef. The steak should be cut into pieces and used to fill the tortillas, flavouring it with the two sauces according to preference.

Po' boys

Fast food like these po' boys are in no way subtle, but are made out of good wholesome ingredients, and go straight to the heart of what you sometimes want, just like a great rock 'n' roll song. When the Americans get fast food right, like this dish, nobody does it better! As the name might suggest, po' boys originated as food for the poor, or at least that's what most of the explanations of the name suggest. The most plausible to me is that it originated in New Orleans in the nineteenth century as an oyster sandwich which was given as charity to the poor. Though oysters were the original filling, po' boys are made with both shrimp and clams as well.

MAKES 6

2 baguettes
Sunflower oil for deep-frying
350 g (12 oz) peeled, raw prawns
175 g (6 oz) *mayonnaise* (page 280), plus extra to serve
2½ tablespoons milk
25 g (1 oz) plain flour
175 g (6 oz) fresh white breadcrumbs
1 small crisp green lettuce
Salt and cayenne pepper

Cut each baguette into three and then cut each piece in half lengthways. Pull out a little of the soft white crumb to make a very shallow dip in each half. Lay them on a baking tray, cut side up, and toast very lightly under the grill. Remove and set aside.

Heat some oil for deep-frying to 190°C/375°F. Season the prawns well with salt and cayenne pepper. Whisk the mayonnaise and milk together in a bowl, put the flour into a second bowl and spread the breadcrumbs over a large plate.

Dip the prawns into the flour, mayonnaise and then the breadcrumbs so that they take on an even coating. Treat them gently once they are done because the coating is quite delicate. Pick them up by their tails, drop them into the hot oil about 6 at a time, and fry for 1 minute, until crisp and golden. Transfer to a tray lined with kitchen paper and keep warm in a low oven while you cook the rest.

To serve, spread the bottom half of each piece of bread with a little more mayonnaise, then put some lettuce leaves on top. Pile on a few of the fried prawns, cover with the tops and eat straight away.

Chicken with coloradito

Coloradito means 'with a little red colour' and is one of the seven famous mole sauces of Oaxaca, in Mexico. It uses dried guajillo chillies, which have a sweet, refined heat and appear in a lot of classic Mexican salsas.

SERVES 4

900 ml (1½ pints) *chicken stock* (page 278)
8 chicken joints (thighs, drumsticks and/or part-boned breasts)
12 dried guajillo (little gourd) chillies (page 283)
25 g (1 oz) sesame seeds
8 allspice berries
5 cm (2-inch) cinnamon stick, broken into small pieces
1½ tablespoons dried oregano
85 ml (3 fl oz) sunflower oil
6 garlic cloves, sliced
1 onion, sliced
1 medium-thick slice of white bread, broken into pieces
1 slightly under-ripe banana, sliced
3 canned plum tomatoes
25 g (1 oz) plain or Mexican chocolate
Sea salt

Bring the chicken stock to the boil in a pan. Add the chicken joints and 1 teaspoon of salt, bring back to the boil and simmer for 10 minutes. Leave the chicken in the stock while you prepare the sauce.

Slit open the dried chillies and remove the stalks and seeds. Heat a heavy-based frying pan and add the chillies. Using a wooden spatula, press them down into the hot pan until a small amount of smoke appears. Turn over and repeat on the other side. Transfer to a bowl and cover with 600 ml (1 pint) of hot water. Leave to soak for 15–20 minutes.

Add the sesame seeds, allspice berries and cinnamon stick to the hot frying pan and turn them for a minute or two until the sesame seeds are lightly toasted. Tip the mixture into a spice grinder, add the dried oregano and grind to a coarse powder.

Heat the sunflower oil in a large frying pan, add the garlic and onion and fry until beginning to brown. Add the bread and banana and continue to fry until the bread has taken on some colour. Transfer to a liquidiser and add the tomatoes, the drained soaked chillies, the dry ground ingredients from the spice grinder and another teaspoon of salt. Blend until smooth. Press through a sieve into a medium-sized pan to remove any large pieces of chilli skin, then bring to a simmer and cook for 5 minutes, stirring frequently.

Lift the chicken pieces out of the stock, remove the skin and add them to the sauce. Simmer for 10–15 minutes, or until the chicken is cooked through. Stir in the chocolate until it has melted and then serve with *steamed rice* (see page 281) or *corn tortillas* (see page 279).

Stuffed Romano peppers fried in polenta with guajillo chilli sauce

Chiles rellenos (poblano or Anaheim chillies, stuffed with cheese, coated in a crisp cornmeal crust and served with a dried red chilli and tomato sauce) is one of my favourite Mexican dishes and the sort of thing that must set the taste buds of every vegetarian alight. It's really hard to get the right chillies, though, so I have rearranged the recipe using Romano peppers, those long, chilli-shaped red peppers that most supermarkets now sell. You might like to add a pinch of chilli powder to the cheese stuffing, to re-create the heat. I've changed the cheese, too, as it's difficult to get the special Mexican cheese for stuffing.

SERVES 4

4 good-sized Romano peppers
225 g (8 oz) Cornish Yarg cheese or mild cheddar
2 eggs, beaten
2 tablespoons milk
50 g (2 oz) polenta or cornmeal
Sunflower or groundnut oil, for frying
Sea salt and freshly ground black pepper
Corn tortillas (page 279), to serve

FOR THE GUAJILLO CHILLI SAUCE:

3 dried guajillo (little gourd) chillies (page 283)
1½ tablespoons sunflower oil
75 g (3 oz) onion, roughly chopped
2 canned plum tomatoes
1 fat garlic clove, crushed
½ teaspoon ground cumin
1½ teaspoons caster sugar
2–3 teaspoons lemon juice

Slit open the dried guajillo chillies and remove the stalks and seeds. Put them into a small bowl, cover with hot water and leave to soak for 20 minutes. Meanwhile, preheat the oven to 220°C/425°F/Gas Mark 7. Roast the Romano peppers for 10–12 minutes. Put the peppers into a plastic bag and leave to cool.

For the chilli sauce, heat 1 tablespoon of the oil in a small pan, add the onion and fry over a medium-high heat, stirring now and then, until richly browned.

Drain the chillies, reserving the soaking liquor. Put the soaked chillies, tomatoes, fried onion, garlic, cumin, sugar and ½ teaspoon salt into a liquidiser, with 120 ml (4 fl oz) of the chilli soaking liquor and blend to a smooth paste.

Heat the remaining ½ tablespoon of oil in a medium-sized saucepan.

Add the paste and simmer for 10 minutes, stirring now and then, until it has reduced to a good sauce consistency. Stir in the lemon juice and some seasoning to taste. Keep hot.

Carefully peel the skin off the peppers, then make a slit down one side, leaving the stalks in place, and scoop out the seeds, taking care not to tear the flesh. Season them well inside and out. Remove the rind from the cheese and cut it into long pieces, about 2½ cm (1 inch) wide and 1 cm (½ inch) thick. Fill the whole length of each pepper's cavity with pieces of cheese, putting a tapering piece in towards the tip. Push them back into shape and tie in 2 places with string, to keep everything in place.

Beat the eggs and milk together in one large, shallow dish and put some seasoned polenta into a second dish. Dip the stuffed peppers in the polenta, then in the egg and milk, then the polenta once more.

Heat 1 cm (½ inch) of oil in a large, deep frying pan to 180°C/350°F or until a cube of day-old bread rises to the surface and browns in a bit more than a minute. Add the peppers and fry them gently for 5 minutes on each side, until crisp and richly golden. Carefully lift out with a fish slice and drain on kitchen paper. Serve with the chilli sauce and warm corn tortillas (see page 279).

Grilled scallops with a pumpkin seed, serrano chilli and coriander sauce

I've had a lot of success serving scallops grilled in their shells; I think the aroma of hot shells adds a lot of excitement. I've never had a dish like this in Mexico, but I'd love to. Using pumpkin seeds to thicken a sauce or a dressing is very popular there, as is the combination of green chilli and coriander.

SERVES 4

50 g (2 oz) pumpkin seeds
1 serrano (hot green) chilli, chopped
A large handful (about 25 g/1 oz) of coriander leaves
2 garlic cloves, peeled
150 ml (5 fl oz) sunflower oil
Juice of 1 lime
2 spring onions, chopped
7 g (¼ oz) parmesan cheese, grated
16–20 cleaned king scallops or 32 cleaned queen
    scallops in the shell
25 g (1 oz) butter, melted
Sea salt and freshly ground black pepper

For the sauce, put the pumpkin seeds, chilli, coriander, garlic, oil, lime juice, spring onions, parmesan cheese and ½ teaspoon of salt into a food processor and blend to a smooth paste.

Preheat the grill to high. Put the scallops on to a baking tray, brush each one generously with melted butter and season with salt and pepper. Grill king scallops for 2 minutes or queen scallops for 1 minute.

Lightly spread about 1 teaspoon of the pumpkin-seed sauce over the scallops (use about ½ teaspoon for the 'queenies') and grill for another 1–2 minutes (1 minute for the queenies) until they are just cooked through and the sauce has just started to colour. Place on 4 warmed plates and serve straight away.

Broiled haddock fillets with succotash

The American word 'broiled' simply means grilled. I've kept it in to add the right atmosphere to the dish. These things matter to me.

Until I went to the southern states of America I had always thought that succotash was some kind of squash-type vegetable, but it's actually a down-home mix of beans, sweetcorn, bacon and cream, finished with chives. Once I'd made it, I knew it was a dead certainty to go with a nice thick fillet of white fish such as haddock. We also filmed this recipe using striped sea bass in America, so a fillet from a good-sized bass would be an ideal alternative; you could also use cod, hake or kingfish. American recipes for succotash normally call for lima beans. These are the same as butterbeans, one name referring to the capital of Peru, where they were first grown, and the other to their buttery, creamy texture.

SERVES 4

175 g (6 oz) dried butterbeans
100 g (4 oz) rindless smoked streaky bacon, in one piece
1 small onion, chopped
1 tablespoon sunflower oil, if needed
300 ml (10 fl oz) *chicken stock* (page 278)
3 whole sweetcorn cobs
50 ml (2 fl oz) double cream
4 x 175–225 g (6–8 oz) pieces of unskinned thick haddock fillet
15 g (½ oz) butter, melted
2 tablespoons chopped chives, plus a few extra to garnish
Sea salt and freshly ground black pepper

Put the dried beans into a pan and cover with plenty of water. Bring to the boil, cover, remove from the heat and leave to soak for 2 hours.

Cut the bacon into 5 mm (¼-inch) dice, put it into a pan and cook over a low heat until the fat begins to melt. Increase the heat a little and allow it to fry in its own fat until crisp and golden. Add the onion (and the sunflower oil, if it looks a little dry) and cook for about 5 minutes, until soft.

Drain the beans and add them to the pan, with the stock. Simmer gently until they are just tender and the stock is well reduced.

Stand the sweetcorn cobs up on a chopping board and slice away all the kernels. Add the sweetcorn to the beans, with the cream, and simmer for 5 minutes.

Meanwhile, preheat the grill to high. Brush the pieces of haddock on both sides with the melted butter and season with salt and pepper. Place, skin side up, on a lightly oiled baking sheet or the rack of the grill pan and grill for 7–8 minutes.

Stir the chives into the beans and season with salt and pepper. Spoon the mixture into 4 warmed soup plates and place the haddock on top. Scatter over a few more chives and serve at once.

Huevos rancheros (ranch-style eggs)

This is the best-known breakfast egg dish in Mexico. As rather a cautious twenty-one-year-old, I found some of the food and drink there distinctly alarming: things like fried grasshoppers, ants' eggs, chicken with chocolate sauce and tequila with a worm in it. I loved the street food though – tacos, burritos and tamales – and I became a real enthusiast for tequila, salt and the bite of a lime: so much so that I seem to have spent too many a morning in Mexico seeking out this revitalising combination of corn tortilla, tomato, chilli and egg, normally served with refried beans and strong black coffee. I still like to cook this on a long Sunday morning after a particularly lively Saturday night.

SERVES 4

8 large, fresh, free-range eggs
Sunflower oil for shallow frying
Salt and freshly ground black pepper

FOR THE SALSA RANCHERO:
2 tablespoons sunflower oil
1 medium onion, finely chopped
4 garlic cloves, crushed
2 medium-hot fresh green chillies, such as jalapeño
½ teaspoon crushed dried chillies
½ teaspoon freshly ground cumin
1 x 400 g (14 oz) can large, plum tomatoes in tomato juice
1 teaspoon freshly squeezed lime juice, to finish
1 tablespoon chopped coriander

FOR THE FLOUR TORTILLAS:
225 g (8 oz) strong white bread flour
50 g (2 oz) lard, or solid white vegetable shortening,
    left to soften slightly at room temperature
A scant ½ teaspoon salt
120 ml (4 fl oz) warm water

For the flour tortillas, sift the flour into a bowl, add the slightly softened fat and rub the two together with your fingertips until the mixture looks like fine breadcrumbs. Dissolve the salt in the warm water and add it gradually to the flour mixture until you have a soft, cohesive dough. Take care not to let it get too wet. Turn the mixture out onto a lightly floured surface and knead for about 4 minutes until you have a smooth, elastic dough. Divide the dough into 12 evenly sized pieces and roll each one into a smooth ball. Place them on a lightly greased baking tray, cover loosely with a sheet of cling film and leave to rest at room temperature for 1 hour.

Meanwhile, for the salsa ranchero, heat the oil in a medium-sized pan, add the onion and garlic and fry for 7-8 minutes until soft but not browned. Add the green chillies, crushed dried chillies and ground cumin and fry for a couple more minutes. Add the tomatoes and break them up with a wooden spoon. Leave the sauce to simmer gently for 5 minutes until slightly reduced and thickened – you want a pourable sauce. Season to taste with salt and pepper and set aside.

Heat a dry heavy-based frying pan or flat griddle over a medium heat. Take one of the balls of dough and flatten it on a lightly floured surface. Roll it out into a 12–13 cm (5-inch) disc, lay in the frying pan and cook for about 1 minute until the dough starts to puff up and the underside becomes speckled with brown patches. Flip the tortilla over and cook for another minute. Remove immediately from the pan or griddle while it is still flexible. If you leave it too long it will start to dry out. Wrap in a clean tea towel and keep warm. Repeat for the remaining tortillas.

When you are ready to serve, gently reheat the tomato sauce and then stir in the lime juice and coriander. Heat some oil in a frying pan over a medium heat, and fry the eggs in batches to your liking, spooning a little of the hot oil over the yolks as they cook.

Slightly overlap 2 tortillas in the centre of each plate and put 2 of the fried eggs on top. Spoon a generous quantity of the salsa ranchero over and around the eggs and serve with the rest of the tortillas and some hot, strong, good quality black coffee.

Hangtown fry

This was apparently the last breakfast for a condemned prisoner in a Western frontier town, who dreamed it up as a dish containing all of his favourite things. The Americans are really good at hearty breakfasts, though, personally, I think this recipe is unlikely to have come from someone who was just about to die. It has all the enthusiasm of somebody enjoying themselves too much for that. Although primarily designed for breakfast, it is great for lunch too, with some sautéed potatoes and a simple green salad.

SERVES 4

8 large oysters
6 eggs
6 cream crackers or Saltines
4 tablespoons sunflower oil
4 tablespoons *clarified butter* (page 279)
3 tablespoons plain flour
15 g (½ oz) chilled butter
3 tablespoons double cream
2 tablespoons chopped parsley
15 g (½ oz) parmesan cheese, finely grated
A little lemon juice
8 thin rashers of rindless streaky bacon
Sea salt and freshly ground black pepper

Remove the oysters from their shells. Beat the eggs and pour them into a shallow dish. Put the cream crackers in a plastic bag and crush them into fine crumbs with a rolling pin. Tip them into a dish.

Heat the oil and the clarified butter in a 20 cm (8-inch) non-stick frying pan. Dust the oysters in the flour, dip them into the beaten egg and finally into the cracker crumbs. Fry for 1 minute on each side until golden brown and then remove from the pan, season with a little salt and keep warm. Drain away the cooking fat from the pan and wipe it out with some kitchen paper. Rub the base well with the chilled butter.

Add the cream, parsley, parmesan cheese and some seasoning to the leftover beaten eggs. Return the oysters to the pan and squeeze over a little lemon juice. Pour the egg mixture around the oysters and cook over a low heat until just set – about 10–12 minutes. Meanwhile, grill the bacon until crisp and golden.

As soon as the 'fry' is set, put the pan under the grill until the egg is browned and puffed up. Lay the bacon rashers on top, take the pan to the table and serve.

A feast of mahi-mahi, tortillas and salsa de tomate verde

Probably my most favourite part of a meal in Mexico is the first course, when a pile of corn tortillas comes warm in a wicker basket, wrapped in a napkin. There is some fish or meat and piles of shredded lettuce, sliced avocados, coriander, chopped tomatoes and onions, and a bowl of tomatillo sauce called salsa de tomate verde. Eating tortillas is a bit like eating Chinese crispy aromatic duck pancakes – you help yourself to whatever filling you want, then roll it up in a warm tortilla and wash it down with plenty of cold beer. The fish I've chosen for this recipe is entirely apt. Mahi-mahi, or dolphin fish as it is also known, is found mostly in the Pacific and Indian Oceans. It is firm of texture and sweet to taste, ideal for grilling, slicing and serving with this hot but very fresh jalapeño-flavoured salsa. Mahi-mahi is difficult to get hold of in the UK but, as well as the monkfish suggested as an alternative in the ingredients list, sea bass would be an excellent substitute, as would John Dory fillets.

SERVES 4

1 Romaine lettuce heart, thinly sliced across
2 avocados, halved, skinned and sliced
1 small bunch of coriander sprigs
3 tomatoes, skinned and cut into small dice (page 283)
1 onion, halved and very thinly sliced
8 fresh *corn tortillas* (see page 279)
4 x 175 g (6 oz) mahi-mahi fillets or monkfish fillets, skinned
A little sunflower oil
Sea salt and freshly ground black pepper

FOR THE SALSA DE TOMATE VERDE:

2 tomatillos or green tomatoes
A little freshly squeezed lime juice, if using green tomatoes
2 jalapeño or other medium-hot green chillies
1 garlic clove, roughly chopped
1 small onion, roughly chopped
1 tablespoon chopped coriander

For the salsa, peel the papery husks off the tomatillos if using. Drop them or the green tomatoes and the jalapeño chillies into a pan of boiling water and simmer for 10 minutes. Then strain and cool slightly. Tip them into a food processor and add the rest of the salsa ingredients and a little lime juice, if you have used green tomatoes instead of tomatillos. Pulse the mixture for a few seconds until you have a fairly smooth sauce with a little bit of texture. Season with salt and spoon into a serving bowl.

Put the shredded lettuce, avocado, coriander, tomato and onion into 5 other serving bowls.

To reheat the tortillas, stack them on a plate, cover with a tea towel and cook in the microwave on high for about 30 seconds. Alternatively, heat a dry frying pan over a medium heat. Add a tortilla and leave it in the pan for a few seconds, then turn it over, adding a second tortilla on top of it. After a few seconds turn them over together and add a third one to the pan. Continue like this until all your tortillas are in the pan, then remove them and wrap them in a napkin. Keep warm while you cook the fish.

Preheat the grill to high. Cut the mahi-mahi or monkfish fillets into short, chunky strips. Toss them with a little oil and plenty of seasoning and spread them out on a grilling tray. Cook them for about 2 minutes on one side only, until just cooked through.

Lift the fish on to a serving plate and take it to the table with all the other bits and pieces. Let everyone fill their own tortillas with whatever they fancy.

American corn 'oysters' (fritters) with bacon and roasted vine tomatoes

Corn oysters are simply deep-fried fritters shaped like oysters. The recipes date back to the 1890s. Many call for the corn to be finely chopped but I prefer it left whole.

SERVES 4

4 strings of cherry tomatoes on the vine (each with about 8 tomatoes)
3 tablespoons olive oil
Sunflower oil, for shallow- and deep-frying
12 rindless rashers of dry-cured smoked streaky bacon
Sea salt and freshly ground black pepper
Maple syrup, to serve
FOR THE CORN 'OYSTERS':
25 g (1 oz) polenta
100 g (4 oz) plain flour
1½ teaspoons baking powder
A large pinch of cayenne pepper
1 egg
120 ml (4 fl oz) milk
200 g (7 oz) can of sweetcorn kernels, drained (150 g/5 oz kernels)
¼ red pepper, seeded and finely diced
4 spring onions, thinly sliced
15 g (½ oz) butter, melted

Preheat the oven to 180°C/375°F/Gas Mark 4. Put the cherry tomatoes into a small roasting tin, drizzle with 3 tablespoons of the olive oil and season. Roast for 10–12 minutes, until just tender.

Sift the polenta, flour, baking powder, cayenne pepper, ½ teaspoon of salt and ¼ teaspoon black pepper into a mixing bowl. Beat the egg with the milk and stir into the dry ingredients, together with the sweetcorn, red pepper, spring onions and melted butter.

Heat some oil for deep-frying to 180°C/350°F or until a small piece of white bread dropped into the oil browns and rises to the surface in a little more than a minute. Drop 4 heaped soup spoonfuls of batter into the oil and cook for 3 minutes, turning them now and then in the hot oil, until crisp and richly golden and cooked through. Lift out with a slotted spoon on to a tray lined with lots of kitchen paper and keep warm while you return the oil to the right temperature and make another 4 fritters.

While you are cooking the fritters, heat a heavy-based frying pan or griddle pan. Add a teaspoon or two of oil and the bacon and cook for 1 minute on each side until crisp and golden.

Put the corn 'oysters' on to 4 warmed plates and place the roasted vine tomatoes and crisp bacon alongside. Drizzle with a little maple syrup and serve.

Barbecued shrimp with coleslaw

You can cook this quite successfully under the grill or on a barbecue, but, if using a barbecue, heat the remaining marinade in a small pan to the side of the rack to cook out any raw flavours left from the marinated prawns. The coleslaw goes spectacularly well with them, but it must be freshly made and crunchy. I can't stand that soft stuff you buy in tubs – make your own!

SERVES 4

150 ml (5 fl oz) olive oil
120 ml (4 fl oz) chilli sauce
3 tablespoons Worcestershire sauce
1 teaspoon salt
4 garlic cloves, crushed
1 tablespoon sweet chilli sauce or clear honey
½ teaspoon Tabasco sauce
900 g (2 lb) unpeeled, raw prawns
FOR THE COLESLAW:
325 g (12 oz) white cabbage, cored and thinly sliced
2 celery sticks, thinly sliced
1 green pepper, thinly sliced
6 spring onions, thinly sliced
3 tablespoons chopped dill
2 teaspoons Dijon mustard
1 heaped teaspoon creamed horseradish
½ teaspoon Tabasco sauce
1 tablespoon red wine vinegar
2 tablespoons extra virgin olive oil
2 tablespoons olive-oil mayonnaise
A pinch of cayenne pepper
Sea salt and freshly ground black pepper

Mix the olive oil, chilli sauce, Worcestershire sauce, salt, garlic, sweet chilli sauce and Tabasco sauce together in a bowl. Stir in the prawns, cover and marinate at room temperature for 2 hours, or overnight in the fridge.

Preheat your barbecue or grill. Meanwhile, make the coleslaw: mix the cabbage, celery, green pepper, spring onions and dill together in a bowl. Mix the rest of the ingredients together to make a dressing. Stir it into the vegetables at the last minute and spoon it into a large serving bowl.

If you are barbecuing the prawns, you might prefer to thread them on to large metal skewers first, which will make things easier when you come to turn them. Cook them for 1½–2 minutes on each side, basting them with some of the marinade. Pile them into a warmed serving bowl. Bring the remaining marinade to the boil in a small pan and pour it over the prawns. Serve them with the coleslaw and plenty of crusty French bread.

Fish tacos from Baja California

Perhaps the most thoroughly irresistible dish in this chapter. I've never been to Baja California in Mexico but I got the idea for this recipe from the television presenter and food journalist, Hugh Fearnley-Whittingstall, who lent me a book on the Baja because I'm very keen on surfing and the waves there are fantastic. He told me about this great dish, consisting of a tortilla filled with deep-fried fish, coriander, chilli, tomato, a little soured cream and some salad. I knocked it all up according to how it sounded to me and it's brilliant. One day I'll make the trip to Ensenada with my big old Malibu and ride the odd small wave that may just happen down there.

SERVES 4

2 sea bream, sea bass or red mullet, weighing about 325 g (12 oz) each, filleted
Sunflower oil, for deep-frying
8 soft flour tortillas
225 g (8 oz) iceberg lettuce, finely shredded
300 ml (10 fl oz) soured cream
Sea salt and freshly ground black pepper

FOR THE BATTER:
225 g (8 oz) plain flour
2 eggs
200 ml (7 fl oz) water

FOR THE SALSA:
1 red onion, finely chopped
5 tomatoes, skinned, seeded and finely chopped (page 283)
3–4 medium-hot red chillies, seeded and finely chopped
1 teaspoon sugar
Juice of 1 lime
4 tablespoons chopped coriander

First make the salsa by mixing together all the ingredients with a pinch of salt. Set aside.

Cut the fish fillets across into strips 1 cm (½-inch) wide and season with plenty of salt and pepper.

For the batter, put the flour, eggs, water and a pinch of salt into a liquidiser and blend until smooth.

Pour the sunflower oil into a pan until it is about one-third full and heat to 190°C/375°F or until a small piece of white bread dropped into the oil browns and rises to the surface in 1 minute. Warm the tortillas in a low oven or a microwave.

Dip the strips of fish into the batter and then drop them into the hot oil and fry for 4 minutes, until crisp and golden. Lift out with a slotted spoon and drain briefly on kitchen paper.

To serve, put some lettuce down the centre of each tortilla, top with the fried fish, then spoon over some salsa and soured cream. Fold in the sides, roll up as tightly as you can and serve straight away, with some cold Mexican beer.

Ceviche of monkfish with avocado

Lara Skinner, who is a effervescent member of our staff at St Petroc's, *comes from Peru and says we can never get ceviche totally right because we don't have the same limes. I think this is a pretty good attempt actually.*

SERVES 6

500 g (1 lb 2 oz) monkfish fillets
Juice of 3 limes
1 medium-hot red chilli, halved and seeded
1 small red onion
6 vine-ripened tomatoes, skinned (page 283)
3 tablespoons extra virgin olive oil
2 tablespoons chopped coriander
1 large ripe but firm avocado
Sea salt

Cut the monkfish fillets across into thin slices and put them into a shallow dish. Pour over the lime juice, making sure that all the slices of fish are completely covered in juice. Cover with cling film and refrigerate for 40 minutes, during which time the fish will turn white and opaque.

Meanwhile, slice across each chilli half so that you get very thin, slightly curled slices. Cut the onion into quarters and then each wedge lengthways into thin, arc-shaped slices. Cut each tomato into quarters and remove the seeds. Cut each piece of flesh lengthways into thin, arc-shaped slices.

Just before you are ready to serve, lift the monkfish out of the lime juice with a slotted spoon and put into a large bowl with the chilli, onion, tomato, olive oil, most of the coriander and a little salt to taste. Toss together lightly.

Halve the avocado, remove the stone and peel. Slice each half lengthways into thin slices.

Arrange 3–4 slices of the avocado on one side of each plate. Pile the ceviche on to the other side and sprinkle with the rest of the coriander. Serve at once.

Strawberry and vanilla shortcake

This is the very essence of afternoon teas. I love my Cornish cream teas, but in strawberry season this classic American cake is hard to beat.

SERVES 8

300 g (11 oz) self-raising flour
2½ teaspoons baking powder
A pinch of salt
100 g (4 oz) chilled unsalted butter, diced
60 g (2½ oz) caster sugar
1½ eggs, beaten (you need 6 tablespoons)
About 2 tablespoons milk

FOR THE FILLING:

400 g (14 oz) strawberries
2–3 tablespoons icing sugar, depending on the
    sweetness of your berries, plus extra to decorate
The seeds from ½ vanilla pod
300 ml (10 fl oz) double cream
25 g (1 oz) caster sugar

Preheat the oven to 200°C/400°F/Gas Mark 6. Sift the flour, baking powder and salt into a food processor. Add the pieces of chilled butter and process briefly, until the mixture looks like fine breadcrumbs. Tip the mixture into a bowl and stir in the caster sugar.

Beat the egg with 1½ tablespoons of the milk. Add to the bowl and stir with a fork, until the mixture starts to stick together into small clumps: if the mixture is a little dry, add the rest of the milk. Gather together into a ball of soft dough, turn out on to a floured surface and knead briefly, very gently, until smooth.

Lightly roll out the dough on a lightly floured surface into a disc 1 cm (½ inch) thick and about 23 cm (9 inches) across. Lift on to a lightly buttered baking sheet (using the base of a loose-bottomed flan tin helps) and bake for 15 minutes, until the shortbread is golden and a skewer inserted into the centre comes out clean. Remove and leave to cool on a wire rack.

Carefully slice the shortcake in half horizontally. Lift the top piece on to a board and cut into 8 even-sized wedges.

For the filling, halve or quarter the strawberries, depending on their size. Add the icing sugar and vanilla seeds, mix together gently, cover and chill until you are ready to serve. Whip the cream and caster sugar together into just-stiff peaks.

Place the base of the shortcake on a serving plate. Spread with the whipped cream and then spoon over the vanilla strawberries. Cover with the shortcake wedges, dust with more icing sugar through a tea strainer or fine sieve and serve, cut into wedges.

Buttermilk pancakes with blueberry and lemon butter

Breakfasts in America are a particular pleasure especially in the trendier places where you'll find dishes like this. I'm thinking Martha's Vineyard, a swim, pancakes, a cappucino and Tom Petty on MVY Radio.

SERVES 4

FOR THE PANCAKES:
50 g (2 oz) *clarified butter* (page 279)
225 g (8 oz) self-raising flour
2 teaspoons baking powder
50 g (2 oz) caster sugar
A good pinch of salt
175 ml (6 fl oz) buttermilk
2 eggs
175 ml (6 fl oz) full-cream milk
1 teaspoon vanilla extract

FOR THE BLUEBERRY AND LEMON BUTTER:
150 g (5 oz) blueberries
50 g (2 oz) caster sugar
Finely grated zest and juice of ½ lemon
100 g (4 oz) unsalted butter, at room temperature

For the blueberry and lemon butter, put the blueberries, sugar and lemon juice into a small pan and leave over a low heat until the sugar has dissolved. Increase the heat, bring to a gentle simmer and cook for 1 minute, until the berries just burst. Add the butter and lemon zest to the pan, take it off the heat and stir gently until the butter has melted and the ingredients have amalgamated, taking care not to crush the berries. Pour the mixture into a small bowl or 4 individual small pots or ramekins and chill for a few hours. The mixture will thicken up but not go completely hard. You can make this the day before, if you wish.

Sift the flour, baking powder, sugar and salt into a bowl. Make a well in the centre, add the buttermilk, eggs and milk and whisk together to make a smooth, thickish batter. Stir in the vanilla extract.

Heat a large, non-stick frying pan over a medium heat. Brush the base with a little of the clarified butter, add 3 large spoonfuls of the batter, spaced well apart, and cook for 2 minutes until bubbles start to appear on the surface of the pancakes and they are golden-brown underneath. Turn over and cook for another minute. Lift on to a plate and keep warm while you cook the remainder.

To serve, pile 3 of the pancakes on to each of 4 warmed plates, top with a good spoonful of blueberry butter and serve hot, straight away.

Basic recipes

Aïoli

MAKES ABOUT 175 ML (6 FL OZ)
4 garlic cloves, peeled
½ teaspoon salt
1 medium egg yolk
2 teaspoons lemon juice
175 ml (6 fl oz) extra virgin olive oil

Put the garlic cloves on to a chopping board and crush them under the blade of a large knife. Sprinkle them with the salt and then work them with the knife blade into a smooth paste. Scrape the garlic paste into a bowl and add the egg yolk and the lemon juice. Using an electric hand mixer, whisk everything together and then very gradually whisk in the olive oil to make a thick mayonnaise-like mixture.

Allioli

This is a punchy garlic sauce from Spain. I first had it on board a fishing boat, stirred into a fish stew, but they also use it as a dip with tapas or as a sauce for grilled fish and rice dishes.

MAKES ABOUT 175 ML (6 FL OZ)
4 garlic cloves, peeled
½ teaspoon salt
1 medium egg yolk
175 ml (6 fl oz) extra virgin olive oil

Put the garlic cloves onto a chopping board and crush them under the blade of a large knife. Sprinkle them with the salt and then work them with the knife blade into a smooth paste. Scrape the garlic paste into a bowl and add the egg yolk. Using an electric mixer, whisk everything together, and then very gradually whisk in the olive oil to make a thick mayonnaise-like mixture.

Beef stock

MAKES ABOUT 2½ LITRES (4½ PINTS)
2 celery sticks, sliced
2 carrots, chopped
2 onions, chopped
900 g (2 lb) shin of beef
5 litres (9 pints) water
2 sprigs of thyme
2 bay leaves
1 tablespoon salt
2 tablespoons sunflower oil (optional, for a richer stock)

For a pale-brown stock, put all the ingredients except for the bay leaves, thyme and salt into a large saucepan and bring to the boil, skimming off any scum as it rises to the surface. Reduce the heat and leave to simmer for 2½ hours, adding the herbs and salt 15 minutes before the end.

For a deeper, richer-coloured stock, heat the sunflower oil in the pan, add the vegetables and beef and fry for 10–15 minutes until nicely browned before adding the water, salt and herbs.

If not using immediately, leave to cool, then chill and refrigerate or freeze for later use.

Chicken stock

Use the bones from a roasted chicken for a slightly deeper-flavoured stock.

MAKES ABOUT 1¾ LITRES (3 PINTS)
Bones from a 1½ kg (3½ lb) uncooked chicken or 450 g (1 lb) chicken wings or drumsticks
1 large carrot, chopped
2 celery sticks, sliced
2 leeks, cleaned and sliced
2 fresh or dried bay leaves
2 sprigs of thyme
2¼ litres (4 pints) water

Put all the ingredients into a large pan and bring to the boil, skimming off any scum as it rises to the surface. Leave to simmer very gently for 2 hours – it is important not to let it boil, as this will force the fat from even the leanest chicken and make the stock cloudy. Strain the stock through a sieve and leave to simmer a little longer to concentrate the flavour if necessary. If not using immediately, leave to cool, then chill and refrigerate or freeze for later use.

Clarified butter

Place the butter in a small pan and leave it over a very low heat until it has melted. Then skim off any scum from the surface and pour off the clear (clarified) butter into a bowl, leaving behind the milky white solids that will have settled on the bottom of the pan.

Corn tortillas

MAKES 36
675 g (1½ lb) masa harina (maize flour)
975 ml (1½ pints) warm water
¼ teaspoon salt

Put the masa harina, salt and water into a bowl and mix together to make a slightly moist dough. Shape the dough into about 36 balls. You need to line the tortilla press with a couple of 15 cm (6-inch) squares of cling film or baking parchment. You'll soon get the hang of pressing out the tortillas and peeling the liner away. Alternatively, roll them out by hand into 15 cm (6-inch) discs between 2 squares of cling film.

Place a dry, heavy-based frying pan over a high heat until very hot. Cook the tortillas in it, one at a time, for about a minute on each side, until lightly coloured with little brown spots. Wrap the tortillas in a clean tea towel and keep warm.

Dashi

MAKES 1 LITRE
1 litre (1¼ pints) water
1 x 10 cm (4-inch) piece dried kombu seaweed
15 g (½ ox) dried bonito flakes

Put the water and kombu into a small saucepan and heat to just below boiling point. Remove from the heat and leave for 5 minutes, then lift out and discard the kombu. Bring the liquid back to a simmer, add the bonito flakes and bring up to the boil. Remove the pan from the heat and leave the flakes to settle for 1 minute. Then pour though a very fine or muslin-lined sieve into a bowl. The dashi is now ready to use.

Duck confit

MAKES 4 PIECES
50 g (2 oz) salt
1 tablespoon thyme leaves
The leaves from 1 large sprig of rosemary
2 bay leaves, thinly shredded
2 garlic cloves, roughly chopped
4 large duck legs
900 g (2 lb) duck or goose fat

Put the salt, thyme, rosemary, bay leaves and garlic into a spice grinder and grind together until the mixture looks like wet sand. Sprinkle half the cure over the base of a shallow dish, put the duck legs on top and then cover with the rest of the cure. Cover and leave in the fridge for 6 hours, turning over halfway through. Don't leave any longer or the duck will become too salty.

Preheat the oven to 140°C/275°F/Gas Mark 1. Rinse the salt cure off the duck and pat them dry with kitchen paper. Bring the duck or goose fat to a gentle simmer in a pan, add the duck legs, making sure that they are completely submerged, cover and cook in the oven for 1½ hours. Then remove, leave to cool and chill until needed. To use, lift the duck out of the fat and wipe off as much as you can with kitchen paper.

Fish stock

You can also make this with 500 g (1¼ lb) of cheap white fish fillet (such as whiting or coley), cut into 2 cm (1-inch) slices, instead of the bones, for a deeper-flavoured stock.

MAKES ABOUT 1¼ LITRES (2 PINTS)
1 onion, chopped
1 fennel bulb, chopped
100 g (4 oz) celery, sliced
100 g (4 oz) carrot, chopped
25 g (1 oz) white button mushrooms, sliced
A sprig of thyme
2¼ litres (4 pints) water
1 kg (2¼ lb) flat-fish bones, such as lemon sole, brill or plaice

Put all the ingredients except the fish bones into a large pan, bring to the boil and then turn the heat down and simmer very gently for 20 minutes. Add the fish bones (or fish fillet), bring back to a simmer, skimming off any scum as it rises to the surface, and simmer for a further 20 minutes. Strain through a sieve into a clean pan and simmer a little longer if necessary, until reduced to about 1¼ litres (2 pints). If not using immediately, leave to cool, then chill and refrigerate or freeze for later use.

279

Goan masala paste

1 teaspoon cumin seeds
1 teaspoon coriander seeds
1 teaspoon black peppercorns
½ teaspoon fennel seeds
½ teaspoon cloves
½ teaspoon turmeric powder
50 g (2 oz) medium-hot red chillies,
    stalks removed then roughly chopped
½ teaspoon salt
3 garlic cloves, chopped
1 teaspoon light muscovado sugar
1½ teaspoons tamarind water (page 281)
2½ cm (1 inch) fresh root ginger,
    roughly chopped
1 tablespoon red wine vinegar

Grind the spices to a fine powder in a spice grinder. Put them into a food processor with the rest of the ingredients and blend to a smooth paste.

Lemon olive oil

MAKES ABOUT 600 ML (1 PINT)

Pare the zest from 1 lemon with a potato peeler. Cut the zest into thin strips and mix with 600 ml (1 pint) of extra virgin olive oil. Leave to infuse for 24 hours before using.

Mayonnaise

This recipe includes instructions for making mayonnaise in the liquidizer or by hand. It is lighter when made mechanically because the process uses a whole egg and is very quick. You can use either sunflower oil, olive oil or a mixture of the two if you prefer. It will keep in the fridge for up to 1 week.

MAKES ABOUT 300 ML (10 FL OZ)
1 egg or 2 egg yolks
2 teaspoons white wine vinegar
½ teaspoon salt
300 ml (10 fl oz) sunflower oil or olive oil

Make sure all the ingredients are at room temperature before you start. Put the egg yolks, vinegar and salt into a mixing bowl and then rest the bowl on a cloth to stop it slipping. Lightly whisk to break the yolks. Using a wire whisk, beat the oil into the egg mixture a few drops at a time until you have incorporated it all. Once you have added the same volume of oil as the original mixture of egg yolks and vinegar, you can add the oil a little more quickly.

To make the mayonnaise in a machine, put the whole egg, vinegar and salt into a liquidizer or food processor. Turn on the machine and then slowly add the oil through the hole in the lid until you have a thick emulsion.

Pilau rice

In Goa they sometimes add crisply fried shallots to their basic aromatic spiced rice. It goes particularly well with the Monkfish vindaloo on page 160 and the Mackerel recheado on page 140. This recipe gives you the option to do it either way.

SERVES 4
6 large shallots, thinly sliced (optional)
350 g (12 oz) basmati rice
2 tablespoons sunflower oil
3 cloves
3 green cardamom pods, cracked open
5 cm (2-inch) piece cinnamon stick
1 bay leaf
½ teaspoon salt
600 ml (1 pint) boiling water

If you wish to add some crisply fried shallots to your rice, heat 1 cm (½ inch) sunflower oil in a large frying pan. Add the shallots and fry them, stirring now and then, until they are crisp and golden. Lift out with a slotted spoon on to plenty of kitchen paper and leave to drain and cool.

Wash the rice in a few changes of cold water until the water stays relatively clear. Drain, cover with fresh water and leave to soak for 7 minutes. Drain once more. Heat the oil in a heavy-based 20 cm (8-inch) saucepan over a medium heat, add the spices and cook gently for 2–3 minutes, until they become aromatic. Stir in the rice, bay leaf, salt and boiling water, quickly bring to the boil, stir once and cover with a tight-fitting lid. Reduce the heat to low and cook for 10 minutes. Uncover, fluff up the grains with a fork and serve. If adding shallots, toss them with a little salt before stirring them into the rice.

Roasted red peppers

Spear the stalk end on a fork and turn the pepper in the flame of a gas burner or blowtorch until the skin has blistered and blackened. Alternatively, roast the pepper in an oven which has been preheated to 220°C/425°F/Gas Mark 7 for 20–25 minutes, turning once until the skin is black.

Leave the pepper to cool. Break it in half and remove the stalk, skin and seeds. The flesh is now ready to use.

Rouille

MAKES ABOUT 300 ML (10 FL OZ)
25 g (¼ oz) slice of day-old white bread,
    crusts removed
A little fish stock or water
3 fat garlic cloves, peeled
1 egg yolk
250 ml (9 fl oz) olive oil
FOR THE HARISSA
1 roasted red pepper (page 280)
1 teaspoon tomato purée
1 teaspoon ground coriander
A pinch of saffron strands
2 medium-hot red chillies, stalks removed
    and roughly chopped
¼ teaspoon cayenne pepper
½ teaspoon salt

For the harissa, put the roasted red pepper, tomato
purée, ground coriander, saffron, chillies, cayenne
pepper and ¼ teaspoon of the salt into a food
processor and blend until smooth. Transfer to a
bowl and set aside. For the rouille, cover the slice
of bread with the fish stock or water and leave to
soften. Squeeze out the excess liquid and put the
bread into the food processor with 2 tablespoons
of the harissa, the garlic, egg yolk and remaining
¼ teaspoon of salt. Blend until smooth. With the
machine still running, gradually add the oil until
you have a smooth, thick mayonnaise-like mixture.
This will store in the fridge for up to 1 week.

Sri Lankan curry powder

2½ tablespoons coriander seeds
1 tablespoon cumin seeds
1½ teaspoons fennel seeds
A pinch of fenugreek seeds
2½ cm (1-inch) cinnamon stick
3 cloves
2 green cardamom pods
6 black peppercorns

Simply grind everything together to a fine powder
in a spice grinder. Store in a screw-top jar.

Steamed rice

SERVES 4

Rinse 350 g (12 oz) long grain or basmati rice in
cold water until the water runs relatively clear.
If using basmati, cover it with fresh water and
leave it to soak for 7 minutes. Drain the rice, tip
into a 20 cm (8-inch) heavy-based saucepan and
add ½ teaspoon salt and 600 ml (1 pint) boiling
water. Quickly bring to the boil, stir once, cover
with a tight-fitting lid and reduce the heat to low.
Cook the basmati rice for 10 minutes and the
long grain rice for 15 minutes. Uncover, fluff
up the grains with a fork and serve.

Tamarind water

Take a piece of tamarind pulp about the size of a
tangerine and put it in a bowl with 150 ml (5 fl oz)
warm water. Work the paste into the water with your
fingers until it has broken down and all the seeds
have been released. Strain the slightly syrupy mixture
through a fine sieve into another bowl and discard
the fibrous material left in the sieve. The water is now
ready to use and will store in the fridge for 24 hours.

Thai red curry paste

5 large medium-hot red chillies, stalks removed,
    then roughly chopped
2½ cm (1 inch) fresh root ginger, chopped
2 lemongrass stalks, outer leaves removed
    and core roughly chopped
6 garlic cloves
3 shallots, roughly chopped
1 teaspoon ground coriander
1 teaspoon ground cumin
¼ teaspoon blachan (dried shrimp paste)
2 teaspoons paprika
½ teaspoon turmeric powder
1 teaspoon salt
1 tablespoon sunflower oil

Put everything into a food processor and blend
to a smooth paste.

Vinaigrette dressing

Whisk together 1 teaspoon white wine vinegar
and 1 teaspoon Dijon mustard, then slowly whisk
in 5–6 teaspoons oil of your choice – sunflower,
olive oil or extra virgin olive oil. Season to taste
with salt and freshly ground black pepper.

Walnut vinaigrette dressing

Whisk together 1 tablespoon white wine vinegar,
3 tablespoons olive oil and 1 tablespoon walnut
oil. Season to taste with salt and freshly ground
black pepper.

Preparation techniques

Butterflied lamb

To butterfly the leg of lamb, find the place where the long bone running down the length of the leg appears to run quite close to the surface. Split open the meat along this bone and cut the meat away from either side. At the fatter end of the leg there is a group of smaller bones. Continue to cut the meat away from these until you have completely opened up the leg and can lift them all out. You should now have a piece of meat shaped like butterfly wings. Trim off any excess fat and open up any thicker areas of the meat so that it is all about 4–5 cm (1½–2 inches) thick. If in doubt, get your butcher to butterfly the lamb for you.

Mussels

Wash the mussels under plenty of cold running water. Discard any open ones that won't close when lightly squeezed or given a sharp tap. Pull out the tough fibrous beards protruding from between the tightly closed shells and then knock off any barnacles with a large knife and give the mussels another quick rinse to remove any little pieces of shell.

Skinned, seeded and diced tomatoes

Plunge the tomatoes into boiling water, or cover them with boiling water from the kettle and leave for about 30 seconds, until the skins split. This will happen more quickly the riper the tomatoes are. Drain, cover with cold water and then peel off the skins. Cut them into quarters and remove the seeds. Cut the flesh into small pieces or neat dice, depending on the dish you need them for.

Squid

Hold the squid's body in one hand and the head with the other and gently pull the head away from the body, taking the milky-white intestines with it. Remove the tentacles from the head by cutting them off just in front of the eyes. Discard the head. Squeeze out the beak-like mouth from the centre of the tentacles and discard. Separate the tentacles if they are large. Reach inside the body and pull out and discard the clear, plastic-like quill. Pull off the two fins from either side of the body pouch, then pull away the brown, semi-transparent skin from the body and fins. Wash out the body pouch with water. The squid is now ready to use.

Specialist ingredients suppliers

I have used quite a few unusual chillies in a number of my recipes because they add a unique, traditional flavour to many of the dishes. These are not always easily available in the supermarkets, but two companies can supply them by mail order:

Seasoned Pioneers (www.seasonedpioneers.co.uk) – for crushed pasilla chillies.

The Cool Chile Company (Tel: 0870 9021145 or www.coolchile.co.uk) – for guajillo (little gourd) chillies, pasilla chillies and jalapeño chillies, as well as tomatillos, masa harina and Mexican chocolate.

Dried kashmiri chillies are available from most supermarkets and all Indian grocers.

For judión beans and all things Spanish: Brindisa, Floral Hall, Stoney Street, Borough Market, London SE1 (Tel: 020 7407 1036); Brindisa, 32 Exmouth Market, Clerkenwell, London, EC1R 4QE (Tel: 020 7713 1666)

If you do not live in London and it is not possible to visit the retail outlets listed, please call the Borough Market stall for stockists in your area.

Visit www.purespain.co.uk for Calasparra rice and other Spanish ingredients.

All Asian ingredients, including paneer, dried shrimps, Thai fish sauce, blachan (shrimp paste), ketjap manis (sweet soy sauce), Chinese fermented salted black beans, sichuan peppercorns, wet tamarind, dried egg and rice noodles and sambal oelek are available from www.theasiancookshop.co.uk.

Japanese ingredients such as bonito flakes, wakame seaweed, kombu seaweed, pickled ginger, keta (salmon roe), Japanese sticky rice, rice vinegar, mirin and Japanese soy sauce are available from www.japanesekitchen.co.uk.

Most of the ingredients are also available from *Stein's Deli* (www.rickstein.com/online shop or 01841 533 250).

Index

INDEX

RICK STEIN

Acknowledgements

I would like to thank Debbie Major for her untiring assistance in putting the book together, testing recipes and making the completely appetising dishes for the food photography, my new commissioning editor, Shirley Patton who saw the sense of a book of recipes as a record of all the parts of the world that have influenced me in my cooking. I'm also indebted to the fresh look of the new book largely brought about by the team work of Alex and Emma Smith the designers, James Murphy, Noel Murphy and David Loftus the photographers and the project editor, Eleanor Maxfield.

Thanks too to Claire Heron-Maxwell assisting Debbie, and to all those who supplied great produce for them, notably, Matthew Watson Smyth for vegetables, Jax Buse for the beautiful asparagus, Billy Freeman for the John Dory and red mullet from Padstow, Matthew Stevens from St Ives for all the other great fish and shellfish. David West for most of the meat and Gary Eveleigh for rabbits, pheasants and wild garlic. Also to Penny Markham for the atmospheric props.

Lastly my love to Sarah, Zach and Olivia who had to put up with yet more single minded cookery book writing and my three sons, Edward, Jack and Charles who took me off on a fly fishing holiday in Scotland during all this to give me a break.

NOTES ON THE RECIPES

All teaspoon and tablespoon measurements are level unless otherwise stated and are based on measuring spoons where 1 teaspoon = 5 ml and 1 tablespoon = 15 ml. Don't be tempted to use a coffee spoon or an old-fashioned serving-size tablespoon instead.

All cooking times are approximate.

All recipes have been tested in a conventional oven. If you have a fan oven, you will probably need to adjust the dial by about 20°C. So for 200°C, set the dial at about 180°C. I always keep an oven thermometer hanging from one of the racks so that I can check the temperature before I start cooking.

Free-range eggs and chickens are recommended in all recipes.

Recipes made with raw or lightly cooked eggs should be avoided by anyone who is pregnant or in a vulnerable health group.

Exact cooking times for pasta and soaked dried beans vary according to the brand and age of the ingredients.